Now this is a rich read! I've long been convinced the healing of our humanity comes through attachment to God. Jim shows you how.

JOHN ELDREDGE, *New York Times* bestselling author

Just when I thought I had extracted all that Dallas Willard had for me, Jim Wilder integrates something fresh from neuroscience into a revised model of transformation. Read this book one page at a time, or you will miss what it has for you and the people you lead.

RANDY FRAZEE, pastor; coauthor of *The Renovation of the Heart* student edition

Building on a classic understanding of the spiritual formation of the whole person with the latest relational discoveries in neuroscience, it is easy to see that this is what we are created for—and what joy the world so desperately needs to see in the lives of Jesus' apprentices. A practical primer for disciples who long for a richer life with God and others.

AMY PIERSON, founder of Burning Heart Workshops; former executive director of the Spiritual Formation Alliance

Transformation occurs as we are renovated from the inside out, formed and reformed emotionally and relationally, changed and developed most powerfully in the context of the community of Christ. It all begins with love for God, from which our characters are healed and redirected toward the active presence of God. How kind of Jim and Dallas (and Jane), for guiding us thoughtfully and graciously toward a radical maturity based in healthy attachment love.

STEPHEN A. MACCHIA, founder and president of Leadership Transformations, Inc.; author of several books, including *Crafting a Rule of Life*, *Broken and Whole*, and *Becoming a Healthy Church*

No one has taught me more about intimacy with God and relational discipleship than Jim Wilder. If he writes a book, I read it. The opportunity to sit in on this cutting-edge discussion between a giant of the faith like Dallas Willard and my friend Jim is a rare treasure. I guarantee this book will open new doors in your understanding and take you deeper in your walk with God.

MARCUS WARNER, president of Deeper Walk International

Jim Wilder offers a genuine hope in *Renovated*. He uniquely combines the truth of Scripture with the truth in developing brain science to give us a path of renewal and restoration.

DUDLEY HALL, president of Kerygma Ventures

A breakthrough on so many levels. Renovated is a must-read for everyone who is serious about discipling people and seeing life transformation.

BOB ROBERTS, global senior pastor of Northwood Church; founder of Glocal.net

There is a fearful lack of intensity and low expectancy for releasing New Testament Christianity in a mad and muddled world today. You just might be holding in your hands the key to a massive return to a world-transforming Christianity, both corporately and personally, as we learn to think with God.

JACK TAYLOR, president of Dimensions Ministries

Dr. Jim Wilder has spent most of his adult life researching, praying about, observing, field-testing, pondering, and validating how God has designed people to mature and Christ followers to be conformed to the image of Jesus. His research and understanding are truly groundbreaking and provide vital missing pieces regarding how so much of Western Christianity has lost its relational foundation and focus. *Renovated* is his most important book to date.

REV. MICHAEL SULLIVANT, CEO of Life Model Works

Elegant, clear and bountiful in hope . . . a magisterial work that weaves together wisdom, application, and most of all, relational connection. If transformation for yourself and of your community is what you seek, I can think of no better place to start.

CURT THOMPSON, author of *The Soul of Shame* and *Anatomy of the Soul*

A gold mine of truth exposing the mother lode of God loving us and sharing love for us to love Him, love others, and love ourselves. Take as much as you want. The supply is eternally limitless.

JIM HYLTON, staff pastor of Northwood Church

An answer to prayer for those asking the question, *How does God transform people into the likeness of Christ?* The answer is found in the way human beings have been created: in attachment love with God and others. I highly recommend this book for anyone working in the field of spiritual formation and for all believers who are seeking guidance and understanding for how God transforms lives.

JOHN Y. LEE, academic dean of the John Leland Center for Theological Studies

A must-read for your continued growth in faith and life.

KEN R. CANFIELD, founder of National Center for Fathering

If the goodness of a book could be measured in how many times I spontaneously smiled or exclaimed, "I'm loving this!" then *Renovated* is *very good*! Dr. Wilder shines in his understanding of the way of maturity and offers practical steps to get there.

JERRY REDDIX, Member Care International and Vineyard Missions, USA

A comprehensive, Trinitarian, and human-friendly way to carry out the great commission. It opens a revelatory door that will empower the body of Christ to actualize a more relational Christianity, even a relational revolution in Church and culture.

DR. TIMOTHY M. JOHNS, founder and overseer of Rock International

For too many people, this will be the book that finally connects their soul to the Father of creation. Dr. Wilder writes with compassion, graciousness, and understanding, all interspersed with bright humor and warm anecdotes about real people. Here is the gentle sharing of a sensitive pastor who is equally at ease in imparting biblical truths and counseling troubled and searching people.

BERNARD FRANKLIN, PH.D., vice president of student life, Mount St. Mary's University

For those of us who consider ourselves to be the most hopeless of cases in spiritual formation, our backs against the ropes, this book rekindles confidence that even spiritual-transformation underdogs have a puncher's chance of becoming more like Christ.

JAMES HENDERSON, cofounder of Ashrei Center for Spiritual Formation, Mexico City

Jim Wilder takes us deep into the heart of the question, *How do people change?* This practical and provoking work is greatly needed today. With many messages on transformation and maturity swirling in the world and in the church, Jim and Dallas together bring clarity and hope for God's people to walk in wholeness. This is a *must*-read!

LINDY BLACK, associate US director of The Navigators

Mining the timeless truth of Holy Scripture as well as neuroscience, James Wilder builds on the profound teaching of Dallas Willard, adding clarifying insight regarding the primacy of attachment love in divine design and in the formation of emotional and spiritual maturity. This excellent book not only reframes prevalent spiritual-growth paradigms but also provides practical guidance to more fully experience the *with-God life*. I highly recommend it.

TOM NELSON, president of Made to Flourish, pastor of Christ Community Church

RENOVATED

*God, Dallas Willard & the Church
That Transforms*

JIM WILDER

NavPress

A NavPress resource published in alliance
with Tyndale House Publishers

NavPress is the publishing ministry of The Navigators, an international Christian organization and leader in personal spiritual development. NavPress is committed to helping people grow spiritually and enjoy lives of meaning and hope through personal and group resources that are biblically rooted, culturally relevant, and highly practical.

For more information, visit NavPress.com.

Renovated: God, Dallas Willard, and the Church that Transforms

Copyright © 2020 by Shepherd's House. All rights reserved.

Lectures by Dallas Willard transcribed and edited from the Heart and Soul Conference, June 28, 2012, in La Cañada, California. Lectures and PowerPoint images from Dallas Willard used by permission of the Willard Family Trust.

A NavPress resource published in alliance with Tyndale House Publishers

NAVPRESS and the NavPress logo are registered trademarks of NavPress, The Navigators, Colorado Springs, CO. *TYNDALE* is a registered trademark of Tyndale House Publishers. Absence of ® in connection with marks of NavPress or other parties does not indicate an absence of registration of those marks.

The Team:
Don Pape, Publisher; David Zimmerman, Acquisitions Editor; Elizabeth Schroll, Copy Editor; Jennifer Ghionzoli, Designer

Cover and interior illustration of geometric pattern copyright © Ozerina/Depositphotos.com. All rights reserved. Cover and interior illustration of plum by May Rivers/Wikimedia Commons/Public Domain.

Author photo taken by Christopher Kamman, copyright © 2015. All rights reserved.

For information about special discounts for bulk purchases, please contact Tyndale House Publishers at csresponse@tyndale.com, or call 1-800-323-9400.

ISBN 978-1-64158-167-7

Printed in the United States of America

26 25 24 23 22 21 20
7   6   5   4   3

To Nemesius, bishop of Emesa (AD 390), the first neurotheologian of the church. His book, De Natura Hominis, written in the fourth century, expressed how God designed the lobes of the brain with different functions. His Doctrine of Ventricle Localization of Mental Functioning stood without peer for over a thousand years.

And to Dr. Lee Edward Travis (1896–1987), who handed me the baton of neurotheology, the science of spiritual maturity.

CONTENTS

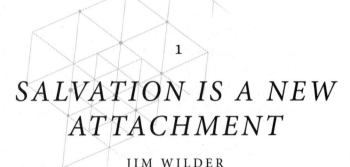

SALVATION IS A NEW ATTACHMENT

JIM WILDER

Dallas Willard sat across from me with tears in his eyes as he looked at the floor. Dallas had only weeks to live, but his tears were not for his own life. "What I have learned in this last year," he told me, "is more important than what I learned in the rest of my life. But I have no time to write about it. I will try to finish the projects I have started." He looked up at me. I wondered if he was thinking about our conversation or something else.

"You need to write about this," Dallas said. His voice was steady but with mounting passion: "I know of no soteriology [doctrine of salvation] based on forming a new attachment with God." He offered no arguments in favor or against the idea. Dallas, for as well as he knew history, could think of no previous proponents. His body slumped back into his chair, tired from the energy of speaking.

I glanced at his wife, Jane, sensing that it was about time for me to leave. Dallas needed rest. A fast message of understanding passed between our minds without words.

Jane was always an astute observer and pragmatist. As both a licensed therapist and spiritual director, Jane had constant contact with people who experienced less success at the Christian life than they had hoped to have.

Traumatized people were not achieving the degree of transformation they expected. She noticed that commonly proposed solutions worked for some people but not as well for others. Good-hearted people were working very hard using both theological and psychological approaches and still not seeing their desired change into the character of Christ.

Jane had been one of my first supervisors[1] after I finished my doctorate. It was her training that brought the presence of God into the healing experience for me. Jane joked that she discovered both Dallas and me, but there is much more to Jane's influence than that. Jane applied the same rigor to psychological interventions as she did to spiritual solutions. Over the last thirty-five years, Jane had challenged both Dallas and me to find broader, deeper, and more complete means of transformation. Dallas wanted to see empirically verifiable effects after encountering God. Jane wanted methods that would work regardless of someone's wounds or maturity, and she expected solutions that were both theologically and academically defensible. All of us wanted means of transformation that were accessible and enduring.

Jane caught my eye. We all prayed together before I headed out the door. My mind went back to 2011, when I felt strongly pressed in my spirit to have a dinner honoring Dallas for his contributions to Christian life. I had been impacted by both his books and his presence. As an author myself, I knew that most Christian books came and went. Few books would be remembered in a hundred years. Yet, I am certain that Christians will continue reading Dallas. People who are serious about godly character will find guidance in his work.

Honoring Dallas would not be easy. While he was as warm and kind as he was brilliant, Dallas did not like attention. He did agree to do a conference with us on the topic of spiritual and emotional maturity, and to submit to a dinner as part of that event. Our goal was to examine best practices to achieve "transformation of character" in contrast to what Dallas called "sin management." The 2012 Heart and Soul Conference would bring together thought leaders who designed and taught methods to achieve transformation and people who had "tried it all." Ordinary Christians would meet brain specialists and theologians, and together we would explore, for the first time, how the brain learns Christlike character. We would examine whether current brain science would change the understanding of human nature that had dominated Christian theology

since the Middle Ages. Would knowing how the brain learns charac
revise how we teach ourselves to be Christian?

Heart and Soul began a discussion between Dallas and me that became this book. How does the brain develop an identity and normal human maturity? The human-identity systems in the brain generate our emotional reactions to life—reactions that often lack Christlike character. Changes in the brain's identity systems will change both our character and our reactions. Dallas and I wanted to compare how the brain changes character with the methods Christians use for discipleship and spiritual formation. Could spiritual disciplines like prayer, fasting, and Bible study be better tuned to produce character change?

Dallas and I began talking about a joint project on the nature of transformation that could become a book. Shortly after the Heart and Soul Conference, however, Dallas discovered the condition that was to take his life. It was clear that I was to take the path ahead without him.

As I drove home, my mind went back to how Dallas acted at the Heart and Soul Conference. I knew he was not well, so we set up a room for him to rest, but Dallas was having none of it. He sat at the front of the auditorium, rarely looking up but deeply engaged with all who asked him questions. Most audience members had been Christians for over thirty years. Many practiced spiritual disciplines, moved in the Holy Spirit, saw a spiritual director, and had been in therapy or inner healing. Many participants were therapists, teachers, spiritual directors, or ministers of inner healing themselves. Their questions revealed a deep desire for better results from their spiritual practices. Few could say "yes" when they applied Dallas's main test for Christlike character: whether one spontaneously responds to one's enemies with love.

Relationships and emotions were frequent issues among Heart and Soul participants. Dallas engaged each person thoughtfully. He was caring for their souls.

The Care of Souls

My mind went even further back. I had opened the Heart and Soul Conference by telling the story of how I first met Dallas. It was 1982, and Jane had just become the director of training for our community counseling center. She thought it would be great to have Dallas speak in our staff meeting. A staff member mentioned that Dallas was a philosophy professor at the University of Southern California. Some of the staff seemed quite excited. I figured this would be a dry staff meeting. The course of my life was about to change dramatically.

"Psychology," Dallas said quietly, "is the care of souls. The care of souls was once the province of the church, but the church no longer provides that care." He paused. "The most important thing about the care of souls is that you must love them."

Love souls! My whole professional training had been one of learned disengagement. I carefully learned not to have any emotional connection with "clients." That very disengagement was strange, had I stopped to think about it. My interest in psychology began during a spiritual crisis at age nineteen when I discovered a loving and relational God. As I searched for what it meant to believe in Jesus, three elements of the Christian life came into sharp focus: (1) dialogue with God about everything, (2) do nothing out of fear, and (3) love people deeply. Dallas was precipitating a collision between my professional training and the very spiritual life that initiated my counseling education.

As Dallas softly declared that we must love souls in order to care for them, this truth shattered my professional persona. I realized that somewhere during seminary, I had stopped dialoguing with God about everything. Sure, I prayed outside the office, but the active presence of God was something I no longer felt. I never taught others to experience God in the counseling hour. I did recommend spiritual practices, but people neither learned nor practiced them in my office.

Meanwhile, down the hall in her office, Jane, my supervisor, was teaching people to find God's presence. Lives were being transformed and traumas were being resolved by God's active presence. Word got out to the church about what Jane was doing. Many responses were not favorable. Some Christians (particularly pastors) were concerned that people claimed to be hearing from God. Was this not some form of "private revelation," demonic deception, or, at best, a psychological delusion?

As a counseling center, we had no shortage of demonic manifestations or delusional people who thought they were speaking for God. When those hearing voices told others, the outcome was predictable. We observed a noticeable lack of peace, an absence of healing, and the production of distress in others. With Jane's group, however, we saw healing, growing love for God, and deepening fellowship with other people.

Providentially, Dallas wrote the book *In Search of Guidance* (later retitled *Hearing God*), arguing that we can be guided by God's active presence in our daily lives.[2]

Over the next years, Dallas continued to explore and develop ways to become aware of God's presence. The spiritual disciplines were his focus. Although spiritual exercises had a long history in the church, their use was not widespread. Dallas explained and encouraged these spiritual practices: The disciplines themselves were not transformative, but they placed the soul in a position to be transformed by God.

While Dallas promoted spiritual disciplines, others of us were developing relational exercises to help people love each other. People with emotional wounds seemed particularly hampered in growing and sustaining loving, joyful relationships. Using the brain science behind secure and joyful attachments, we trained people how to build and sustain loving relationships with the people God placed in their lives. This science of character formation helped people thrive and became part of the Life Model—a guide to joyful, godly maturity.

Both the group doing people-with-God exercises[3] and the group doing people-with-people exercises showed promising growth. Each method slowly increased Christlike character. Each approach had observable limitations. People doing spiritual exercises with God often struggled in their relationships with others. People working on relationships with others often had difficulty sensing God. Neither group did overly well at loving their enemies. Were we missing something in both groups that made transformation of character go deeper and spread farther?

Could it be that deep spiritual and relational maturity requires something that was missing from the exercises and disciplines we were using? Was there an additional factor or factors that Western Christianity had yet to recognize? Or could our limited success be due to a need to combine the two approaches into one? Going one step further, perhaps spiritual and emotional maturity were one thing, not two different issues.

Dallas changed my life with his teaching about loving souls. I return the favor by telling him about attachment love in the human brain.

Attachment Love

The only kind of love that helps the brain learn better character is attach-ment love. The brain functions that determine our character are most pro-foundly shaped by who we love. Changing character, as far as the brain is concerned, means attaching in new and better ways.

This realization brought Dallas to tears. If the quality of our human attachments creates human character, is it possible that when God speaks of love, "attachment" is what God means?

God is described over two hundred times in the Old Testament as being חסד "hesed/chesed," a quality God also desires from us: "For I delight in loyalty [hesed] rather than sacrifice" (Hosea 6:6). The Hebrew word *hesed* is translated as "devoted," "faithful," and "unchanging love." Could God be speaking of an attachment love that sticks with us?

Dallas's mind raced ahead of mine in our conversations about attach-ment. He wondered, "Is salvation itself a new and active attachment with God that forms and transforms our identities?" In the human brain, iden-tity and character are formed by who we love. Attachments are powerful and long lasting. Ideas can be changed much more easily. Salvation through a new, loving attachment to God that changes our identities would be a very relational way to understand our salvation: We would be both saved and transformed through attachment love from, to, and with God.

Although months passed after Dallas first suggested a soteriology of attachment, he never produced arguments for or against the idea. Salvation through attachment was not something he had previously considered or taught. Had I suggested salvation through God's will, the intellect, emo-tional experiences, ritual, good deeds, or attachment to a group, Dallas would have been full of comments. Western Christianity has long taught that we are changed by what we believe and what we choose—that is, by the human will responding to God. Attachment to God would functionally replace the will as the mechanism of salvation and transformation.

We know that loving God and loving others are the two greatest charac-teristics of a godly life. Yet, I had never considered that where Scripture spoke of love, it might mean "attachment." I had never thought about how I could learn to love in attachment ways. Dallas was proposing a practical shift in theology that would change our Christian methods for developing spiritual maturity. Christians have tried forming character through beliefs, experiences, and spiritual power. I knew how churches changed people's beliefs but not how churches grew attachments. I knew I was to (a) love God and (b) love others, but I didn't know how Christians develop attachment love.

I considered how I was taught of God's great love for me. We meditated on how much torture God asked Jesus to endure on our behalf. I was impressed by the greatness of God's love but, at the same time, not drawn toward closeness with God. Thinking of the Cross did little to enhance my attachment to God.

Neither was I drawn much toward Christian people. I did like my friends. Yet, attachments to friends did not always help me develop good character and often pulled me away from being Christlike. My reactions became more like the people in my identity group and conflicted with my beliefs. For example, my friends and fellow Christians didn't spontaneously love their enemies, although I believed I should. How would I develop spontaneous attachment love for my enemies?

What delightful harmony emerges between neuroscience and theology if building attachment love is the central process for both spiritual and emotional maturity. Suppose we focused spiritual exercises and human-relationship exercises less on changing our beliefs or choices and more on building attachment love with God and with people. Would that yield the kind of character transformation we yearn to find? The brain's need for love-that-equals-attachment could explain why spiritual practices sometimes disappoint diligent Christians. A focus on attachment would have profound implications for our understanding of human character, fellowship, and spiritual formation.

I concluded that my relationship to God needed more attachment love. My relationships with people needed more of God's character. How would this happen? Frankly, I did not expect hesed from church people if my character were to be exposed. Christians had not provided strong enough attachments for me to expose what went on in my brain. So I kept my Christian face on in church. But unless I had strong attachments with God and people at the same moment, I could not reasonably expect to see much transformation into the character of Christ. Reconciling the church's practices of transformation to how the brain works will be our topic for this book.

Dallas passed on, but not before urging the ongoing discussion of salvation as hesed. His understanding was that salvation *should* produce disciples who spontaneously exhibit the character of Jesus. His acknowledgment was that salvation as we conceive of it too often doesn't. Dallas saw in attachment love a possible remedy.

The Heart and Soul Conference, from which this book emerges, gives us a day with Dallas. His first talk addresses the question of how spiritual wholeness and emotional maturity are related. Let us begin there.

2

SPIRITUAL AND EMOTIONAL MATURITY

DALLAS WILLARD

It fell to me to introduce Dallas at the Heart and Soul Conference. A great deal of gray and white hair from well-known Christian thinkers was evident in the sanctuary. Spiritual-formation and neuroscience leaders sat in the same room. There has not always been harmony between psychology and Christian thought, but I was hopeful that what we have learned about human identity from neuroscience would explain why great thinking and faithful spiritual practices can work so gradually. At the same time, I hoped that spiritual practices would lift the ceiling for the rapid character change produced by relational practices and yield a more Christlike character.

Jane sat beside Dallas in the front row, showing no sign of the concerns she carried for Dallas's health. The two of them represented the issues this conference wished to resolve. Dallas, the philosopher and theologian, was a practical realist who sought reliable spiritual solutions for people's formation and discipleship. Jane, the psychotherapist, had sought spiritual solutions for wounded and traumatized people for whom classic Christian practices did not always seem to work well. I smiled their way and began with the story of how Jane taught me to unite heart and soul. Here is the short version.

When I was nineteen years old, learning to interact with God about everything, I found a summer job as a counselor in a Salvation Army camp. One afternoon, a massive thunderstorm hit, and I ran for shelter. At first, I thought I was alone in the building, but soon, I saw a figure curled up on the floor. I ran to see and discovered a woman who was also a counselor. She was breathing but otherwise unresponsive.

"Jesus, help!" I said aloud.

She opened her eyes and asked what was happening. I quickly told the story. She replied, "Ever since I was a baby and lightning struck a tree outside my bedroom, this happens to me. People tell me that I am curled up and unresponsive just the way they found me in my crib that day. What is happening now?"

"I said 'Jesus, help!' and you opened your eyes and stood up," I answered. "You have never watched a thunderstorm?" She shook her head, "No."

"This is the biggest one I have seen in my life. Come and watch."

When I returned to college, I changed my major from biology to psychology and religious studies. I learned from my studies about how this woman came to be in the fetal position. But nothing in my coursework explained "Jesus, help!" I went to graduate school for a PhD in psychology and an MA in theology. Still no answer.

One day, as I worked at Shepherd's House under Jane Willard, she said to me, "I don't know if I should tell you this since you are a psychologist and all, but down at my end of the hall, we are inviting Jesus to join us and watching amazing healing take place." That is what I had been seeking!

A fifteen-minute introduction of Dallas left me no time to tell the audience how Jane helped people form an attachment with Jesus. Nor was there time to explain how abused women who could not form an attachment to Jesus (because He is male) would form an attachment with Jane, who would then "stand in" for Jesus as they began to heal and form their own attachment to Him. Jane's experience suggests a kind of overlap between how we form attachment love with people and with Jesus that we will return to later in this book.[1]

I *did* have time to speak about Dallas's book *In Search of Guidance* (later revised and retitled *Hearing God*), in which Dallas reflected on the practice of interacting with God, and his successive work on spiritual disciplines that help us commune with God. Now, at the conference, we were asking Dallas to address why people sometimes remained emotionally immature after their trauma was healed and even after they practiced spiritual disciplines. What was the relationship of spiritual maturity to emotional maturity?

Dallas rose and leaned on the podium, a large cross and shiny organ pipes lighting the space behind him. He launched directly into his theme—how humans become like Jesus. Here is what he said.[2]

• • •

In the Bible, God has put together a picture of reality, the sourcebook of a civilization of which we are a part. The content of the Bible is meant to be used as instructions in how to live.

These instructions may be tested empirically, in real life: It is a demonstration of the Bible's authority that you may go to bed saying, "Jesus, help!" and then wake up to find yourself helped.

When you read in the Bible, "The kingdom of heaven is at hand,"[3] you can put such a statement to the test. For example, when Jim was trying to help the young woman curled up in the fetal position, he invoked the Kingdom of God, which is at hand: "Jesus, help!" It's very interesting that this kind of invocation is usually more effective when you don't know what else to do. If Jim had had a theory about how to help this woman, he might not have said, "Jesus, help!" But such an invocation also usually proves effective.

Let's put a passage of Scripture to the test: "Blessed are you who are poor."[4] Have you seen any poor people that were blessed? How many of you have known poor people that were blessed? To consider that passage, you must study what "blessing" consists in. As you do so, you begin to enter a fuller understanding of blessing—and perhaps even pass it on to others.

Now, every time you put Scripture to the test, you are going to come into incredible opposition. Others do not believe the Scriptures true in the sense of being empirically verifiable. If they believed as much, their lives would be radically changed. But if we understand that the Bible is a record of reliable experience with God, then it is a *major* player in the field of how to live. In order to fully appreciate it, you have to put it up against all the other books and recommendations that come along.

For example, some time ago, there was a book called *The Secret*. The lady from Australia who wrote it is now well off—she certainly found the secret. But I can tell you, if *The Secret* worked, the world would now be in an entirely different economic condition. *The Secret* can be tested as reliable instruction on how to live but will be found wanting.

You must be aware of the tendency to just hold to something—the Bible or *The Secret* or something else—without testing whether it works. As our time together unfolds, I am going to use teachings from the Bible, and I want to encourage you to not just think, *Well this is authoritative because Paul said it, or Jesus said it, or Moses said it.* I want you to say, "Let's put that to the test."

For example, the Bible addresses the problem of how to live in the real human situation. To do so is to bring on all comers—psychology, brain science, evolution, whatever it is. You put each down beside what the Bible teaches. And you test it as an alternative. What does transformation in the manner that Jesus and the Scriptures teach about—a manner that has been observed repeatedly through the ages—look like in real life? What does, say, emotional maturity amount to in the Scriptures? What does spiritual maturity amount to in the Scriptures?

There is an interesting story in the Gospel of John. Jesus has just said some tough things, and people are turning away in droves. He looks at his closest followers and friends and says, "Are you going to go away too?" Peter's response to Jesus is the most important question for us to ask continually: "To whom should we go?"[5] You can't understand and appreciate the teachings of people like Jesus and Paul unless you measure them against the possible alternatives. That's what we have to do with the Bible. I hope you will think about all of my references to the Bible, and the teachings that I will be taking from it, in that respect.

My talks will unfold over the course of four big ideas. First, we're going to deal with the questions, "What is spiritual wholeness in Christ? What is emotional maturity? And how are they related?" We are going to be a little picky at some points—for example, I really do want to talk about the *function* of emotions, which will mean discussing feelings, emotions, and desires. An emotionally immature person is being governed by their feelings, desires, and emotions.

I also want to contrast *emotional maturity* with a picture of *spiritual maturity*—how someone who has grown up spiritually acts, and conversely, how someone who has not grown up spiritually acts. That's our first job.

My second session [chapter 4] is about the dimensions of human life, from which the notions of maturity and immaturity arise:

- the will (very important);
- the mind, which includes thoughts and feelings;
- the body, which is our little power pack that God has given to us to allow us to have a decent kind of life;
- our social connections (which are essential); and then finally,
- the soul.

These dimensions don't always function as they should. And by understanding what these dimensions are and how they work—or don't work, when they malfunction or otherwise don't do what they are supposed to do in relation to one another—we see how a person who has grown up physically might still be a squawking baby, emotionally and spiritually. Frankly, that's where most of us in our world are—babies emotionally. And we've never come to grips with that reality.

Now, theologically, that fundamental immaturity is the effect of sin. And it's very serious business. If you can't talk about sin, you're like a farmer who can't talk about weeds and bugs: The bugs get fatter and the weeds get taller. So we have to talk about sin, because sin is a matter of the will's distortion of the whole person.

My third session [chapter 6] is about our view of salvation and the gospel, which, unfortunately, keeps the church at large from dealing with spiritual maturity. It is not at all uncommon that a church is caught up in tiptoeing around leaders who are babies emotionally. I don't think this is intentional, but the fact is that our churches don't focus on formation as the central issue; consequently, we deal with emotional and spiritual immaturity as a cultural norm far too often.

We don't have to live there—and we haven't always lived there, thank God. We have, through the ages, seen people stepping up to champion emotional and spiritual maturity. I'm thankful that this conference involves responsible, bright, well-prepared people who are seriously dealing with emotional and spiritual immaturity. We have to deal with it, and we have to get past views of salvation and the gospel that think it's not important to do so.

Some wonderful people have called for us to live lives of maturity. To do so, they've had to find their way beyond fear. Fear is one of the pervasive, motivational forces in human life. The Bible often includes the phrase "Fear not" because even when we're met by God or an angel, our initial response is "Aaaugggghh!" Our lives are based on fear, and we must confront that fact.

The focus of the church is not generally on emotional and spiritual maturity. But you know what? If we refocus on maturity, maturity will happen. It's not a mystery. It's not magical. It is a matter of development that we can understand, devote ourselves to, and communicate to others.

Now, it's not mechanical, and we ought to understand that the Spirit of God is involved in all the instrumentalities of the Kingdom. But we're not *waiting* on the Spirit of God; the Spirit of God is already there. Much of our theology, especially in American religion, would give you the impression that we're all just sort of waiting around to see if the Holy Spirit will strike us and turn us into paragons of Christlikeness. But when we *do* observe Christlikeness, the Holy Spirit is always involved. Our part is to learn, intelligently and carefully utilizing all the resources that we might have.

What we're talking about, then, as we pursue emotional and spiritual maturity, is bringing people to Christlikeness. But we're also talking about bringing people to a place of health. Health—the condition of a fully functioning human being—is alignment of all the parts that make us up (will, mind, body, social connection, and soul) in a way that allows us to say that we "follow Christ." That's what Paul said, you remember? First Corinthians 11:1: "Follow me as I follow Christ."[6] Just that simple.

You say, "Follow me as I follow Christ? How could you say that, Willard?" Well, it takes some understanding. "As I follow Christ" is the saving clause. In honesty and humility—because I don't have anything to hide—I'm happy if people will find out where I'm wrong and then help me get it right. That's a part of stepping into the companionship of Christ and growing in this way. We'll explore an understanding of salvation and the gospel that has emotional and spiritual maturity as its outcome.

My final session [chapter 8] will be on instrumentalities for becoming spiritually and emotionally mature.

I want us to have a picture of what spiritual and emotional maturity looks like. To do so, I'll start by taking you to a jailhouse, a very unpleasant jailhouse. From there, the apostle Paul is giving advice to the Philippians about how to live their lives, and he says, "Rejoice in the Lord always. Again I say, rejoice!"[7] That might be a mark of a spiritually and emotionally mature person, don't you think?

"Let your gentleness be known to all men. The Lord is near. Be anxious for nothing."[8] There's the fear, which all of us contend with, and yet the assurance "the Lord is near." The Lord's nearness is the source of our gentleness. Freedom from anxiety is sourced in the contrast that follows: "But in everything by prayer and supplication with thanksgiving let your requests be made known unto God."[9]

This is Paul we are talking about, and he's pointing us to spiritual *and* emotional maturity. "The peace of God, which surpasses all comprehension, will guard your hearts and your minds in Christ Jesus."[10] The ultimate source of maturity, spiritually, is the immediate tie into Jesus Christ and His Kingdom—which is right there, where you are. "The Lord is at hand."

Interestingly, that is the same Greek language that shows up when Jesus comes to proclaim the gospel, for example, in Matthew 4:17: "Repent, for the kingdom of heaven is at hand." It doesn't mean it's about to come—it's there. So the path to spiritual and emotional maturity is rooted in the practice of the presence of Jesus.

Such a life lived in the presence of Jesus is incompatible with a life of sin. But wait—some people will say, "You know, if I don't sin, life is going to be very boring. What am I going to do if I don't sin?" Well, Paul tells us here:

Whatever is true, whatever is honorable, whatever is right,
whatever is pure, whatever is lovely, whatever is of good repute,

if there is any excellence and if anything worthy of praise, dwell on these things.[11]

That's what the spiritually and emotionally mature person's life is filled with. That is a list of all of the wonderful and good things that are available to human beings once they get pulled out of the unfortunate position of trying to take God's place in running their life, when they move from emotional and spiritual infancy toward maturity. Then they can accept and dwell in the good things that are all around them.

The emotionally mature person is not the one with a starved, deprived existence, but rather one that reaches out and embraces and furthers all that is good—everything that is good. And that's a long list. You can start just with simple beauty. It's very hard to be grumpy when you're looking at a beautiful rose—try it. It's turning to what is good that fills out the life of the emotionally and spiritually mature person. As you step into spiritual maturity, you step into the wonderful world of God so rich with good things that we won't have enough time to concentrate on them.

This is, in the classic language of the church, holiness, sanctification. I have to acknowledge that the way many people present holiness and sanctification is a very pinched view of life. It's very starved, because they have not been encouraged to turn themselves loose into the fullness of God's presence and all that is good for them to invest their lives in. That is not commonly thought of as a part of holiness. We have to correct that, and much more can be done with that. But I give you these verses from Paul to help you have a picture of what we are aiming at when we talk about becoming spiritually and emotionally mature people.

See, most people who remain emotionally immature are hung up on a lot of really bad stuff. And that often expresses itself in a secret life that they have to hide from others. But healthy people—people who are spiritually and emotionally mature, people who are following Jesus—don't live there. So Paul can say in verse 9 of Philippians 4, "The things you have learned and received and heard and seen in me, practice these things, and the God of peace will be with you."

Okay then, here's a picture of the emotionally and spiritually mature person. And Paul writes this from a miserable Roman jail. And look at these wonderful things that he says in what follows: "I have learned to be content in whatever circumstances I am."[12] Where did that come from It came from the richness of the life he was living, *in jail*. That's the life instruction on offer in the Scriptures, put to the test empirically in the life of Paul. That life is available to all of us when we learn to turn to the Kingdom of God and put our confidence in Jesus and then learn by experience the reality of that kind of life.

Over and over and over in the Scriptures, this is presented.[13] But we normally encounter it not as an opportunity to be explored so much as an ideal no one realizes. So you read 1 Corinthians 13 and just feel bad about yourself. We read "Love is patient, love is kind," and more often than not, we wind up frustrated and discouraged. But the text doesn't say, "I do all these wonderful things"; it says love does. And so 1 Corinthians 13 is in fact a proposition: If you will receive love into your life, over time, out will come the things that 1 Corinthians 13 says are true of love.

That's the structure we have to learn. We don't try to do those things— we *become the kind of person* who does those things. If you try to do those things, it will just kill you. But if you receive love as the principle of your life in all dimensions of your being, then you will see love: Love is kind, love does not envy, and so on all the way down the line. And having received love, you will be transformed into a person who loves.

Emotional and Spiritual Maturity

We have discussed emotional maturity and immaturity as something we want to distinguish. And yet the phrase itself—"emotional maturity"—is a little misleading because our emotions are only part of the puzzle. The area we're concerned with covers a range of human essentials: our feelings, our desires, and of course, our emotions. Those are different and must be considered differently.

Feelings determine much of human behavior. We find it difficult to stand apart from them so that we can deal with them authentically. And meanwhile, they've been granted a place of privilege; they've been glorified in society. You know, we even have this song,

Feelings, nothing more than feelings. . . .
Feelings, wo-wo-wo-wo, feelings.[14]

Think about that song. Feelings are right at the center of human life, according to that song, and unfortunately that's pretty truthful about human life. You see a lot of feeling manifested in mob behavior. Sometimes, the mob is a square in Cairo filled with people who are jumping up and down and all of that stuff, but just as often mob behavior manifests in a committee meeting.

Feelings are blind. Very often, when you feel something, you don't even know why you feel it. Now, I believe that God has given us feelings—I don't think feelings are bad. It's just that if you try to live by your feelings, you're dead. You can't do it. They're not enough.

That's also true of desires. Desires are focused on determinate objects. When you have a desire, you desire some particular thing. If you are hungry, you desire food; if you're sleepy, you desire rest; and so forth and so on. One of the things that characterizes desires is that they don't pay attention to each other. Desires are essentially conflictual. That's why James says in chapter 4 of his little letter, "Where does war come from?"[15] He says it comes from your desires. Desire does not address the issue of what is good. It simply says, "I want that." And it neglects everything else.

In our culture, one of the things we are most apt to miss is the difference between desire and will. The will is meant to be the arbitrator of desires. That's why when we speak of the will, we often think of deliberation. Think about that word: *de-liberation*. It's the work of the will that frees you up. It gives you a choice. Desire doesn't care anything about choice; it cares about a particular thing. It has focused on a determinate object: "I want that."

Children are dominated by desire. One of the things the parent has to say now and then is, "No, Johnny, you don't want that." To which Johnny responds, "I *do* want that." Sometimes we have to give in so that Johnny will learn that he didn't want something after all. That's us training a child's will: We help them learn how to deliberate. The will is designed to make a choice.

Desire alone, divorced from the will, ruins peoples' lives time after time. In our public life and even among leaders of our denominations or church organizations, time after time we see a desire that has been harbored and protected—nursed instead of deliberated—ruining the life of the person or group that they are leading. Your desires are not your friends.

That's the most shocking thing I believe I say to my students. They are great believers in desire, and yet if they allow themselves to be dominated by their desires, their lives will be ruined. But ask them, "Well now, suppose you have a choice between studying for the exam tomorrow or going to the movie with your friends." And they will immediately recognize that if you do what you want—if you allow your desires to dominate—you are going to be in serious trouble. The whole point of ethics as it has developed in the human scene from the beginning is to give you a reason for not doing what you want to do and for doing what you don't want to do. And anytime you find a person with any degree of any success in any area, it will be because they have known *not* to do what they wanted to do and *to do* what they don't want to do.

Can you identify with that? See, doing what you don't want to do is the key to emotional maturity.

Emotions are a third force—things like love and hate and shame. Emotions are deeply rooted in who you are in your identity and in your character. But they, too, are conflictual. And if you try to live by your emotions, you will ruin your life.

Now emotions are great—you have to have them, and in fact, emotional richness is the key to emotional maturity. But you have to be very careful and not just be the plaything of your emotions, or, like desires and feelings, they will ruin your life. And they are going to make people around you miserable too. If you live in a family with emotional babies, it's not a good place to be. We all need people around us who are able to have emotions and feelings and desires under the governance of what is good.

The emotions, the desires, and the feelings are manifestations of "flesh." Biblically, *flesh* refers to the natural powers of human beings. Flesh is not bad. But you can't allow flesh to rule your life. To the extent you do allow it to rule your life, you get the fearsome list of things in Galatians 5: the works of the flesh.

> The deeds of the flesh are evident, which are: immorality, impurity, sensuality, idolatry, sorcery, enmities, strife, jealousy, outbursts of anger, disputes, dissensions, factions, envying, drunkenness, carousing, and things like these, of which I forewarn you, just as I have forewarned you, that those who practice such things will not inherit the kingdom of God.[16]

We look at that list and probably just want to turn away. But what Paul is doing is listing what shows up in ordinary human life. He is giving us an account of what the natural human abilities, left to themselves, will produce. And he winds up by saying those who do such things do not inherit—they don't come into interactive relationship with, they don't live in—the Kingdom of God. And because they don't live in the Kingdom of God, they have no alternative to a life dominated by emotions, desires, and feelings.

Of course, Paul goes on quickly to talk about the fruit of the Spirit: love, joy, peace, and so on. It's this fruit that's the mark of the person who is emotionally and spiritually mature. Emotional maturity refers primarily to having our feelings, desires, and emotions under the guidance and control of what is good. The will deliberates about what is good, speaking to our natural tendencies and saying, as needed, "No, that's not good." Living for what is good is what characterizes the emotionally mature person.

Sometimes this is called self-control, by which we mean that the self has a broad view: not just what is wanted, but what is good. To be emotionally mature is to be in a position to control what is wanted in terms of what is good. Where this dwells in the person, we talk about in the next lecture.

Secular thought has not succeeded in solving this problem. And so today, in our culture, there's immense confusion on such things as what is good and what is right. It has become a political contest.

Consider how often we find ourselves waiting for the word to come down from the Supreme Court on a particular law. We tend today to make of the Supreme Court the ultimate arbitrator of what is good and what is right. But each Supreme Court decision is not a statement of what is good and right but what our politics affords us. Even in the church, there are real problems with asserting simple goodness and rightness. Don't steal, don't lie—"Well, really? Maybe, you know."

We've lost confidence in our knowledge of what is good. Secular thought has proven itself unable, over a period of about two hundred years, to answer the question of how you direct the factors of emotion under what is good, because it has lost confidence in what is good. The emotionally mature person, on the other hand, is able to direct their "wants," to speak simply, in terms of what is good. The spiritually mature person is someone who has chosen the Kingdom of God—God's reign over them—as their guide to what is good. And not only that, but the Kingdom is understood as what will enable them to achieve and live for what is good. They have developed the knowledge and habits that keep them constantly turned toward and expectant of God and God's action in their life. This is the primary source of direction and empowerment for all that concerns them and their world.

For example, the spiritually mature person will look at some wrong-doing and say, "Why would anyone want to do that? Let's bless instead of curse." They can do that because their mind is turned constantly to the world of God and God's presence with them.

The Lord's Prayer is a typical expression of the spiritually mature person. It starts out, "Our Father who art in heaven." Now, biblically, that means, "Our Father always near." So that's the vision. "Our Father who is always near . . ."

"Hallowed be Thy name." This first articulation is a recognition of the goodness of God. I don't know what the word *hallowed* does for you—not much for most people. It simply means to think highly of, to regard as precious. God is near and God is good—that's our starting point.

"Thy Kingdom come" is not a prayer about end times. It's a prayer about this time. "Thy Kingdom come" where I am. "Thy will be done *on earth*," where I am, "as it's done in heaven." How would you say it's done in heaven? Pretty well, wouldn't you think? So, I'm asking that God's will would be done in my life, where I am now, in what I'm doing, wherever I am and whatever that involves, that the Kingdom of God would come into that.

"Give us today our daily bread and forgive us our debts, as we forgive our debtors." We are acknowledging our needs for basic provision and forgiveness for wrongdoing. These are desires that have passed through the deliberative work of the will. We know this because we've not simply sought forgiveness but have committed ourselves to living in a context of forgiveness.

"Lead us not into trouble, but deliver us from everything that's bad." We begin the prayer acknowledging that God is near—nearer to us than trouble—and that God's goodness can deliver us from everything that's bad. This is the prayer that expresses the emotional and spiritual maturity of Jesus. This kind of prayer characterizes emotional and spiritual maturity. Indeed, to pray this prayer is to set out on the path of maturity.

I want to take a moment to describe the Kingdom of God, because it is sometimes presented in a way that is puzzling. You can't be secure in spiritual and emotional maturity unless you understand the Kingdom of God.

Living in the Kingdom of God

The only thing that allows you to live without fear is to live in the Kingdom of God.

The Kingdom of God is God acting—what God is doing. It is His reigning—where what God wants done *is* done. It is the range of God's effective will.

Those are different ways of describing the same thing. Basically, the Kingdom of God is God in action, and He's in action many ways. One of the reasons why nature is so wonderful is because it is God in action. People often don't know why they are so refreshed when they go into nature; it's because they are experiencing God in action. I am often amazed myself. I can look at a huge pile of earth and rock called a mountain and somehow be reassured. Isn't that strange? Well, actually it's because it expresses the greatness of God, the majesty of God. And perhaps we don't know what it is, but it's there just the same.

The Kingdom of God is not political or social reality; it is not even the church. For many centuries, the church thought it was the Kingdom of God. But you don't have to look at most churches for very long until you see that, well, it isn't where what God wants done is done. Churches at their best are like hospitals, where people are drawn in to be helped and sent out with a wholeness that they didn't have before. But churches are not the Kingdom of God. And that's very important for us to understand.

That doesn't mean we downgrade the church. We just have to recognize what it is. The Kingdom of God is different. And when Jesus says the Kingdom of the Heavens or the Kingdom of God is at hand, He doesn't mean the church is at hand. It may or may not be at hand, but that's a different kind of question.

The Kingdom of God is an everlasting metaphysical reality. God and His reign are the natural home of the soul. The Kingdom of God invites us to live in it and call it home. What does that mean? To live in the range of His effective will.

Once you understand that, you can begin to see the point of many of Jesus' teachings—teachings that have to do with complete trust. I read the passage from Paul, "Be anxious for nothing," but that's Jesus' teaching, isn't it? Don't worry about the provisions for life. Paul declares it, but Jesus points us to flowers and birds and things of that sort and assures us that if we are in the Kingdom of God, it is a perfectly safe place for us to be.

It's really important for us to hold on to that when we're in times of trouble, because sometimes we can't see it, and we need to remember Paul's words: "Everything works together for good to those who love God and are inducted or called into what God is doing."[17] Everything works together for good in God's Kingdom. How can this be? It's because, in the Kingdom of God, we have a future for good in which even things that are not good by themselves will be redeemed. Paul does not say everything is good. He says everything works together for good, to those who love God and are called into His purposes—who are caught up in His life. Being caught up in the life that God is now living on earth is a good way of thinking of salvation. In such a life, everything that happens to us is redeemed—even the things that happen to us that in themselves are not very attractive. They don't look good. We're not here to call things that don't look good "good" by themselves; rather, we refer them to the larger context of the Kingdom of God.

It's in the Kingdom of God that the spiritually mature person has learned to live. To choose to live in the Kingdom of God is to live from resources that enable us to not do what we want to do. All temptation takes the form of "If you don't do this, you're going to miss out on something that's very good." It always presents itself in that way. And if we harbor desires that are wrong, we are holding on to a promise that there is something we really need to have. But the Kingdom of God comes and says, "No, you are abundantly provided for. If you don't get what you want, you are still in a world where what is good for you will prove to be what you really want and will come to pass."

It's essential for us to have our understanding of ourselves redeemed. How do you think about yourself? If you are unable to see yourself living

.. ωe Kingdom of God, you will constantly be troubled by the things you wanted and the things you didn't get. And you will be tempted to take things that are not good for you. When that doesn't work, you will be disappointed and hurt and angry, and you will probably reject yourself and others around you. You will not be able to love those who are in your presence. You will be filled with fear because you are trying to run your own kingdom.

It is the Kingdom of God that is the source of integrated life—a life that is able to find in the provisions of God what is adequate to their souls. So if you're going to be a spiritually mature person, you have to think of yourself in a different way.

I want to try out some wording and see if you can identify with it: "I am an unceasing spiritual being with an eternal destiny in God's great universe." Say that yourself: That's the understanding of yourself that will make spiritual maturity possible. You are an unceasing spiritual being with an eternal destiny in God's great universe.

When we come to talk later about the role of the disciplines in spiritual growth, we will talk about the role of the mind. If you in your mind don't have an adequate conception of the Kingdom and of yourself, it will be impossible to lead a life of integrity around the character of Jesus Christ. And as a result, you will probably be incapable of emotional maturity as we've described it. So, maybe you could just practice standing before the mirror in the morning or the evening and telling yourself, "I am an unceasing spiritual being with an eternal destiny in God's great universe."

Now, when we say those words, we need to check: *Do I really believe that?* We don't talk much about such things in our churches. It makes a lot of people uneasy. But you cannot rest in the purposes of God for your life unless you understand who you are. How you think about who you are enables you to deal with life in a way that is emotionally and spiritually mature. The Kingdom of God allows you to step into a future that involves your continuing life with God and with others forever.

Take a look at Revelation 22:5 and meditate on what you're going to be doing a thousand years from now. Do you have plans for that? We often sing the great old hymn, "When we've been there ten thousand years, bright shining as the sun, we've no less days to sing God's praise than when we'd first begun." Now, actually I think there's going to be a lot going on other than singing. You may want to put some thought into that for your future life in the Kingdom of God.

The life of the spiritually mature person in Christ is one freed from domination both from those internal dominations of emotions, feelings, and desires, but also from the traditions and habits of our fallen world. For most of us, domination comes to us automatically as we are born and we're living with a family and then with playmates and neighbors and going to school and growing up through life. The push for domination by feelings, emotions, and desires is overwhelming for most people because they have nowhere else to stand. It's by recognizing that you have a place in the Kingdom of God that you are allowed to say, "I don't need to be a part of that."

"The world," in one of the main senses that it's used in the Bible, refers to the order of activity that comes out of flesh—emotions, feelings, and desires—getting organized and systematically pursuing its ends. When you look at the way things go in the world, you have to recognize that this is something that developed over time; the old trilogy of the world, the flesh, and the devil is a real, hard-bitten reality. John says in his letter, "What is in the world is the lust of the flesh, the lust of the eyes, and the pride of life."[18] Stepping into alignment with Jesus begins the renewal of your mind. Then you can recognize another way of living.

Lust is an encompassing word, ἐπιθυμία (*epithumia*), for the kinds of desires that tend to run people's lives. The lust of the flesh—the natural desires of the embodied, socialized self. The lust of the eyes—the experiences of looking and being looked at that we find ourselves craving. It's an amazing amount of human life that runs on "How do I look?" and "How do you look?" For example, calling a little child stupid or wicked or some other negative thing (or, by contrast, making much of a child's good looks or great intelligence to the point that it becomes for them a solely defining characteristic) can shape how they see themselves and then how they act, and sometimes it follows them through their whole life. Entering the Kingdom of God enables them to break out of that and to back away and look and say, "Well, there are just three things going on here: the lust of the flesh, the lust of the eyes, and the pride of life." Pride of life is essentially domination of others or being dominated. It is reducing a person's identity to their relation to some other person. Think what a tremendous role that plays in ordinary human life.

Life with Jesus in the Kingdom of God relieves us of this kind of envious and resentful comparison with others. As you step into alignment with Jesus and your mind begins to be reworked, you begin to recognize another way of living. It's by recognizing that you have a place in the Kingdom of God that you are allowed to say, "I don't need to be a part of that."

As we arrive at this understanding, then our emotional and spiritual maturity increases, because we are no longer trying to run the world by how we feel. We are rather orienting ourselves to the Kingdom of God. And the Scriptures become our instruction guide to that end. If we observe someone doing beautifully in sports or business, or whatever it is, the lust of the flesh and of the eyes and the pride of life might steer us toward resentment. But we have stepped into a future that involves our continuing life with God and with others forever. And what are we taught to do in this continuing life? Rejoice with those that rejoice. Do not envy. Do not resent. As we embrace these instructions, we are freed up into an additional dimension of personal integrity, because we can now, in love and understanding, admire what needs to be admired and care for what needs to be cared for without all the negative stuff that comes with the lust of the flesh, the lust of the eyes, and the pride of life. Now we have a different place to live.

It's here where the fruit of the Spirit takes the place of the works of the flesh. Fruit comes from nature, which distinguishes it from both work and even gifts. The fruit of the Spirit comes forth in us not as an outcome of our works or even as a manifestation of our core giftedness; it comes as a natural expression. We have been increasingly transformed away from the domination of our feelings and all that goes with that in fallen reality, and we are moving more and more into the harmony of truth that characterizes the Kingdom of God. Love, joy, peace, long-suffering, gentleness, goodness, kindness, meekness, faithfulness, self-control are the natural expressions of that Kingdom—they are the natural expression of our Kingdom nature.

And so, when we talk about the person who is spiritually and emotionally mature, we are thinking about people with natures other than what is natural to the world around us. And in our next lecture [chapter 4] we will go into this in much greater depth. But at this point, we just want to emphasize that when you live from the Spirit, the light of the Kingdom floods your life.

One of the things that characterizes the emotionally and spiritually mature person is that they are not hiding. That doesn't mean that they just pour themselves out on every passing person. It means that they are honest, straightforward—when they meet you there's nothing behind their back.

When I am living under God, I leave you free to be who you are. Meanwhile, I am free to be who I am. I am trusting myself to the Kingdom of God that surrounds me. That's where my confidence is, and as a result, the constant contact with God frees me up from the chaos and destructiveness of the works of the flesh.

That contrast between the lusts and the freedom that comes from surrender to and redemption with God is set out in 2 Peter 1:2: "Grace and peace be multiplied to you in the knowledge of God and of Jesus our Lord." Knowledge is true representation of how things are. I realize that is a little complicated, but if you have knowledge, then you understand and are able to represent things as they are. Among other things, we know from the Scriptures that God is love—"God so loved the world, that He gave His only begotten Son," and so forth.[19] And Jesus Christ is a manifestation of the love and presence of God in our world. That knowledge of God and of Jesus enables us to act in trust.

Look at the abundance of provision here: "His divine power has granted to us everything pertaining to life and godliness."[20] It blows your mind, doesn't it, when you think about it? Everything pertaining to life and godliness. How many things does that leave out? Nothing. That's the abundance of life in the Kingdom that comes to the person who is spiritually mature. It enables them to be mature in every respect—spiritually and emotionally.

"True knowledge of Him who called us by His own glory and excellence."[21] Note that this knowledge is emphatic—"true."

Now, watch the next one here: "For by these He has granted to us His precious and magnificent promises, so that by them you may become partakers of the divine nature, having escaped the corruption that is in the world by *epithumia*."[22] We don't really have a good English word to translate that, so most of the translations say, "the corruption that is in the world by lust." Corruption means a breaking apart, a loss of integrity. Things don't fit together. Corruption refers to the failure of function: The parts of the fallen human being don't function well. So, for example, you have people who don't know what the will is, and they think their desires are their will. If they do that, they are not going to function well because they are dominated by desire, which (as James reminded us) leads to all sorts of conflicts and failures. Their will isn't working, and their whole system is in a state of breaking apart—it's *corrupt*. That's what characterizes the emotionally immature person.

The spiritually mature person has the resources and knowledge to enable them to function well with every part of their being—their body, their social relations. They are following what is right and what is good, not simply what they want (or what someone else wants, which is a different and very serious problem).

"You may become partakers of the divine nature, having escaped the corruption that is in the world by lust."[23] Partakers of the divine nature have escaped corruption—we're not dominated by emotions. The only way to have a rich emotional life is to not be dominated by emotions, but rather follow what is good with your emotions, your desires, and even your feelings. A rich emotional life is a life caught up in truth and beauty and goodness in the concrete details. It might be just the devotion to some important cause in society, of education, or politics, or art, but life is rich when it is directed by what is good—because you are living in the Kingdom of God. You have been born into it, you have allowed things to grow so that progressively every aspect of your life is taken over by the Kingdom of God. And the provision that is made for us is more than adequate for every need that we have.

When we speak this way of the Christian life, sometimes people think we are just sort of puffing something up. But you cannot know the reality of this Kingdom life except by living in it. Living a life of emotional maturity is how we come to have solid knowledge of the goodness of emotional maturity. It allows us not to be captured by what is wrong and not to make others miserable by how we are behaving in relationship to them. Having stepped into a future that involves our continuing life with God and with others forever, we have availed ourselves of the absolute sufficiency of the present God, Jesus Christ, for every need that we have.

So let me just say once again: The emotionally mature person is one in whom all of the tensions of desire and feeling and emotion are resolved in the sense of goodness that guides their life. All of their feelings, desires, and emotions are under the guidance of what is good. They don't find themselves overwhelmed by their desires; they do what is good.

That is, in fact, what people without reference to Christianity tend to regard as a good person. But how do you manage that? By being spiritually mature—by taking assurance from God that what is good will be provided to them not only now but forever.

. . .

With that, Dallas sat down. People began lining up to ask him questions. I wanted a conversation with Dallas as well, but this was not the time. I spent the next year preparing for that conversation. The BIOLA Center for Christian Thought had received a grant for a fellowship year integrating neuroscience with theology under Dallas Willard. With Dallas's encouragement, I applied, but Dallas did not make it there. In the next chapter, you will read the conversation on neurotheology that never happened.

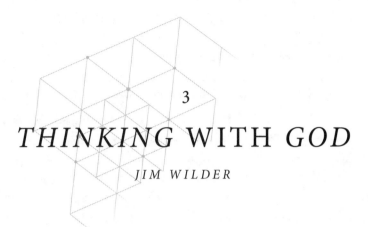

3

THINKING WITH GOD

JIM WILDER

Dallas was sitting on the front pew by the time I reached the front of the church. A line of conference participants wrapped around the end of the pew and down the aisle. Jane was standing at the other end of the pew, waiting to take Dallas to the speaker's room. He sat looking down at the floor, answering questions and hearing the comments from all who came. When he spoke, his voice was soft and warm.

Jane (and the group that sets Dallas's schedule) had agreed to this conference on the grounds that I would allow Dallas to rest. I would provide a nearby room with a place to lie down, eat, drink, and such necessities. According to these terms, it fell to me to get Dallas some rest. He was having none of it. He had just said, "See, doing what you don't want to do is the key to emotional maturity." A live demonstration was underway.

Standing between the Willards at the front of the church represented a position I had filled occasionally over the twenty-five years we had known each other. I had one foot in each of their worlds. My PhD—my "doctor of philosophy" (Dallas's world)—is in psychology (Jane's world). We studied very little philosophy in school, but I avoided total ignorance by reading the philosophy books suggested by my brother Timothy, who did his graduate work in philosophy and theology. We had many long, critical, and fruitful talks. My training in theology was supplemented by his love for translating theology from original-language sources.

Under Jane's leadership as director of training at Shepherd's House, we counseled a steady stream of immature people. Jane tested what Dallas taught in the troubled waters of people's lives. In her counseling "lab," Jane and I soon discovered that when people were traumatized, they stopped maturing in the area of their identity altered by trauma. Traumas come from two sources: bad things that should not happen and necessary, good things that did not happen. Both sources left people alone with critical needs at critical times. It proved relatively easy to resolve trauma from bad things that happened.[1] Insuring that the person was no longer alone in their troubles converted trauma (alone and frozen in pain) back to suffering (how life experiences an evil world). It was much harder to correct trauma caused when crucial good things did not happen. For example, seeing a murder was resolved more easily than never having been loved.

Even once a trauma was resolved, a person was still no more mature than they were before. Maturity development must be restarted from where growth was stopped by trauma. Think of a child who breaks a hand. While he or she is in a cast, the class learns to play piano. When the hand heals, the child still cannot play music like all the others. The child must now learn to play. Learning may be harder because of limitations with the healed hand.

On this conference day, the conditions with Dallas provided a graphic, and very human, illustration of the tension between spiritual and emotional maturity. Dallas had just lectured that the mature person is governed by the will and not by desires, feelings, and emotions. He was providing a clear illustration of this maturity. Rather than going to get a drink, take care of his body, or rest, he was willfully engaging with everyone in line. His willful purpose was to care for others. This was what he had just taught.

Dallas demonstrated, and very well, the triumph of will over desire. But the will was exactly what was not working for immature people in the counseling "lab." Just when wounded and immature people needed their will, it was not there. A strong will gave evidence of maturity, but willpower failed repeatedly as a method to *produce* maturity. Dallas would soon tell us that developing maturity based on willpower produces endless failures. We will return to this issue in chapter 5, once we have read Dallas's next lecture on the components of a human person.

Neuroscience and Mutual Mind

A careful observer at the front of the church would have noticed something in the neurological activity of the group gathered there. What was not being said provided an unexpected explanation and solution for developing spiritual maturity. While I fretted about helping Dallas rest, I noticed that all the people to his right showed signs of concern, while most people on his left seemed oblivious. How did I know?

Dr. Daniel Siegel would call my awareness "mindsight."[2] Most of us might call it "body language." Yet, it is not the language we must consider but rather, how we decode what others are thinking. How does the brain know what is going on in another brain?

For instance, I saw Jane was standing rather than sitting as she glanced from Dallas to the exit. My mindsight decoded this as "Jane wants Dallas to rest." This "knowing" what others are thinking, while they are still thinking and before they have said anything, has a profound impact on us. Indeed, we are often influenced by what others think even when they are not present or have long since died.

When two minds tune their mindsight on each other it creates a state of "mutual mind." Dr. Allan Schore uses the classical term *intersubjectivity* when describing mutual mind and how it creates our identities.[3] Mutual-mind states synchronize human thought, motivation, energy, and activities by helping two brains experience the same internal state of activation, together and in real time. Without this synchronization, any kind of cooperative effort would fail. Everything from teamwork to intimacy depends on mutual mind between humans.

A mutual state of brain activation is illustrated by running together while passing a ball. The mind must sense our speed and intentions along with the speed and intentions of others and change our pace accordingly. For this coordinated action to work, the brain must be able to speed up and slow down the energy for each player, so they move together. Whatever part of the brain creates mutual mind can regulate our energy.

What Dallas called "emotions, feelings, and desires" are relational-energy states of the mind. Mature character can regulate these energy states and do what is good instead of whatever we desire. The brain system that creates mindsight and mutual mind is the same one that regulates our relational energy. This mechanism that creates mutual mind begins operation when we are five months old. As this relational-engagement system grows, it learns to self-regulate.

What Dallas calls emotional maturity, then, is self-regulation. And for the brain, self-regulation—emotional maturity—is deeply relational.

What of spiritual maturity? Dallas just said that spiritual and normal, human emotional maturity regulate our emotional energy. Spiritual and emotional maturity must then use the same brain functions. Appropriate emotional regulation in relationship to others requires that we understand what others are experiencing in the moment. Regulating our emotions in relationships requires a working mutual-mind state. How well we regulate ourselves in relationship to others is what we call *character*.

The connection between mutual mind and character raises new possibilities. Under the right conditions, human brains create a mutual mind with each other and learn how to respond to life. Are mutual-mind states only possible between humans? Can we have a mutual-mind state with God?

Dallas had spoken passionately about the nearness of God. Is God so near that we could share a mutual mind? For God's will to be done on earth in "real time," human brains would need some sort of mutual-mind state with God. A mutual-mind state with God would be possible only if God is with us and limited divine thoughts to a form we could understand. Without a "real-time" mutual mind with God in each situation, we will not respond as God would respond. Without mutual mind, we will fail to react as God is reacting. Only in retrospect will we think of what God wanted when things happened. By that point, we already will have responded without the character of Christ.

There is a large difference between thinking *about* God being with us and thinking *with* God about our reality. Mutual-mind states *with* God could produce a *with-God life*. We would think *with* God rather than simply *about* God. When we think back about what God wanted in a past moment, we can feel remorse, but thinking *with* God changes our *initial* reactions—it changes our *character*.

Does God intend to use the mutual-mind system He created in the brain to help us think more like God thinks and regulate our responses to match His? Such intimate character training requires us to accept a very relational gospel. We will need to explore the nature of mutual-mind states and how they are produced before we can answer.

Creating a Mutual-Mind State

As I stood in front of Dallas, I looked toward Jane. I said no words, but my face said, "I am trying to get Dallas to go rest." Jane's mind created a mutual-mind state with mine in less than a second. Twenty-five years of relationship with Jane and memory of conversations before the conference combined faster than I could think consciously. We communicated far faster than words. Her head tilted slightly, and her face answered, "I know. That is how he is." Jane's smile didn't change from her social smile so I knew leaving Dallas here was not okay with her. We were in a mutual-mind state. I knew what was in her mind that moment. I was thinking *with* Jane rather than *about* Jane. Mutual mind shaped the character of my responses.

As soon as we say "thinking," our minds lock on to conscious thought. Yet what we monitor consciously is a very small part of our mental process. There has been speculation about subconscious and preconscious thought, but until the 1990s, very little was known about mental processes that are faster than conscious thought. Some part of the mind creates our sense of who we are, what is around us, and how we will react before we begin a conscious analysis. A sudden loud sound behind us, for example, finds us in the air well before we can consciously think it through:

> *Hmmm. There is a lot of motion in my eardrums just now. I bet that is a loud sound. Loud sounds, unlike soft sounds, have a higher-than-average probability of being from something powerful. Now, as I consider what might be behind me, try as I might, I don't remember seeing anything powerful. So, the sudden appearance of something powerful requires attention. My best preparation for an encounter is a sudden dose of adrenaline—where is that release valve? In case the powerful thing is big, I will also jump, so I appear*

bigger than I am. Following that, it makes sense to turn quickly and investigate. Maybe quickly exhaling and making a loud noise will also help. Go!

A supraconscious brain process stays ahead of conscious thought. Because we cannot consciously catch up with the faster process, we do not see it running above conscious awareness. When we think about thinking, we ignore where most thinking happens. For example, we simply assume that we always know who we are. We are unaware that the brain is constantly calculating the answer to *Who am I now?* The fast calculator's answers to *Who I am now?* become our spontaneous responses.

The brain's fast-track processing grows in, and is dominated by, the right brain. At the center of the fast-track system is the right cingulate cortex, which synthesizes mutual mind "on the fly." We have already seen hints that this same system regulates our energy for emotions, feelings, desires, and impulses—both internally and externally—in relationship to others.

Mutual-mind states are produced through visual cues and voice tone rather than words. Most visual cues come from the left side of the face we are observing. The emotional state of the fast track in the right brain is displayed on the left side of the face. Because of our eyes' optics, the left side of the face we are observing shows up on the left side of each retina. Signals from the left side of both eyes are sent to our right brain. This is the right-brain-to-right-brain communication path. Our observing right brain returns a message. The original sender receives back a visual message about the state of our right brain.

It takes about 165 milliseconds (a sixth of a second) for a full round trip from one right brain to another right brain and back again. It will take our conscious mind 15 milliseconds longer to become aware that we have seen someone's face. By then, a second round is already underway. Through this fast-track "thinking," the minds of two people begin to synchronize. In a matter of seconds, they are using the same circuits, matching chemistry, experiencing similar energy levels, and sharing one experience.

Right-brain-to-right-brain communication is rapid, authentic, and quite a bit faster than conscious thought can track. Consciously, we are too slow to fake our messages. Each person feels like the state was created by the other. "You make me smile!" or "You are making me mad!" or "You started it!" are all signs of a mutual-mind state.

Spiritual Disciplines and Mindfulness

Mutual mind is not the same as the increasingly popular concept of mindfulness or the experience of mindsight I mentioned earlier in this chapter, although the three ideas are quite related. *Mindfulness* makes us aware and present in the moment. *Mindsight* lets us know there is a mind behind the face we see. *Mutual mind* connects us mind-to-mind with another in that moment. Mutual mind develops in a mindful state. If we are not mindfully aware in the present moment, we cannot "read" what another mind is thinking (mindsight). Without accurate mindsight, we cannot manage to synchronize our mental state with someone else. Mutual mind comes from the same brain structures that produce mindfulness and mindsight.

Standing third in line to see Dallas, a woman looked mindlessly at me while she rummaged inside a large purse. Her eyes drifted vacantly as she dug deeper. She didn't see me right in front of her, but I watched her agitation increase as she failed to find what she was seeking. She was not mindfully present at all. She told me all this without intending to because I tracked her mind visually. In this case, I was tracking a lack of response to my face that told me she was not mindfully present by using the same fast-track brain system that would make mutual-mind possible if she had been.

Mindfulness is the basic state needed for relationship. Numerous writers give special attention to ways that mindfulness affects prayer. Dr. Charles Stone combines cognitive neuroscience[4] and spiritual disciplines. He blends Christian traditions with practical steps for Christian mindfulness. Dr. Gregory Bottaro teaches mindful awareness of the present moment in the context of Catholic prayer practices.[5] These (and many other) writers carefully distinguish Christian mindfulness from Eastern religious practices and stay in harmony with the spiritual disciplines Dallas encouraged.

Similar to what Dallas will soon tell us about the spiritual disciplines, mindfulness cannot be considered a righteous act.[6] Mindfulness and spiritual disciplines are preparations for encountering God. Goodness is not found in the preparations but in the encounter they help facilitate.

In his work on mindfulness, Dr. Curt Thompson, who spoke at the Heart and Soul Conference, combines neuroscience and spiritual practices with special attention to the effects of mindfulness on relationships.[7] Curt was not content to give lectures but made a special point to connect relationally with the other speakers. He understood that spiritual maturity is developed, tested, and observed by the way our spiritual practices influence relationships. He makes a very significant point. Christian mindfulness is relational and is based on attachment to God and others. Talking with God grows from loving attachment with God in which each party genuinely cares about the other's point of view.

MINDFULNESS, MINDSIGHT, MUTUAL MIND, AND MEDITATION—WITH AND WITHOUT ATTACHMENT

We can distinguish mindful and meditative practices that are (a) without mutual mind, from those (b) created by mutual mind. One must be careful when reading brain-scan studies of "spiritual" states to notice if they are studying unattached mindful awareness or a mutual mind with a living God. "Spiritual" sounds righteous, but the two are not the same.

Mindful states tend to produce a decreased sense of self. In nonattached mindful awareness, the mind fills with the present reality. We can be such a small part of that reality that it seems we nearly cease to exist. Typically, "transcendent" is used to describe this experience. While we may feel "one" with everything, a transcendent state does little to shape character.

In a mutual-mind state, where there exists a loving attachment with the beloved other, the mechanism that reduces the sense of self operates differently. In a mutual mind, mindful, and meditative state, we are caught up in the love, joy, peace, or even distress of the beloved one. In mutual mind, we cannot consciously be sure which are our thoughts and feelings and which come from the beloved other. A mutual-mind state touches our relational identity through attachment.

Limits of Conscious Activity

It is quite easy to mistake *understanding ideas* for a *mutual-mind state*. Let's say three theologians—a Muslim cleric, a Jewish rabbi, and Christian seminary professor—explore the idea that Jesus is God. The three theologians can come to a very clear agreement about the idea and its implications and yet not be of one mind. When it comes to their persons and identities, their mutual understanding of an idea has not become mutual-mind.

Ideas are communicated at the speed of words, but mutual mind is nonverbal—usually visual. A look, like a picture, can speak a thousand words. As Dallas sat answering questions, he kept his gaze on the floor. He did not make eye contact with the woman in front of him even as he thoughtfully and carefully answered her question. Dallas and the woman were both mindfully present—Dallas was directing her conscious attention to conscious ideas. The two were in a state of joint directed attention. Dallas did not look up to see the look on her face, which indicated she was following his thoughts and words with delight.

Even with this deep level of engagement, the two were not in a mutual-mind state. The physical means of visual communication was interrupted. Their energy levels did not match as they would in mutual-mind. The lady was in a very high energy state of excitement with rapture on her face. When her face lit up in response to something Dallas said, he showed no change in his pensive, measured delivery. He was in a state of focused conscious attention but they were not in mutual mind.

The brain system that forms and changes character runs under mutual-mind but not under focused conscious attention. In practice, that means that while Dallas was engaging the woman and helping her understand him, the conversation in and of itself was not formational to her character.

The focused conscious thought system that Dallas was using allowed him to focus on deep ideas. At the same time, it limited the scope of his attention. The fast-track system I was using allowed me to tell a great deal about the maturity of each one in line to talk to Dallas. At a moment's glance it was clear who was mindful, who was self-absorbed, who saw the needs of others, and who was being swept away by their emotions at that moment. Dallas was not using his eyes for communication, so this information was not available to him.

Western education and Christian life have come to rely on conscious thoughts formed in the slow-track systems of the brain. A soteriology of attachment shifts Christian life to the fast track, as we will see. Our methods become face-to-face and eye-to-eye.

The conscious mind must, by its design, focus attention on details.

Our conscious mind is like a dog with a cone on its head that limits what it can see. Consciously, we are unable to fully grasp reality. This is not a case of being *out of touch* with reality—we can grasp reality in our faster-than-conscious mind. The problem with conscious thought is that *it is not aware of being unaware* of what it fails to notice. (Yes, I did say that!) The philosopher of science Michael Polanyi once said, "Unbridled lucidity can destroy our understanding of complex matters,"[8] which is another way to say that when we focus on details, we miss reality. He called what we know faster than conscious thought "tacit knowledge."

Dr. Iain McGilchrist calls the conscious mind the "emissary" for the brain.[9] Although this emissary does exceedingly well with investigating details, it cannot grasp the whole picture. The business of the conscious emissary is coordinated using the slower brain systems of the left brain. Dr. Marcus Warner and I have called those conscious systems the "slow track" of the brain.[10] What McGilchrist has called the "master" system, we have called the "fast track" of the brain because it runs faster than conscious speed and is managed from the right brain.

THE FAST TRACK AND SLOW TRACK IN THE BRAIN

To help us understand the difference between the fast-track (right-brain dominant) process and the slow-track (left-brain dominant) process, picture yourself outside on a dark summer's night. You are taking in the whole experience. Fireflies, stars, warm breeze, grass that could use mowing, rustling leaves, realizing dinner is in the oven for another twenty minutes, the children are happy, a mosquito bite itches, family visits to your grandparent's farm come to mind with the games there at dusk. You find yourself humming and taking a deep breath that brings with it the faint smell of paint drying on the deck. Your fast track takes everything in, incorporating your current moment with your people and memories of your past.

Something large moves in the darkness among the trees. The fast track remembers that bears are large, dark, and among trees. You don't think of this as remembering because by the time you are conscious of the noise, you already are reacting with fear and your attention is focused on a spot. The fast track has sent its emissary to grab the flashlight and shine it in the woods. Gone is the reality of the stars, fireflies, mosquito bite, and your grandparent's farm. Like the flashlight, your attention is focused on a very small part of the world. The flashlight cannot capture the reality of the night. It can see only a tiny bit. The two eyes looking back from that tiny spot in the woods becomes its world.

Behold! Your neighbor has a cow.

This conscious mind (slow track) cannot grasp reality. Like the flashlight, it sees only a bit at a time. The conscious mind cannot even fully grasp that it cannot see reality because it only knows what has gained its attention. Sometimes, like when we are engrossed looking through a telescope at the night sky, someone comes up behind us and scares the daylights out of us. At those moments, the conscious mind realizes that there is more reality than what we noticed. The conscious slow track will select a detail that has its attention as the explanation. Soon, its attention will shift to something else.

When our Christianity is only in our conscious mind, our attention shifts from one virtue or sin to another but forgets to monitor the rest of our character. We will focus our conscious attention just in time to see our sinful reactions.

Unlike the emissary (slow track) that cannot understand reality because it sees trees and not forests, the master (fast track) system refuses to be focused. The fast track considers all input and all related memory at once. The goal of the fast track (master system) is to establish our reality at this moment and answer what we (and our people) do under these conditions.

Character reflects what we have learned to be when things get "like this."

Maturity is the sum of our memories of what we and our people do when things get "like this."

A properly trained and uninjured fast track performs many identity functions: individual identity; group identity; social engagement; attachment to our important people; awareness and understanding of other minds; providing moral thoughts and values; remembering important lessons from our past; finding and remembering our role models; maintaining joyful relationships; preserving our shalom/peace; taking action when peace is missing; regulating emotions, feelings, and desires; and more. By comparison, the slow track focuses on details and finds if they are important, explains what things are and how they work, solves problems, matches words with experience, develops procedures to get results, and keeps a narrative of our conscious experience.

While Dallas was putting his slow track and its words to good use, the fast tracks around him held numerous, almost instantaneous conversations. The slow track used words to convey many good ideas; people's character and maturity was displayed in the fast-track communication.

The second woman in line was becoming increasingly irritated. She glanced back and forth between Dallas and the woman at his feet. Dallas was taking way too long to answer that question! The seated woman with the blissful look was disregarding the rest of the line—letting Dallas go on and on like that. How inconsiderate! She shot me the "Can't you do something?" demand look. She said nothing aloud. But now you know how I knew.

Fourth in line, a man was wondering if he should come back later. He glanced at me. His eyebrow lowered, and he looked at Dallas. He looked back at me, concerned. I glanced at my watch and shook my head slightly. The man understood. He turned and attempted to take the next man in line with him. "We should go and let him rest," he said, but the next man eagerly stepped into the open place in line—mindsight failing.

Fast Track and Character

Character is not only displayed and communicated by the fast track; it is also learned and changed for the better or worse by the fast track. Character is housed and remembered in the fast-track structures. Character and maturity are not separate for the brain. Both are aspects of identity.

Since identity (including character and maturity) runs in a brain system that is faster than conscious thought, the fast track produces a reaction to our circumstances *before* we have a chance to consider how we would rather react. What happens before we have a chance to think about it is the source of what we call character. Our reactions will reveal our character.

This suggests that if we are to learn Christlike character, it would be best learned in the ways that the right-brain, fast-track mind thinks and learns. The mechanism for building and changing character in the fast track is mutual mind. We need to think *with* God, not simply *about* God. Learn. to think with God carries major implications for spiritual-formation practices if we want to create a Christlike character that spontaneously responds with love for our enemies.

Seeing how fast- and slow-track systems operate differently illuminates how the brain develops maturity and character. This neuroscience raises some questions about developing our character. Can the brain only learn character from other humans? Could brain processes be employed by God to develop mature, Christlike character? Can God use the fast-track master system? Does God develop our character without engaging us with other people? Does God add something to our best human maturity and character that we could not add ourselves? Does following scriptural practices train the fast track of the brain? These are the questions of neurotheology. Yet every item above requires that our salvation forms a new, hesed love attachment—through Jesus—with a God who is present and interacts with us.

FAST TRACK LEARNS IDENTITY, CHARACTER, AND MATURITY

If there is so much going on in the fast track, why don't we see more character change? There is a big reason: The fast track only allows "my people" access to the character settings.

Identity is a rather protected brain function. We do not easily allow any other mind to change who we are. Access to establish or change identity is limited to those who are attached with us. Thus, our significant attachments (the people we love) shape our character. Attachment love (what Scripture calls "hesed," as noted in chapter 1) is the key to access our character. No hesed means no access. Attachment is the foundation for developing character.

For Christianity to change identity and character, we need God's direct communication to the fast track. The channel used to form character is that of mutual mind with the one we love. A mutual mind with God capable of changing our identity and character requires a love attachment (hesed) with God. Through mutual mind, the fast track learns to respond like Jesus. The identity that grows as a result becomes the fast-track master system guiding our reactions, which would display Christ's character, including spontaneous love for our enemies.

Hesed Attachment for Hard Times

To develop character, we need the kind of hesed attachment that does not come apart when things get rough. Developing character requires attachments with someone who stays mindful even during suffering. That is some strong hesed. Another way to say "staying mindful during suffering" is to say that we stay attached even when others begin to act and feel like our enemies. If we wish to exhibit Christlike character, we must not let suffering turn others into our enemies. But how is this mature character acquired?

THE FAST TRACK NEEDS BOTH INDIVIDUAL AND GROUP ATTACHMENT

Maturity requires attachment and mutual-mind practice time with greater minds. Do you remember the disciples in a boat during a storm while Jesus was asleep? The lesser minds lost all their peace and awakened Jesus. This began a tug-of-war between minds. Would Jesus become as alarmed as the disciples, or would they become calm like Jesus? Which was the greater mind?

Now, asking which mind was greater when one side is *Jesus, the Father, and the Holy Spirit* and the other mind is *a group of disciples* may seem confusing. Yet, the brain can create a group mind with "my people." This group mind runs in the fast track using mutual-mind states. Group mind is kept together through attachment love (hesed).

Mutual mind starts with a mindful attachment figure. Jesus was present and mindfully aware of the storm and His disciples. Jesus' mind was peaceful. Whether the disciples could stay in a mutual mind with Jesus depended on the strength of their attachment love to Jesus. The disciples had some strong doubts about Jesus and His hesed, so they asked, "Don't you care if we die?"

Jesus removed the threat to show that yes, He cared. Even so, the disciples were not attached to Him: They didn't even recognize Him. They were terrified and asked each other, "Who is this?"[11] Without attachment from the disciples, Jesus had better results quieting the storm than quieting the disciples.

This passage of Jesus with the disciples illustrates the individual and group attachments that form identity and character. The disciples were able to connect as a group mind with one another. They had an attachment and group identity as fishermen from Galilee who knew this lake and one another. They would put ultimate effort into saving one another from a storm. This is a strong attachment and sense of working together as one. Their group mind was terrified, and that made sense. They were of mutual mind.

Mutual mind with Jesus (an individual with a greater mind) offered the disciples a new fast-track identity. This new identity (the character of Christ) would become only as strong as their love attachment to Jesus. We can see that Peter's attachment grew in time because in the next storm story, he can walk on the waves when he has his eyes on Jesus. (Direct, eye-to-eye contact provides the best conditions for mutual mind.)

In this first storm story, the disciples' fast-track identity looks at Jesus and sees shalom/peace. The fast track then checks this mutual-mind moment with Jesus against reality as seen by "our people" (the other disciples). The stronger attachment wins. We know that uneasy feeling when someone wants us to believe something our people do not believe. "Our people do not get in boats with God," the disciples' group identity told them. Consequently, the group identity canceled any character change for the disciples that day. They stayed scared.

For character development, the brain needs joyful and loving attachments both with a greater mind (in this case, Jesus) and with a people (other disciples). Had the disciples and Jesus all seen this event the same way, all of them would have been peaceful. Everything was working together for their good. This harmony is what Scripture calls "shalom."

FAST TRACK AND MATURITY

In brain terms, we call the harmony of all parts working together *synchronicity*. We are mindfully present. We have good mutual mind with others. We stay relational. Maturity is the measure of how well the fast-track system can maintain relational synchronicity (shalom) both internally and externally (with others) as pressure and suffering increase. Maturity is the ability to maintain a relational state under pressure: We stay loving even when others turn against us.

Trauma creates a nonrelational, desynchronized state. Other people begin to feel like our enemies. Our brain loses synchronicity in the fast track. We lose our shalom. Even the presence of Jesus might terrify us, as it did the disciples. The fast-track system that produces mutual mind is severely disrupted by trauma, poorly developed by relational neglect, and easily interrupted when two people lack a significant attachment. This suggests an answer to the issue that troubled Jane—*Why do people with trauma backgrounds experience inconsistent results when applying Dallas's teaching?* Could traumatic disruptions of our relational identity cause these deformities in maturity?

Maturity, to the brain at least, means treating others like "my people" no matter what happens. The central function that unifies the fast track is identity.[12] Our identity is fundamentally relational. When the fast track is running well, identity is coherent and we experience shalom. Coherent identity, not the will, is in control of feelings, emotions, and desires.

FAST TRACK AND TRAUMA

Trauma creates a disruption of the brain's master fast-track processing.[13] An incoherent or shut down fast track produces a lack of self-control. Trauma weakens our ability to stay "with" others and God by disrupting our mutual-mind states. Without a coherent sense of identity (that can maintain relational connections in the face of distress), our feelings will not be regulated. Recall that being unable to regulate feelings, emotions, and desires was Dallas's description of immaturity.

The ability to stay relational and coherent develops through thinking *with* others in mutual mind. Mature people have had extensive practice using mutual mind. Substantial practice keeps this social-engagement system running smoothly and well. The well-trained brain has learned how to stay relational under pressure. Better developed relational stability makes it harder to traumatize adults compared to children or infants. Mature adults are more stable relationally.

When the master system cannot answer the question *What do I and my people do under these conditions?*, it sends the conscious, slow-track mind out with its flashlight to find a solution. This will be a slow search. A slow but focused system is needed. If the fast track is still running, the answers that the slow track finds with its flashlight will be tested against all we know about ourselves and our people. This is a character check.

When the master system has been disrupted (as after trauma), no character test is performed. People react according to their desires, feelings, and emotions. Reactions will be aimed at whatever is directly in the beam of the conscious flashlight. This generally results in blaming whoever is directly in front of us.[14] We saw an example of a "blaming reaction" in the irritated woman who was second in line to see Dallas. She has lost her hesed for the lady sitting in front of Dallas.

RELATIONAL MATURITY

All immaturity exhibits poor regulation of emotions, feelings, and desires. Yet we need to make a distinction (philosophers love to make distinctions) about what causes the immaturity Dallas observes—being ruled by emotions, feelings, and desires. We use the word "immaturity" two ways. One meaning, the one intended by Dallas, is that someone has failed to develop. A second meaning is that someone is young. The immaturity of children comes from an undeveloped self in the fast track. The immaturity of children is usually mindful, joyful, and peaceful. Children with loving attachments are open to developing identity.

The immaturity shown by adults with traumatic, incoherent identities is rarely mindful and lacks a sense of loving attachment. The immaturity after trauma is both undeveloped and incoherent. Brain studies demonstrate that after trauma, the brain no longer runs in smooth synchronicity.[15] Not only does the fast track not run smoothly but the fast and slow tracks are out of synchronization with one another, as well. A disrupted identity also occurs with children who lack secure, loving attachments.

Restoring a secure, loving attachment where there are traumatic memories not only resolves the trauma but resynchronizes the fast track. Where there was once an incoherent identity, stability is restored. Now the brain can mature and develop an identity capable of regulating emotions, feelings, and desires. This restoration depends on acquiring a loving attachment.

Becoming Relational

As I looked to Dallas's left and right, I saw the difference attachment brings to mindsight. The people lined up on his left believed in Dallas, had fa in Dallas, had accepted Dallas as a personal teacher and, judging by the books in their hands, had read Dallas's words. They were eager to see what Dallas would do for them and what truth he might reveal.

Jane and company were to Dallas's right. They had deep attachments to Dallas and knew him relationally. Their mental state was quite different from the people in line on his left. People with attachments didn't simply know about Dallas, they *knew Dallas*. Because of their attachment bond with him, the minds on the right saw reality far differently from the minds on the left.

Although it is possible for most of us to "read" body language of complete strangers (mindsight), mutual-mind states that create identity and character only develop when the brain has an attachment to the person with the other mind. If we don't attach, we will not let others build our identities. They are not "our people." The social-engagement system of the fast track in the brain opens itself to changing identity and character only with those we hesed. Who we love has far more impact on character than what we believe. Who we agape dominates the master fast track. What we believe runs through the emissary slow track.

The human brain yields far different "access rights" for those we know through attachment (of a family sort) and those we know in an informational/thinking way. The impact of "my people" could hardly be more different and separate from "not my people." To change human character, we need to experience mutual-mind states with our attachment figures and our people. To work the way a brain is designed, Christianity would require extensive practices that promote a loving attachment with Jesus and develop loving attachments with the rest of His family. Like ducklings following their mother, a deepening attachment love creates a mutual-mind way of life.

Jane's practice of spiritual healing centered on creating attachments to Jesus and to His people. Jesus and Jane became "my people" for the traumatized. This attachment proved to be the solution to trauma. Once people became aware that Jesus was present with them in their painful event, they were no longer alone. A mutual-mind state with Jesus and Jane helped traumatized people discover how their people would act in the presence of their enemies. Mutual mind with Jesus and Jane began to change their identities and character. Once the master fast track was back in operation, maturity development could resume.

The Science of Spiritual Maturity— a Neurotheological Perspective

Could the science of attachment and emotional maturity also be the science of spiritual maturity, once we add mutual mind with God and God's people? Neurotheology suggests the value of

1. attaching to God;
2. thinking *with* God;
3. becoming one of God's people; and
4. thinking *about* God.

Thinking *about* God has very different outcomes than thinking *with* God when it comes to character. Without attachment, we will not think *with* God. Without attachment, we will have spiritual ideas but our reactions and character (in the face of emotions, feelings, and desires) will change very little. We will be far more shaped in this world by the people we call "our people."

Thinking *about* God has value. If we do not think *about* God, we will have great difficulty recognizing that (1) God's thoughts are not like our thoughts, (2) God's character is not like our character, and (3) God's ways are different from our ways. We will not even notice that (4) our loving attachment to God is making us more like Him.

Salvation that produces a new attachment love between us and God makes a mutual-mind state with God possible. Could part of the meaning of Isaiah 1:18—"Come now, and let us reason [יָכַח, yakach] together"—be "let us come to a mutual mind"? God expects yakach to teach us to do good because the previous verse (17) says, "learn to do good" (לָמַד, lamad, or become skillful). We will be practicing a skill when we yakach. In the following verse (19), God adds that all will be well "if you consent" (אָבָה, abah). Abah can mean to synchronize or go along with. If yakach is mutual mind, then our identity (in the master fast track) will become increasingly like God's character.

Could loving attachment to God be how salvation saves us from our sins? Dallas once told me that we would most likely call "sin" a "malfunction" in modern language. Character and control of emotions, feelings, and desires are disrupted by whatever causes the fast track to malfunction. A fast-track malfunction, along with a poorly trained fast-track identity, cause a failure to regulate emotions, feelings, and desires—not to mention our reactions. Dallas has just said that "immaturity is the effect of sin." Salvation through hesed attachment could be a very specific solution to sin and its effects on our identity and character.

Spiritual Maturity and the Human Brain

Dallas told us that both spiritual and human maturity are demonstrated by having feelings, desire, and emotion under the guidance and control of what is good. Persons who are not spiritually mature are under the guidance and control of feelings, desires, and emotion. Neuroscience indicates that, in operation of the brain, the fast-track master system centered in the right brain regulates emotions, feelings, and desires. Spiritual maturity, like emotional maturity, must modify this fast-track system.

Emotional maturity represents how far we can take maturity using only human models. What God's Spirit and people add to normal maturity, we call spiritual maturity. Spiritual maturity is not a separate phenomenon but rather emotional maturity plus more. Jesus says that even the pagans can love their neighbors. This is a good deal further than many Christians bother to go. Spiritual maturity is indicated by the ability to love our enemies spontaneously from the heart.

The social brain is profoundly sculpted across the life span by who it loves. The quality of all relational interactions shapes the development of identity and character. Loving relationships grow from joyful and thankful interactions. When we grow beyond loving only those who bring us joy, we begin to act Christlike. To love our enemies, we surely need a mutual mind with God.

Dallas's first lecture told us of the immediacy of God's presence. Neuroscience has us ask, *Is God immediate enough to create a mutual-mind state with us?* If the answer is yes, then neuroscience has us add: A mutual-mind state might provide guidance with someone we don't love,[16] but it will only change our identity and character if we have significant hesed (attachment love). When we have enough attachment to think *with* God rather than *about* God, the access rights to our identity go much deeper.

The fast-track system develops coherent identity (mature character) through mutual-mind practice with "my people" who have the loving-attachment "rights" to tell me who I really am. Jesus and Jesus' family need to be attached to me as "my people" by deep attachment love to shape the character of Christ in our identities. Practicing mutual mind (through God's Spirit) allows us to develop better character than we could from the best collection of humans. At the same time, if that character does not show itself with humans (particularly our enemies), how can we claim that we are being saved?

Dallas emphatically stated that living in the Kingdom of God should transform people. He decried the current state of the church and indicated that whole churches spend their time tiptoeing around immature leaders and members. He proposed a method of apprenticeship to Jesus for transformation of the whole person (including the will) by grace through the Holy Spirit. We will see that, for the brain, attachments are stronger than and quite separate from what we think of as the will. We must ask, *What is the basis for maturity and Christlikeness? Is it the will, or is it attachment love?*

Our break time ended while Dallas answered questions. He used his conscious will to override his emotions, feelings, and bodily desires. Dallas could and did demonstrate that a mature will can overcome desires. What Dallas means by "the will" might surprise us. Our day with Dallas continues with his teaching about the parts of a human person in our next chapter.

Exercise: Nine-Minute Sunset

The following exercise provides steps to become mindfully present, activate your attachment love to God, and enter a mutual-mind state while enjoying a sunset together. The third part of the exercise (sharing your facial expressions with God) is difficult for the slow track of the conscious mind to understand. How do I share a smile with someone? How can God be in my face? We remember the disciples wondering, *How can God be in our boat?*

But God is there, and as you experience God's presence, you can begin to let your brain and body (your face) discover and express that reality.

Do this exercise during sunset.

This exercise has three parts, each three minutes.

Begin by asking God to lead you.

1. Think of gifts from God that you appreciate. Notice how your body reacts as you focus on your appreciation and gratitude.

2. Remember times when God seemed particularly close to you. Notice the effects of God's presence on you.

3. Share your face with God, so that your face shows God's expression and your eyes reflect God's response to you, the sunset, and any people around you. Speaking is not necessary.

4

COMPONENTS OF THE HUMAN PERSON

DALLAS WILLARD

Dallas's second lecture illuminates the way his model of human persons works. The psychology and structure of persons that he presents has been part of philosophy and theology since before the Middle Ages. We will notice that Dallas uses the terms *will*, *heart*, and *spirit* interchangeably. The equivalence is understood if we use a medieval psychology of persons. The words, particularly the *will*, have quite different meanings for most people now. Philosophers tend to define a word and expect the reader to not confuse the writer's definition with whatever the reader might think the word means (on this, Dallas is no exception). Thus far, Dallas has used words like *desire* and *will* in ways that differ from common usage. We can understand Dallas more easily when we consider that what we think a word means might not be how he uses that word. Here is Dallas.

• • •

We want now to go into more detail as to the kind of transformation we hope to see in the person who is becoming emotionally and spiritually mature. To do so, we first need to more fully examine the concept of maturity itself.

Maturity refers to a process of growth. Immaturity stands at one end of that process, maturity at the other. And the growth process that results in maturity involves the essential components of the human being and some of the dynamics of their interaction.

Recall our essential idea: You don't become spiritually or emotionally mature by willpower. This is one of the hardest things, I think, to get over. We tend to reproach people for their failures by attacking their intentions. I guess we think we can brace that out by attacking them at that level. You have to learn how to use your will, but your will has very little power. You maximize the effect of your will by using it to direct yourself into experiences that will change your mind, and your body, and your social relations, and your soul. Then those changes interact with one another—it's not a very tidy package to think about, actually. We want to beware of someone who comes along with a neat package for spiritual or psychological change. But the will, nevertheless, is something that has an order to it, and we can understand that order and capitalize on it to change.

Now, again, I emphasize that the Holy Spirit is constantly active in this process, as are all the instrumentalities of the Kingdom of God. So you're not alone in it; this isn't a solitary trip. And indeed, a major part of our process of growth is our relationship to other people. God has intended it that way—set it up that way—because all of this growth is captured in a single word that is essentially relational: *love*. We'll deal with that shortly. But for now, we must emphasize that the process of growth into emotional and spiritual maturity requires that we learn to use our will—and yet, willpower is not the key to spiritual maturity. If we make it the key, we will wind up in hopelessly bound legalism.

Meanwhile, if we mistake our will as the key to our maturity, we will also see a constant stream of failure. Notice the difference between what Peter understood about himself when he said to Jesus, "I will not deny you," and Jesus said, "Yes, you will. Yes, you will. Yes, you will."[1] Peter was thinking about his will, his intentions. But there was much more to Peter than he himself realized, and Jesus knew it. In particular, Jesus knew that Peter's body was loaded with readiness to act in certain ways—ways that would trap him.

That's the story of Romans 7 also. Paul here talks about "the things I would, I don't do" and "the things I would not, I wind up doing."[2] This passage is very analytic; Paul is realizing that his body gets ahead of his intentions. There is nothing more important to realize, to understand about spiritual growth, than that fact: Until it hits your body, it hasn't hit you. Righteousness and maturity have to take control of us, and that involves a lot of things, one of which is having enough space to recognize what is happening as you live.

See, Peter didn't have the space. So, when the little girl said, "You are one of them," he didn't have the space to say, "Oh, I know what is happening here, and I know how I am going to react." It was right on him—like that.[3] Our body, because of its ingrained habits, is frequently what is in charge in the moment during day-to-day life. So we want to use our will to train our body in ways that will ready it to respond properly when that moment comes.

So we can talk about things like spiritual maturity, but probably we should talk rather about spiritual *maturing*, which at some future point arrives at spiritual maturity. But I'm a little concerned about that because I recognize that I don't fully know all the things that are in me. I'm in the process of learning that. I've learned a lot—thank God, because boy, I have been a mess. I look back at my teenage years and say, *Who was that? How could I ever have thought like that?* And I was only a moderately wicked young man, as things go. When we reflect backward, we can start to see how nearsighted we are about our future, such that Peter could not accurately predict how he would respond when confronted in his connection to Jesus. We do better, then, to focus on maturing rather than on maturity—especially when we're attending to our own growth.

So now let us look at the essential dimensions of the self and how we can change those dimensions. Sometimes in the Scriptures it will come down on one thing—for example, Romans 12: Devote yourself; your body a living sacrifice.[4] What does that mean? When we get serious about the process of spiritual and emotional growth, whether it's for ourselves individually or we're thinking about a church context, that's where we really have to think about the details. What does it mean to consecrate your body as a living sacrifice? Or consider another famous passage from Paul (which, by the way, I have never heard a sermon on): "I buffet my body."[5]

What does that mean? You are training your body in such a way that it will not get the jump on you in living.

Most people's lives are run by automatic response. Our social context, by and large, dictates our choices. And we have to get out of that pattern. We do that by looking at the particular dimensions of human beings and changing what is in those particular dimensions.

As we reflect on what we've already discussed, we want to ask questions such as "Where does emotional maturity show up in the person?" It isn't just a quality that sits on your head or something. It results from a combination of the way our minds work, our feelings, and so forth, through all the other dimensions of the person. As we look at that, we can begin to understand how this works, and we can begin to plan on it.

Suppose I have a temptation that I am dealing with all the time, and maybe at some occasion it gets the best of me and breaks out into a besetting sin. Or perhaps I just have a weight. Hebrews 12:1 distinguishes between sin and a weight. Not everything that bothers us is a sin. Did you know that? Some of it's just stupid. Maybe how I'm spending my time or money. (I often encourage people not to attribute anything to evil that can be explained by simple stupidity.) As we investigate that besetting sin or stupid habit, we can really begin to make a change. We see how we can lay out our body as a living sacrifice and what that has to do with things like time and energy. Then we begin to see how that goes back to issues that really are in the domain of sin.

For example, you can't love in a hurry, any more than you can sleep in a hurry. So rather than asking, *How can I love more or sleep more?*, we ask the more basic question: *How can I get out of being in a hurry?* And we discover that a lot of our hurry is bodily and social.

Consider the image of the person as a series of circles. Outside of the circles is the infinite environment, a reference to that which is outside of us. Let's consider, then, how these circles relate to one another, and how they interact with our infinite environment.

Here you have a picture of the whole person, and we start from the inside. There are various perspectives on this, but I tend to see the will, the spirit, and the heart as one basic component of the human being. I place this component at the center partly because it is, I think, the smallest part of us, but also because its role is central in a way that really nothing else is.

INFINITE ENVIRONMENT

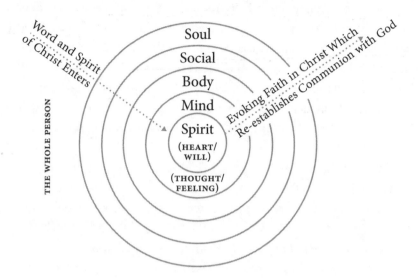

The circle around our will/spirit/heart is "thought and feeling." I put these together; if you wish, you may call them "the mind." This circle represents our capacity to think about things. The will and the mind don't work independently from one another—in fact, none of these things work independently from the rest.

The person—what we are analyzing here—has various dimensions, and we need to look at each one. The next circle is the body, an essential part of the human being. Without your body, you can't act. Often, your body acts on its own, and that's a good thing.

Outside of the body is the social dimension—your relationships with others. These again are essential. The social dimension starts with your parents and others in your family and goes out from there. In terms of who we become and how we act, those social relationships are essential and fundamental.

I put the soul at the outside because it's the most inclusive part of you. Your soul even spills over into the space around you. The basic function of the soul is to put all these parts together and make one life out of it. And if it's not a broken soul, it will do that. But souls often are broken, so the parts of the life don't function together as they should. The way we express that in common language is a *loss of integrity*. Integrity is a matter of things being integrated. They fit together in a certain way. The simplest way of losing integrity is to not live in the truth. When you depart from the truth, then you are running different lines of life.[6] The ordinary human life has an uneasy relationship to truth. For much of our lives, we are in hiding, and very often, that starts in the family and the breakup of the personality that comes from living in a family where certain obvious things have to be denied—terribly destructive of the soul. Maturing, for this soul, involves a healing from that destruction, a reintegrating of these essential parts.

The overall tendency of the self is what we refer to as our character, and our character is fleshed out in our actions, which are born out of some interaction of these various parts. If we are concerned with our actions, we have to look beyond the actions themselves to consider how the different parts of the self are involved. A human being is a very complicated system; the dynamics are of endless fascination. What makes good fiction and even good nonfiction so interesting is the interplay of the factors that go into the personality.

By the way, if you ask, "Where did you get that analysis?" consider when Jesus was asked on one occasion, "What is the great law?" He just rattled off those parts: "You love God with all your heart, with all your soul, with all your mind, and with all your strength, and you love your neighbor as yourself."[7] I think that's more helpful than Dr. Freud or Dr. Jung or Dr. Dry-as-Dust, or whoever. Jesus doesn't spell it all out (He left a lot of that for His followers, and besides, He had a lot of other things to do). But He draws on His tradition to give us this cogent analysis of what is important in the human being.

The Will

Now let's look more deeply at each of these parts. Each part is a particular dimension of abilities. The will (which I equate with spirit and heart in biblical terms)[8] is the central capacity to create and originate things and events. It is meant to be creative under God for good. We love to exercise our will in doing good. Little children do that without being told. And of course, we want to do that as we go through life. When it comes down to the end, we want to be able to say things like, "I left the world a better place." That's a deep human need that comes from the Creation covenant in Genesis 1:26: "Let us make human beings in our likeness."[9] What is that likeness? It is responsibility—"dominion," as some translations render the second part of that verse. Of course, the dominion God extends to human beings was for good and was over creation. You were created to be a creator. And that's why you love to create. The will is a creative capacity for good. I would say that for most of us, our best days are our most creative days.

Now, the primary act of the will is to rely upon God, and in reliance upon God, to bring about what is good for everything that you are in touch with. We are responsible for God's creation. When the will is alienated from God, however, it has to go on its own, which is a tough road to follow. You become responsible for your own life—and, of course, that's a good deal more than almost anyone can take care of. But we can return to the kind of dominion that God intended for us. At this point grace is introduced as the way in which we are able to function and accomplish what God has for us to accomplish. A wonderful statement about the interplay between man on his own and man under God—a splendid introduction to the concept of grace—comes in Romans 5:17: "For if by the transgression of the one, death reigned"—that is, if alienation from God leads to separation from God—"much more those who receive the abundance of grace and of the gift of righteousness will reign in life through the One, Jesus Christ." By grace, we are restored to our relationship with God through the work of Jesus Christ.

Notice the promise: "Reign in life." It isn't just God who has a Kingdom; you have a kingdom. We may not feel like this is where we are, but it is inherent to the personality of a human being to have a domain of responsibility, an arena of governance in which we express our effective will. That's the basic position we are designed to live in. In alienation from God, we can't make it work, but when we are reunited with God through Christ, we "reign in life through the One, Jesus Christ."

The secret to the will is that it can do so very much—like someone using one of those big earth-moving machines: All they are doing is sitting there pushing a button or moving a little lever. They have integrated their will with the powers built into that machine. Our development as human beings includes having dominion—moving beyond the power of our will to master other great powers in creation. The spiritual life works essentially in the same way: People can accomplish great things in the spiritual life if their will is properly applied, first of all in trust and thankfulness to God.

The will is meant to make us count *for good.* That's why we hold it as such a precious thing. Most of us would agree that it's wrong to buy and sell human beings. We have even encoded that into our laws. That's because a human being has no equivalent value in any other thing—not even another human being. Your will makes you a thing of incredible value—so great that even God Himself seems to hold it as precious—so precious that He will not override it. Now, He certainly works with it, talks with it, presents it with things that are important to understand. But God will not override your will. And a person who is resolved to stay away from God will be permitted by God to do just that.

Now I personally don't believe that God sends anyone to hell, but I think He permits people to go there if they want. Hell is basically a matter of being away from God. You can say, "How could anyone want to do that?" Please understand that if you don't like God, it would be hell for you to be in heaven. Just imagine, you go to heaven and you can't avoid Him. The turn to liking and loving God is what makes it a good thing to be with Him—here, as well as afterward.

I know I'm treading on a lot of difficult issues here, but I am trying to emphasize how important the will is. It is your capacity to initiate creatively what is good in things and events. And of course the human will has capacity to do great harm also.

The will is meant to be surrendered to God—to depend upon God in the creation of good. Some of the greatest artists who have ever arisen among human beings attribute the greatness of their work to God. Some of the greatest scientists have done the same thing. That's a natural and good sort of thing. A parent with some children in a family can do that same thing. They attribute the good and the beauty that comes in their children and their loved ones and friends and in the fellowship of the church to God, and they look to Him as the One who will sustain and direct it. The will that is not surrendered to God is in a hopeless condition. It cannot achieve the good it was designed to achieve. It can still do some good things, no doubt about that. And the more, the better—because the Christian wants there to be as much good as there can be under whatever circumstances. Nevertheless, the main thing we want to look for as a mark of emotional and spiritual maturity is the surrendered will. A will that is surrendered to God is the center of the redeemed person.

That's why we see such a stress on thankfulness in the Psalms and the New Testament. Thankfulness to God is central to the organization of the person who is fully devoted to God. It is a mark of a will surrendered to God, a will that acknowledges God's provision and care for us. First Thessalonians tells us to be thankful *in* everything because this is the will of God concerning you.[10] Possibly the greatest expression of faith is the readiness to be thankful for the things we don't particularly like. That is an achievement of an emotionally mature person, and you can only have that, I believe, in a spiritually mature person.

The Mind

The will is the capacity to initiate creatively. The mind is centered on the will. Consider this: If you think wrongly about God, are you more or less likely to surrender your will to Him? Our comprehension of the image of God is so extremely important. I often say that all human evil comes from thinking wrongly about God. We pick it up just by living—we unconsciously adopt a misunderstanding of who God is. But it is also possible to really *want* to think wrongly about God.

When I am engaged in a more or less academic setting with someone who wants to talk about the existence of God, and I see that they are serious, then one of the things I am apt to ask them first is, "Would you like for there to be a God?" Very often, they will say, "No, I wouldn't." There isn't much point in proceeding with the discussion after that because no matter what you present them with in the way of argument and evidence, if they sense that the existence of God is coming around the corner, they will dodge. And of course, there is no end to how much distortion you can introduce to an argument or the presentation of evidence. Consider the so-called popular atheists: It's often stunning how illogical they are. Consider the idea that the physical universe could have come into existence without a cause. You ask them, "Have you seen anything physical come to existence without a cause? A cup of tea, for example? Say there was nothing and then there was this cup of tea!"

The mind works from evidence and reason. It does so naturally. But the will is already in the mix, and it has to be a will for the truth—a will that says, "I will accept the truth. I will abandon my beliefs or my hopes, if necessary, to accept the truth." The will and the mind work together. The mind has to provide some sort of representation in order for the will to work. If the will is bent away from the truth, however, it will not represent things as they are. So there is an interaction there.

Feelings and emotions and desires also get in the mix here. They determine often what we will or can think. Our choices about where we put our mind, then, become substantial in determining how we are going to mature emotionally and spiritually. For example, in personal relations, how I think of other people is often a choice. I have to decide whether I am going to think about them in purely economic or sexual terms or as whole persons. It isn't too much of an exaggeration to say that our basic freedom is where we put our mind. It's not unlimited; we can be captured by thoughts. But our choice as to where we put our mind is what most determines where we go.

That is why Paul says, "Be renewed, be transformed by the renewing of your mind."[11] He's thinking about using your body to direct where your mind is focused. That may mean going into solitude. Or it may mean going to church—which, by the way, is a good idea. If we go to church in order to help us keep and put our mind in the right place, who knows, it might break out into worship—and that will affect your whole life.[12] The choice of where we put our mind is a major part of what determines our emotional and spiritual maturity.

The most important thing we do is to think about God. That wonderful passage in Romans 12 where Paul is talking about presenting your bodies a living sacrifice starts out like this: "Therefore I urge you, brethren."[13] What's the "therefore" there for? Well, you have to go back to verse 36 of chapter 11: "From Him and through Him and to Him are all things. To Him be the glory forever. Amen." That's where the understanding has arrived, by the time we reach Romans 12. "Since your mind is there," Paul continues, "I urge you therefore, brethren, to present your bodies as a living sacrifice."[14] Right thinking about God—as our source and provision—is the starting point. If you didn't think of God like that, you might not go on presenting your bodies a living sacrifice. And it might well be that if you don't do that, your mind won't be renewed; you won't be transformed.

Here, then, is the interconnection between these dimensions of the self. What is in the mind and what is in the feelings and what is in the will is going to be determinative of my whole life. And thinking wrongly about God is the greatest mistake I can make. That is why I need to hear the gospel. Someone needs to tell me that God is really good, that He is really all-powerful. I need to have someone *say* that to me because if someone didn't say it to me, I might very well never think the thought. And if I don't think the thought, then my whole life is going to go in the wrong direction. It really is *important* that we bear witness to the gospel. It has never been more important than in our day, primarily because of how the gospel of Jesus has been abused. We need to be able to present true knowledge of God to people, let them hear the thought, hear the Word. To do so is one of the greatest things we can do for other human beings.

The Body

Now, your mind is not the same thing as your brain. It's often shocking to people when I tell them that God doesn't have a brain. And he doesn't even miss it!

The brain is part of the body, the next dimension of the person in our diagram. People all over the world are working to change human character and life by way of the brain. Will they do that under God, or will they do it without Him?

In many instances, such as dealing with pornography or addiction, we have to work with the body and the mind together. But the brain is a part of the body and so in many respects we can engage our brains directly and holistically as we do with the body—what is called *strength* in the great commandment.[15]

The body is sometimes (wrongly) thought of as evil or bad. It's not. It's good—a wonderful creation of God. I like to think of the body as God's little power pack that He has given to each one of us to act from. Even if we choose to act contrary to God, He gives us that ability. Your body is the primary place you can redirect your life. Every spiritual discipline, even things like memorizing Scripture, involves physical energy or power: You engage your body in it.

Your body is designed to enable you to act without thinking; if you couldn't act without thinking, you couldn't do anything worth doing. Most people act without thinking, for example, when they are driving a car. If someone had to think about everything they did when they were driving a car, you wouldn't want to ride with that person. They would have to think about when to put on the brakes rather than putting on the gas, when to turn and when to go straight. We are blessed with a body that allows us to act without thinking.

Consider what it takes to speak a language. You might recall a time you had to think about everything involved in speaking a language—picking the words, conjugating them properly, matching subject to verb to object. What a relief when you don't have to think about it anymore! Or when you have someone new on the job and they stand around waiting to be told what to do. You want them to learn what to do, so they're ready to do it without a lot of thinking. Jesus initiated His disciples into the category of "friend" because He said, "now you understand what I am doing."[16] They had progressed in their work and ministry so that it was in their bodies; they did what Jesus commanded without having to think about it. (It seems to have taken Peter most of his life to get there, but he did get there! Read the wonderful letter of 1 Peter and see the maturation of his growth.)

See, we want our bodies to come to the place where they do instinctually what is good and right. Unfortunately, they have been pretty thoroughly harmed by learning how to do the things that are wrong without having to think about it. Our bodies have to learn new instincts. Romans 6 is a wonderful statement on this: "Therefore do not let sin reign"—there's that word again—"in your mortal body so that you obey its lusts."[17] Don't let it do that! You see, your body is set up in a certain way by our living in a fallen world. But Paul says, "Do not go on presenting the members of your body to sin as instruments of unrighteousness; but present yourselves to God as those alive from the dead, and your members as instruments of righteousness to God. For sin shall not be master over you, for you are not under law but under grace."[18]

The body is what enables you to have a life. That's the basic thing. And it does that by serving as a source of energy and strength, but also by incorporating good habits or traits so that you don't have to think about doing what is good—you're already doing it. If that doesn't happen, then you will already be doing what is wrong before you've thought about it. Growth in maturity, then, involves changes for the body.

Psalm 104

The Social

Social relations require us to live with others. Aristotle says that anyone who lives alone is not a human being. They may be a god or they may be a monster but they are not a human being.[19] But once we grant that to be human is to live with others, we have to contend with how we engage with one another, which often includes attack and withdrawal.

One reason why fear is so pervasive in our world is because we know how much attack is part of human life. Attack may come quietly, in how someone is thinking about us, but thoughts hurt—and all the more so when those thoughts are given expression. Attack and withdrawal must be eliminated from our social relations and replaced by care for, love of, and identification with those near us.

We are, in fact, made to live together, to care for one another. That's natural and something we expect, enough so that we feel sadness when we hear reports that a child is not being cared for. We sense that it is not the way it is meant to be. But that's not the way it's meant to be between adults, either. Our social relations nourish us when they are receptive and loving. We are built up by such social relations.

Attack and withdrawal is the normal characterization of human lives in a fallen world. But these can be replaced by care and identification. The idea of compassion is "feeling with," so that when I'm with another person, I am feeling how they feel. I have sensed their interests, their hopes and fears, and all of that. Consequently, I am able to live with them and let them live with me in love and caring. Marriage can be a beautiful picture of what social relations are meant to be like, and I think God intended it to be that way. But many marriages are harmful places— wounds are delivered and suffered from, wounds so serious that you cannot escape them. It's heartbreaking to think about how often care and identification—compassion—is missing from our families. We were made to love together, to care for one another.

Rejection by others is perhaps the immediate source of most evils in human life in human terms. What do we need to have in order to replace rejection? Well, we need a safe place to stand, to know the words of Hebrews 13: "God has said, 'I will never leave you or forsake you.' Therefore we can boldly say, 'What shall I fear that men can do unto me?'"[20] Or Romans 8: "If God is for us, who can be against us?"[21]

If we're not able to do that, then we lead a shrunken life. Shame, for example, is one of the most brutal things for the human being—a kind of internalized rejection where I have somehow projected onto myself the rejection that has been cast on me. Shame goes back to emotions (in the mind circle); it has a lot of pain in it because it's rooted in how we think about ourselves. But we also need to look at shame, pride, and so on, in the social context. When Paul says in Philippians 2, "Let each consider the other person better than themselves," he is helping us to resist the temptation to reject others, to cast shame on them.[22] Note that Paul doesn't say, "Believe they are better"—sometimes they aren't better—but it does say to treat them as better. We can do so in love if we have received a place of love in which we dwell with the Lord.

The Soul

Finally, the soul. The soul is that part of the person that integrates all the other dimensions to make one life. Very often, we experience the soul as a sort of stream of energy and direction that is flowing inside of us. It's very hard to conceptualize the soul. But we do have a sense of when it is strong and when it is weak.

Restoration is a need of the soul. One of the promises of the Great Shepherd in Psalm 23 is that "He restores my soul."[23] Then in Psalm 19:7, "The law of the LORD is perfect, restoring the soul." You may never have thought of the law in that connection, but in actuality the law of God is simply God's ways. When we identify with God's ways, we come in touch with a deep source of direction and energy. And it restores our soul. That's why the man or woman who meditates daily, constantly in the law of the Lord is like a tree planted by the river of waters, whose leaf doesn't wither, that brings forth its fruit.[24] That person's soul is tied in to a deeper source. Consider Joshua 1:8, where God commands, "This book of the law shall not depart out of your mouth, but you will meditate day and night therein that you may observe to do all that is in it." You line up your soul with who God is. And that restores your soul.

The restoration of the soul, its direction and its energy, is essential to its work: to pull together all the aspects of your life and make it one life. Paul's testimony in Romans 7—"The things I would, that I do not," and "the things that I would not that I do"—is a typical expression of a broken soul. That's not one life; it's a bunch of stuff running in various directions. What we're working on here is an approach to Christlikeness that leads to spiritual competence and spiritual maturity, with a restored soul functioning in harmony with the Kingdom of God.

Choosing to live in deception and falsehood makes integrity impossible because it splits the self. The self is then acting contrary to what it knows. Feelings do not accord with reality; the body is opposed to the will and the emotions. The things that people do that are so horrible in this world are consequences and evidences of broken souls. Much of their brokenness may be due to what they themselves lived through as children— we all know that abused children are statistically more likely to become abusers themselves. Why? They have broken souls. There is a vital conflict between what they know to be right and what they do. That's the condition of a broken soul. And it has to be healed by coming into union with the Kingdom of God.

When Jesus says, "Seek first the Kingdom of God and its kind of righteousness,"[25] He's primarily talking about bringing the whole soul into union with God's ways of living and acting. The soul is restored by that contact. Now, we know that that comes through putting your confidence in Jesus Christ and allowing the Spirit to come and move in your heart and your mind and give you new thoughts, sometimes deliver you from feelings or giving you different feelings, perhaps sometimes enabling your body to do things which it could never do on its own, and, of course, the transformation of social relations. The divine assistance comes when we set ourselves to bring the whole structure of the self into harmony with God's will. We not only seek the Kingdom of God but we begin to find it. That is where we move toward spiritual maturity.

• • •

Dallas has presented his view of human persons and how they work. How will this compare with the way our brain creates and maintains a human identity? This is the subject of our next chapter.

5

NEUROSCIENCE AND DEVELOPING CHARACTER

JIM WILDER

As Dallas and the audience leave for lunch, you and I can have a conversation about what he has just said. These imaginary conversations have a long tradition in philosophy. Let me recommend we talk at the popular Mexican spot nearby. Of course, there will be a line, but June in Southern California is beautiful. We won't mind standing outside.

Our conversation goes straight to why Dallas seems so positive about the will and so negative about willpower. His opening remark was, "Recall our essential idea: You don't become spiritually or emotionally mature by willpower." Then he added, "We must emphasize that the process of growth into emotional and spiritual maturity requires that we learn to use our will—and yet, willpower is not the key to spiritual maturity. If we make it the key, we will wind up hopelessly bound in legalism."

"As bad as legalism is," you tell me, "willpower has another problem. It does not work reliably. Half the time when I need it, my willpower seems to be in the Bahamas. Even if willpower did work reliably, Dallas says that it would only make legalists of us."

Everyone in line by the restaurant seems to have come from the conference. The lady in front of us turns and says, "Willpower is a popular concept and not a precisely defined philosophical one. It is a new idea, as ideas go. You might as well call it stubbornness or determination. You can be pigheaded all day, and it is no virtue."

"How does the will work if not by willpower?" you ask.

"Or maybe it is not the will doing the work at all," she says. Just then, her party gets seated, and we are left to think high and lofty thoughts.

Our thoughts over lunch will deviate from the way Dallas has told us the components of a human person work together. We will examine an alternate explanation that Dallas would have called a "soteriology of attachment." He told me in a later discussion that he knew of no soteriology based on attachment and claimed none for himself. Based on his statement, we can be sure that what he just presented in his lecture was not a soteriology based on attachment theory.

Soteriology is the explanation of how salvation works. What about us is saved and what is the mechanism? In biblical language, the central part of humans is the heart. At the very least, salvation must save the heart. A heart cannot save itself, so it must respond to God in some way.

By what mechanism does a heart respond to God's salvation? The most common answer we hear in churches today is *the will*, which Dallas places at the center of the human being. A soteriology of attachment, which I am proposing, replaces the will with *attachment.* In this chapter we will discuss the changes a soteriology of attachment produces in what Dallas just presented.

Neuroscience tells us that the brain functions around attachment, not will. Because attachment is relational, it can be surmised to exist in Dallas's fourth (social) circle where we are connected to other people. But we are not saved by belonging to the right group or family. Attachment that saves is in the heart. We must move attachment to the center, then, where our heart is found, where attachment becomes the mechanism through which the heart responds to God and develops Christlike character.

The will, consequently, must move to a secondary place somewhere between the mind circle and the body circle. Our will is logically connected to our mind and physically part of the brain. Will and choice operate in the vulnerable, cortical gray matter of the body.

"Doesn't moving the will leave us in some kind of determinism?" you ask as the hostess guides us between crowded tables.

"Not a bit. Attachment is the ignored but active motivator of human life. It is a free and active force. Attachment grows and dies in its own way, but who we form attachments with is not predetermined. Attachment also cares very little about what you consciously choose, as anyone whose marriage is failing can tell you."

We nod and smile at people we recognize as we get seated. We are greeted by smiles in return as the fast tracks in those brains all around us briefly lock minds with ours using only visual signals.

"I see Dallas's teaching solidly in the mainstream of Christian understanding," you tell me when I look your way once again. "He has very carefully arranged his thoughts, applications, and arguments around the whole person in intimate relationship with God in keeping with everything I have read or heard."

"Yes, that is true. Both theology and philosophy have long histories around the will. Dallas has carefully developed his ideas on the will in ways we will not consider here. Yet, since we are about to replace standard soteriology, we should see how mainstream Western Christian thought developed."

How Western Christianity Placed the Will at the Center

In the days when great thinkers debated whether objects fell because angels pushed or pulled them, theology was the provider of answers for how people operate. Greek philosophy shaped this medieval model of human psychology. According to the Greeks, people had many "faculties," or abilities. Christian thinkers took that list of faculties and assigned some to the heart, soul, spirit, mind, or body. This classical view of human persons has gone through thousands of adjustments and upgrades but has formed the core of theology and Christian practice since the Middle Ages—even before.

Until the Enlightenment, no one gave much importance to human activity. God's will dominated all options. During the Romantic period, thought leaders began focusing on human choices. Simultaneously, the American colonies were enjoying independence. The Second Great Awakening was sweeping through the United States. Salvation was understood, particularly among Baptists and Methodists, as a decision to follow Jesus. Making Jesus Lord, therefore, became a matter of submitting our will to God. To harmonize with older theology, what people thought and chose were attributed to a faculty called the "will." The will emerged as a central feature in American theology. Packaged with the Second Great Awakening, the will and choices appeared quite powerful.

FACULTIES AND VIRTUES

Philosophers as far back as Plato and Aristotle were selecting which human abilities constituted a faculty. Faculties included the intellect, affections, passions, imagination, perception, intuition, reason, memory, and so on. Since these faculties could be used for good or bad things, virtues were used to explain good behavior (courage, generosity, and such) and desirable intellectual properties (wisdom, contemplation, and the like). Christians felt they needed to identify where in human persons these faculties and virtues operated. The options, using biblical language, were: the spirit, heart, soul, mind, and body.

The Christian context raised other questions about faculties. Which faculties are sinful? Which faculties can be saved? The body, emotions, feelings, desires, and will are all fallen and incapable of saving the soul. But *something* must respond to God and be saved. Logically, this must be whatever part makes a choice. Many people concluded that the will could be saved but the rest of the human being would only take us to hell. (Not everyone agreed, of course.) Fallen faculties would not produce godliness, the argument went, so God must work through the will. Since Scripture says that God saves the heart, it could only be that the will and the heart are the same thing.

We have already heard Dallas say, "Your desires are not your friends" and "The body is sometimes (wrongly) thought of as evil or bad. It's not," or "Often, your body acts on its own, and that's a good thing." His general conclusion is that none of the faculties of a human are bad in themselves. Nevertheless, being controlled by the body, desires, feelings, and emotions always ends badly.

As soon as we begin to ask how each of the many faculties of a human person work, we are left to conclude that they all require "thinking," or they are not faculties at all. Without some sort of thinking, actions are only physical events created by chance or natural laws. My brother Timothy summarized it this way, "The problem with every faculty psychology is that in explaining a particular faculty completely, you have to introduce both will and understanding into it, and then it ceases to be a distinct faculty."

With the arrival of the Enlightenment came the idea that what makes us human is our intellect ("I think, therefore I am").[1] This new psychology created the need to widen what could be saved to include the faculty of intellect. The will also needed to know truth. Memory became an important faculty so we could remember truth. Reason should be saved so we could reach truth. Much of the mystery of faith was left behind and relegated to mystics. Other faculties did not fare as well. Artists and other creative people led lives that suggested imagination, desires, and the body were unredeemable workshops for the devil.

Being right increasingly dominated theology. Many of those who were "right" made unpleasant company, but they held sway. Pulpits went to whoever was right, as did seminary positions. By being "right," many wandered from the faith.

Godly life, spiritual and emotional maturity, and developing the character of Christ were left to the one faculty that is behind all others—the will. What we can do with the will (under the influence of the Holy Spirit) becomes our only hope. Unfortunately, as Dallas tells us, "You have to learn how to use your will, but *your will has very little power*. You maximize the effect of your will by using it to direct yourself into experiences that will change your mind, and your body, and your social relations, and your soul."[2]

"I sometimes feel discouraged at how slowly I change," you comment. "Part of why I come to conferences is to find ways to speed up my spiritual life and take my growth deeper. I hate to hear that my will or spirit can do little about it."

"You are in for some good news when we consider how attachment could replace the will as the center of spiritual life," I answer. Spiritual disciplines and classical Christian practices are not known for their speed, Dallas has always been clear that they are strategic, helping us make changes that the will cannot achieve directly by effort. He will tell us more about how that works in his last lecture this afternoon.

THE RISE OF VOLUNTARIST THEOLOGY

Why all this attention on the will? The guiding figure for the group that came over on the *Mayflower* was William Ames. He and the system he presented in his book *The Marrow of Theology* represented a minority view in his day,[3] but for those early settlers in the American Colonies, his book and the Bible were considered all that was needed for a pure Christian life.

As the Enlightenment unfolded, the faculties of the will and the intellect became the focus of both theology and philosophy, explaining what made one both human and Christian. From this perspective, the Christian life was based on truth and good choices. Sin was understood as a choice made to disobey God, salvation as a choice to accept Jesus as personal Savior. Truth came to dominate the imagination, as education (more truth) became the staple solution to every problem, and denominations split over disputes about who had the truth. Preachers urged people to memorize truth, focus on truth, understand truth, and use truth to make decisions. This development has become known as *voluntarism*, from the Latin word for the will.[4]

Voluntarism is the prevailing undercurrent of an American Christian worldview. The mechanism for change, then, under this system has been to (a) use conscious thoughts (in the slow track of the brain) to (b) focus on truth so (c) we make better choices.

It is hard to see how so much truth could go wrong. Yet, the failures of Christian character by some of the biggest proponents of truth have all but demoralized the American church. The stream of moral failures by leader after leader, who knew truth and understood what choices to make, has not been limited to big names. The voluntarist solution for such failure is to focus more time, more energy, and more attention on truth and choice: Choose to think more about God.

If we propose to answer the practical question of how to develop the character of Christ in our lives, the differences between voluntarist and attachment thought become clearer. With voluntarist thought, we would expect to be told to study the Bible and obey what it says. We must correct our faulty beliefs and choose to obey—these actions should produce Christian character. What truth we should know and what Scriptures we should obey might vary from tradition to tradition, but they all flow from the underlying voluntarist worldview.

Attachment love is central to an older path to Christian character. Saint Clare of Assisi (1194–1253) spoke of attachment in a proverb widely attributed to her: "We become what we love and who we love shapes what we become." Neuroscience would add that the beloved one becomes our life, our desire, and the one who sees us as we truly are. "As the deer pants for the water brooks, so my soul pants for You, O God."[5] Without you near me, I die. You define me!

Voluntarist thought concludes that good thinking about God leads to love. Bad thinking about God leads to bad character. But what if the reason we don't know God is that we do not love God? Are we so poorly attached to God that we cannot see or share God's character? God did not say, "This is my chosen believer; understand what he will explain." God said, "This is my dearly loved Son, who brings me great joy. Listen to him."[6]

A Soteriology of Attachment Changes Our Model

You have just heard a hugely simplified version of two thousand years of philosophy and theology in the West. There are at least two serious problems with this classical model for understanding humans. First, applying the model does not produce the kinds of transformation we would expect from Christian practices. Second, the classical model does not match the way the brain works. The brain has attachment love—not our will—as its central feature.

"Since we are discussing a relational-attachment model as well," I say with a grin, "one of the central elements of an attachment model is that we attach to the one who feeds us and gives us our drink. Human history went wrong when Adam and Eve let the serpent, rather than God, feed them. That new attachment did not do us any good. Attaching to Jesus means He becomes the One who feeds us and gives us drink. His people should have meals together if they plan to attach to one another. I will let you order your food and drink before we go on. I am having the lunch burrito special and lemonade. Then we will thank Jesus."

After we have ordered, you say, "Could you go over how replacing the will with attachment is going to modify what Dallas said about the parts of a human person? That might help me sort this out."

THE WILL

Dallas says, "I tend to see the will, the spirit, and the heart as one basic component of the human being." An ancient understanding of the will comes close to the notion of "our complete or deepest identity." Recent discoveries about the brain challenge this premise:

First, the will is about as far from our deepest identity as the brain can separate things.

Second, before our conscious will comes into play, our identity system (fast track) has already determined the options our will can consider.

What we would currently call "the will" would be located in the conscious-thought section, which places the will in the rather fickle cortex. The brain has many "wills" on the cortex that are very hard to separate from desires. We want to get more exercise, eat less sugar, talk more kindly, get out of the chair and away from the TV. We really do! At the same time, other bits of "will" keep us in the chair, watching TV and eating carbs. We sit there knowing what we are choosing to do.

Western theology usually has the will doing all the heavy lifting. In *Life without Lack*, Dallas concludes that Jesus' victory over temptation in the garden of Gethsemane proves that "Jesus' will was invincible."[7] Yet Jesus is saying here, "Not My will, but Yours be done."[8] Jesus was in the process of *resisting* His own will.

Typically this complexity has been addressed by suggesting that Jesus was submitting His will to the Father. Given what we now know about the human brain, we must consider a different explanation. Jesus was using a human brain, and the strongest force in the human brain is attachment. Attachment love will carry parents into burning buildings. It may have been the strength of Jesus' attachment love for His Father, not His will, that was invincible.

Since the immediate text in the Gospel narratives does not tell us how Jesus stayed faithful, our attention goes to Hebrews 12:2, where we discover that what drew Jesus to victory was joy.

"I was following you up to there," you interject as we wait for our food. "You suddenly switched from attachment love to joy as Jesus' motive."

"So I did! This is where neuroscience gives us another hint. Dr. Allan Schore would tell us that attachment develops through joy. When we are truly glad to be with someone, the energy of that joy strengthens our attachment. When we share joy, we become attached." We both smile.

Joy is relational. Relational joy builds attachments. We are happy to see one another. We rejoice that we are together. Joy is the celebration of attachment love. Dr. Schore would also explain that joy builds identity and character in the brain.[9] Joy gives us self-control. Joy is our strength. Joy lets us suffer well when we must suffer.

What joy would Jesus have seen from the garden? His joy was attaching to us and restoring God's family. He has just instructed His disciples to abide in His love,[10] using the metaphor that we are parts of one vine to explain joyful attachment to Him.[11] It would be consistent with the entire narrative of Jesus' arrest, trial, and crucifixion (including the upper-room discourse) to attribute victory to Jesus' attachment love for the Father and for His disciples.

Jesus saw joy ahead because, after the Cross, nothing could ever separate the family. Tribulation, sword, famine, things above and things below, none of it could separate God's children from the love of God. This is hesed, secure attachment with joy. Joy and attachment provide powerful explanations for Jesus' character and victory.

ATTACHMENT AND IDENTITY

When we think consciously about identity, our brain's slow track builds identity from what it can see and quickly identifies our conscious will as its most useful tool. Our will, we know, is one of the easiest things to change, one of the first things to disappear when we are tired, distracted, or have a few beers. The ability to choose is a very flimsy cortical function located on the outside of our brain, where it is tossed about by every novel thing we see and every chemical that washes through.

At the same time, our relational fast track has its own sense of who we are, based on our attachments. Relational identity begins in the brain stem and is cemented through attachments that are nearly impossible to break or change. Consider how hard it would be to really convince you that someone else was your mother. Our identity is still present regardless of how tired or distracted we are (or how much we've had to drink).

The entire fast track of the brain (the master system) is designed to create and maintain identity. Our identity is almost impossible to override. Would you eagerly talk to a crowd? Wear a pretty dress? Drop your pants? Sing a solo? Live on a vegan diet? Identity makes these actions possible or impossible.

Attachments, at a brain level, create an identity that operates faster than conscious thought. Calling that identity *the will* drags our concept of identity into the slower conscious realm. If we use the word *identity* instead of *will,* most of what Dallas says still applies to attachment-based salvation. Only the mechanism has changed.

Dallas describes the will (by which he means the central heart/will/spirit component of the person) this way in his talks:

1. We must emphasize that the process of growth into emotional and spiritual maturity requires that we learn to use our will.

2. The will is the central capacity to create and originate things and events.

3. The primary act of the will is relying on God.

4. Each person has a kingdom, a domain of responsibility, an arena of governance in which you express your effective will.

5. You maximize the effect of your will by using it to direct yourself into experiences that will change your mind, body, social relations, and soul.

6. The will is meant to be surrendered to God.

7. A significant mark of emotional and spiritual maturity is the will surrendered to God.

8. Thankfulness to God is a mark of a will surrendered to God.

9. The mind is central to the will.

10. The mind works from evidence and reason.

11. Our choices about where we put our mind, then, become substantial in determining how we will mature emotionally and spiritually.

12. The choice of where to put our mind is what most determines where we go.

13. The most important thing we do is thinking about God.

14. What is in the mind and what is in the feelings and what is in the will is going to be determinative of my whole life. And thinking wrongly about God is the greatest mistake I can make.

15. If I don't think rightly, then my whole life will go in the wrong direction.

CHANGING WORDS FROM WILL TO HEART

"Be careful! Hot plate," the waiter says, as he sets down your fajitas.

You look my direction. "Explanations of the will have become rather convoluted," you tell me. "Could we use the word *heart* instead of *will* for clarity?"

"Yes. We find our true identities through a heart that has been given new life in Christ. Our current meaning of the word *will* is so far from classical meanings that we should replace it with *spirit* or *heart*, as you suggest."

We should also avoid equating the biblical view of the heart with any part of the brain. Neurotheology has debated for decades whether there is a "God receptor" somewhere in the nervous system. The reticular activating system was a favorite with my professor Dr. Lee Travis. "The cortex is far too fickle," he would say. But no part of the brain matches everything Scripture says about the heart.

It seems to me that God can interact with humans in every human part, function, and location. On the other hand, how coherently the fast track in the right brain is running has a clear impact on how well we think *with* God. Without attachment, this fast system slides dangerously toward seeing others as our enemies. I propose that the coherence of our relational identity (maintained through loving attachment and mutual mind with God) creates Christlike character in our spirit, heart, mind, brain, body, soul, and group identity in synchronicity.

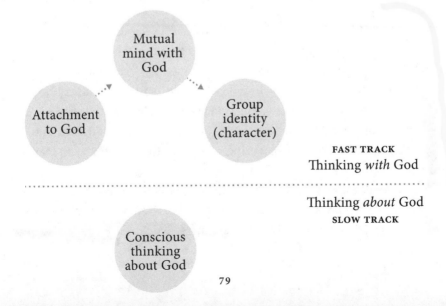

Mutual mind with God

Attachment to God

Group identity (character)

FAST TRACK
Thinking *with* God

Thinking *about* God
SLOW TRACK

Conscious thinking about God

"We have talked a good deal about the heart," you say, glancing at your watch. "What about the other elements of the human person as Dallas described them? Certainly, the mind and body should fit rather nicely with the brain. In fact, the social self probably has a lot to do with attachment, as well."

MIND, BODY, AND BRAIN

Salvation by attachment brings a harmonious element to our understanding of persons. If the heart is changed by attachment love, we certainly find that the physical brain is formed and transformed by the same attachment process. However, when we talk about the mind we often only think about conscious thoughts. Since salvation is about the change of identity and character into the image of Christ, we want to know how the mind of Christ comes to operate through the human brain. Attachment would use the fast track and the conscious will would use the slow track.

Two abilities of the conscious mind are to (1) focus attention and (2) think about something. The slow track of the brain can focus attention, and it is very helpful for solving things that puzzle us. We discussed the fast and slow tracks of the brain in chapter 3. The slow track thinks about things. The conscious slow track can be focused but is unable to grasp reality or change character. The only time that the conscious slow track directs its attention any way it wants is when it has "gone rogue." This rogue condition constitutes a good deal of what we call immaturity and happens when the fast track that controls character has momentarily lost coherence.[12]

It is specifically this slow-track focus that Dallas says will "be determinative of [our] whole life." We can all agree that where we focus our attention is huge, and yet, focusing our attention is a very indirect way to change the mechanism that controls where we focus attention.

When we focus our attention to change our character, we encounter three massive problems in our brain. First, focused attention works too slowly to form character. Focusing is done in the slow track; character develops in the fast track.

Second, the fast track of the brain (right-brain dominant) cannot be focused.[13] The fast track considers all it knows about identity and reality at once. Rather than focusing, the fast track synchronizes *with* another, (ideally) greater mind. If an attachment has been established, the greater mind can change the identity and character of the lesser mind.

Third, the fast track always comes before the slow track. The fast track is primary, both through speed and through the direction our experience moves through the brain. Nerves are one-directional devices. Nerve signals do not run both directions the way telephone lines do. While the brain has many feedback (reentry) systems,[14] these are synchronization and regulation signals, not backward traffic.

Why does one-way traffic matter? If we want to change character, we must change character where it happens in the brain. Trying to change character long after it has expressed itself only results in what Dallas calls "sin management." When we correct the character-creation process, we change all the activity from that point onward.

Correcting character in the brain is a bit like what happens when my wife eats her favorite shepherd's pie from the big warehouse store. Kitty will not eat mushrooms. The big store's shepherd's pie has mushrooms. Kitty picks out each mushroom with great care, but the next shepherd's pie also has mushrooms. Telling the checker at the warehouse that she does not like mushrooms does not remove them from the next pie. Similarly, in the one-way flow of mental activities, correcting character in the conscious slow track of the brain is way too late to correct our next reaction. We can try to pick through reactions we do not like, but that does not change our character the next time we react. No matter how much we point our conscious attention at the "mushrooms," they will be back in the next pie.

Even if Kitty could find the baker and tell him or her that she does not like mushrooms, there would still be mushrooms in the next pie. Why? Because Kitty lacks the proper relationship (attachment) with the baker to have the authority to make a change. Only when the person the baker knows as "my boss" with the attachment provided by "my paycheck" says, "No more mushrooms," will the pies change from that day forward.

Is Transforming the Mind through Attachment Scriptural?

Salvation begins in the heart, but the heart has limited impact on character through directing conscious attention. The heart could have a huge effect on character through building attachment love. What would happen if the art moved its mechanism of influence from the conscious slow track that thinks *about* God to the fast track that thinks *with* the Beloved?

Does Scripture support this idea of the heart being directed and driven by attachment love? Paul tells the Ephesians that Jesus dwells in our hearts through faith that is "rooted and grounded in love."[15] This teaching is in harmony with neuroscience if (and that is a very big if) the love that roots and grounds us is attachment love. If love is a choice, there is little love can do. In an attachment-love model, the means by which Jesus influences our lives is not primarily the conscious, focused attention of the will. We are guided (from our very spirit on out) by the most importantly powerful thing the brain knows—who we love! Let's read Paul:

> For this reason I bow my knees before the Father, from whom every family in heaven and on earth derives its name, that He would grant you, according to the riches of His glory, to be strengthened with power through His Spirit in the inner man, so that Christ may dwell in your hearts through faith; and that you, being rooted and grounded in love, may be able to comprehend with all the saints what is the breadth and length and height and depth, and to know the love of Christ which surpasses knowledge, that you may be filled up to all the fullness of God.[16]

HESED AND AGAPE AS ATTACHMENT LOVE

What sort of love will root and ground us? What love will send us into burning buildings to find a child? What love will search for decades for a missing loved one? What love will remember people who are long gone? What love will open the door to a prodigal child, or search through the wreckage from tsunamis, avalanches, or earthquakes that threaten to collapse the building, or swim through floods? What love will face wild beasts, freezing winds, and certain death? We are talking about attachment love, which comes from the heart.

Dr. Marcus Warner and I have argued elsewhere[17] that the Hebrew word *hesed* and the Greek word *agape* mean attachment love. Paul uses the Greek word *agape* to translate the Hebrew "hesed attachment" but finds the word *agape* inadequate. In 1 Corinthians 13, he devotes considerable effort to expanding the meaning of agape for his Greek-speaking audience.

Many a voluntarist preacher has said of agape, "This love is commanded and therefore must be an act of the will." Agape as a choice sounds logical, since all the will can do is make choices. Agape could also be commanded because it is possible in unity with Jesus. Peter walked on the water because of God in him. Attachment love is commanded because God loves (He is hesed) and all who share a mutual mind *with* God will also love.

The results of making love into a choice have been dismal in actual church life. Splits, divisions, unresolved conflicts, and divorces all underline what Dallas says about the will—it has very little power. Commanding agape by acts of the will has done poorly in marriages, churches, families, denominations, pornography addicts, and traumatized people.

Love as a choice (but without attachment) has preceded many divorces. Yet the very parents who could not stay married by choice fight like tigers to keep their children due to attachment love. Attachment has a lot of power compared to will and choice. It even appears that the pain of lost attachment turns those who were previously lovers into enemies. This does not generally lead to loving enemies either!

Joy is the energy that builds strong attachment love. Joy means "I am glad to be with you!" In fact, most marriages come apart because partners lose the energy of attachment (joy) and form new attachments with someone who gives them joy. Even prominent church leaders who are low on joy can fall scandalously when they encounter someone whose eyes say, "You are special to me." Despite the truth these preachers have preached and the choices they know are right, the power of an illicit joy builds an illicit attachment that costs them everything.

SOCIAL

"You are now discussing the social aspect of human life," you say to me. "Dallas places the social aspect close to the outside of a person. He just said, 'All of this growth is captured in a single word that is essentially relational: *love.*' That means that maturity comes from growing our love."

"Some of the best overlap between *choice* and *attachment* models comes in the social area," I agree. "The social-engagement system in the brain has mechanisms that match what Dallas has mentioned. The difference in a soteriology of attachment is that we move love to the center."

The force that creates human character is relational. Brain science would tell us that we do not become human by thinking *about* people or God. Our brain becomes human by thinking *with* those we love in an attachment way. Salvation by attachment leads us to a life of thinking with God about people.

Dallas says that to move toward emotional and spiritual maturity, "attack and withdrawal must be eliminated from our social relations and replaced by care for, love of, and identification with those near us." Both attack and withdraw impulses demonstrate a lack of love and Christlike character. We attack or withdraw when others begin to feel like enemies. We begin to think like predators and prey. The brain has a matching mechanism in the fast track that accompanies attack and withdrawal, rendering the other person no longer a resource that will help us—he or she becomes "not my people." We have an enemy.

When we are attached to others by love, however, our mind treats them as "my people" and will neither attack nor withdraw. Emotions may go up and down. We may stop to rest before we try again, but this is all aimed toward bringing us together once again. When attachment love is missing, the fast track goes into a predatory kind of enemy mode. When we spot a weakness we can exploit, we attack. If our weakness creates vulnerability, we withdraw.[18]

The resolution of attack and avoidance flows from attachment love (agape) for our enemies. We must see an angry Sanhedrin, a Roman mob, an oppositional child, or a furious spouse as our people. Our brain will not attack or withdraw from our people because we are attached. What happens to them is something we will share and feel as well.

But how does one learn to love enemies? Enemy mode is governed by the "group identity" processes in the brain. Our group identity (in each individual brain) will see others as "my people" or "our enemies" depending on the limits "my people" place on our hesed. Who do we see as one of us? Who is one of them? If our group mind says "one of us" when our individual mind says "enemy," we have a chance to learn to love our enemies. Mother says, "I know she broke your toy (enemy) but that is your little sister (one of us)." We are learning she is one of us. Learning spontaneous love for enemies requires the fast track to practice leaving enemy mode and returning to relational mode.

Just because my mother ("my people") is attached (hesed) with my little sister, I will still attack or withdraw when my fast track goes into enemy mode with my sister. What will bring me back to hesed? I may slowly return to being relational by indirect means. Long walks, sitting quietly, and eatin comfort food help me withdraw and slowly recover. A direct return to being relational is provided through encountering people who do not feel like enemies at the moment. The smiling face of someone I love—like a child, lover, dog, or grandchild—brings me back. But I have not yet learned to love when I am in enemy mode, only to get out of it. If an attachment person who loves me also loves my enemies, then I can learn to love those enemies too.

Learning to love enemies is learned from a people who love enemies. Here are the requirements: (1) Someone who feels like my enemy right now. (2) A teacher who is attached by love to my enemy. This teacher (a) sees these "enemies" as "my people" and (b) knows that "my people" love our enemies. (3) A love attachment with my teacher. (4) A mutual-mind moment with my teacher while I am in enemy mode, where I can experience attachment that lets enemies become "our people." (5) Repeated practice attaching to enemies in the company of "my people" because that is the kind of people we are. With practice, it becomes harder and harder to fall into enemy mode. Fewer and fewer people feel like my enemies. A spontaneous attachment produces the desire for enemies to know what God and God's people know about hesed love. I develop both emotional and spiritual maturity.

"I have never been anywhere that people practice that!" you exclaim. "What a different sort of church that would be. I'm not sure I would like it. But you still have not connected the implications of attachment with the soul. Does the soul also reflect relational neuroscience?"

SOUL

Dallas describes the soul as "that part of the person that integrates all the other dimensions to make one life." The brain happens to contain a structure whose function is the integration of all internal states and external connections with others. The cingulate cortex (in the right brain) synchronizes mental-energy states internally and externally. When Dallas describes our experience of the soul as "a sort of stream of energy and direction that is flowing inside of us," he could hardly have described the cingulate in clearer terms. We met the cingulate before when we discovered that it creates mutual-mind states.

For such harmony to happen in real time, we need the soul to have a mutual mind with God in real time. The brain has a place for mutual minds with people.[19] Could this brain function also be intended to create a mutual mind with God?

If our soul is as involved with our character as our cingulate cortex, we would need a significant love attachment with God for a mutual-mind state to transform character. Could the cingulate serve God's purposes? If we are to love the Lord our God with all our soul, then loving attachment extends from end to end of what it means to be human persons.

"If I understand correctly," you say, "training the soul to develop Christian character would require teaching the master system in the fast track. Most of our Christian practices don't go there."

We call for the check and we notice that our server today has been Jesús #26. "Does that mean that Jesus was feeding us today?" you ask with a smirk. "What do we tip Jesús?"

Centrality of Attachment Love

"Can you summarize for me how you would describe the heart, mind, body, social, self, and soul based on salvation through attachment and hesed love?" you ask.

"Sure! I will try to do that while we walk back."

THE HEART/SPIRIT/WILL

When we become new creatures in Christ, we find Jesus in our heart. Jesus is attached (θεμελιόω, grounded)[20] in our hearts by hesed/agape love. Our hearts can know God and be filled by the fullness of God through this attachment love. With a new heart from God, we can see and hear what God wants us to see and hear. When we see God's great hesed for us, even while we are yet in our sins, we have joy. Joy with God builds hesed love from us back to God—the source of our life.

THE MIND

Philosophers, theologians, and scientists were not able to observe the faster supraconscious track in the right brain until the last twenty-five years. While its "faculty" of intuition has been known for millennia, the conscious attention of the slow track is usually what we mean by "mind."

Both fast and slow tracks must connect the mind and the brain. The fast-track master system is developed and operated through attachment love. The slower, conscious track is an emissary sent to correct malfunctions. Useful corrections require true beliefs. For example, bloodletting was once considered the solution for many problems and diseases. When bloodletting was the cure, doctors faithfully drained bad blood out of the sick and wounded. In the same way, if our slow track (conscious thought) expects more truth will transform character, then we will think about truth to try and change character by truth alone.

Salvation through attachment to Jesus proposes a different solution. Transformation comes when our mind goes beyond correcting our beliefs to practicing attachment love. False beliefs certainly need correction, but we cannot stop there without correcting our loves. We remember that the One who holds the seven stars told the church at Ephesus that they had their beliefs right, "But I have this against you: that you have left your foremost love."[21]

THE BODY

Our brain is built, maintained, and transformed by attachment love. The physical brain is part of the body. Attachment is most centralized in the thalamus, where our sensory data enters the brain and where our brain makes sense of our reality. The brain thus filters everything that comes in from a personal-attachment point of view.

FAST-TRACK THINKING WITH GOD

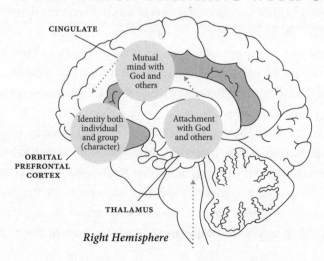

Joy is an energy created by attachment. Joy builds and drives every healthy relational activity of the brain's master fast track. Our identities as individuals and groups ("my people") grow through relational activities—through mutual mind and attachment. Coherent identity requires coherent attachment relationships for a lifetime. As Dallas says, "Growth in maturity, then, involves changes for the body."

Attachment is a drive built into our bodies. So is fear. When there is trauma and neglect, attachment is suppressed and fear is elevated, so fear drives the body/brain. When fear drives the body, we seek to make the other lose and call that winning. When attachment (joy) drives the body, we seek to make others "our people." For the body to learn the character of Christ, it needs joyful love attachments in the presence of our enemies.

THE SOCIAL

It is not a big step to see how "our people" and attachment love are central to our social identities. In the brain, our social identities are at the core of character formation. As Dallas says, "Rejection by others is perhaps the immediate source of most evils in human life in human terms." Brain scans reveal that the pain of rejection and abandonment is attachment pain down in the thalamus. Broken attachments upset the thalamus severely.

Attack and withdrawal are signs of a brain in enemy mode. Enemy mode is the fast track operating without attachment. When the fast track has a broken attachment (with lots of attachment pain), it can become cruel (as often happens when couples break up) or even very dangerous. Consider how many news stories of a shooting are traced to a rejected partner, how many suicides follow a broken relationship, or how much gang violence is tied to revenge. These crimes would not happen if the perpetrators had loving attachments to their victims. Attachment is central to restoring our social selves.

Dallas used loving our enemies as a benchmark to measure spiritual maturity. Learning to spontaneously love our enemies has proven to be very elusive, even a hopeless dream, for many Christians in the Western church. Yet many Christians living under persecution continue to see the government agents who imprison them, the guards who torture them, the killers who murder their family, the neighbors who despise them, or the religious zealots who hunt them down not as enemies but as those who need to become God's people.

I have observed Christians loving their enemies. I grew up in a persecuted church in Colombia. My travels teaching about trauma recovery let me learn from those who suffer. The survivors of the Rwandan genocide in my friend Father Ubald's church[22] are learning to become loving family members with the very ones who attacked them. The wives of the Colombian pastors who were martyred for their faith[23] and the families of the twenty-one Coptic Christians who were killed by ISIS[24] display spontaneous attachment love toward their enemies. Learning to attach to people who would kill us requires both a strong attachment to the God who loves enemies and attachment to the people of God who also love enemies. Where Christians know themselves as people who love our enemies, we find Christian character growing.

THE SOUL

The soul integrates our identities and directs the energy of everything it means to be human. The brain can create this integration using the cingulate cortex. The process of integration produces a state of mutual mind with significant others. But the brain reserves the mutual-mind states that create our identity and character for people who share attachment love. These are "my people."

Coherence

Could it be that at every level of the human person, we are both created and made new by attachment love? Are we being saved when God becomes our Beloved and God's people are our beloved people? Is this why Paul uses attachment love as a test for true faith? He tells the Thessalonians,

> For this reason, when I could endure it no longer, I also sent to
> find out about your faith, for fear that the tempter might have
> tempted you, and our labor would be in vain. But now that
> Timothy has come to us from you, and has brought us good news
> of your faith and love, and that you always think kindly of us,
> longing to see us just as we also long to see you, for this reason,

brethren, in all our distress and affliction we were comforted about you through your faith."[25]

We are transformed by who we love more than what we believe. We should neglect neither but make attachment love our priority. The means and mechanisms for developing a Christlike identity in a human brain are tied, at every level, to the need for loving attachment. Restoration is a relational process. Salvation gives us a new heart and a Lover for our soul.

Trauma and deprivation hinder or block the development of maturity by teaching us to be enemies rather than God's family. By healing through the Holy Spirit, these blockages to maturity are removed. Fellowship with the rest of "our people" trains our brain to grow what has been missing. With a loving attachment that will not let us go, we can develop a fully formed, joyful, and Christlike character.

"Thanks for sharing my lunchtime," I say joyfully.

We arrive back at the conference, ready to hear Dallas give his two afternoon lectures. Dallas will examine what the church is doing that does not work. He will tell us where change is needed and what kind of change is required. This is going to be good!

Exercise: Nine-Minute Meal

Do this exercise during a meal you share with someone.

This exercise has three parts, each three minutes long.

1. Begin by thanking God for feeding you. Since we attach to the One who feeds us, thank God for everything you taste and like on your plate. Thank God by mentioning what you like about the food. Thank God also for those who prepared or brought the food to you. (This exercise is even better if you arrive quite hungry.)

2. Tell a short story of a moment you might have sensed God's smile.

3. Smile at each person sharing the meal with you and bless them with one thing that comes to your mind that God likes about them.

SPIRITUAL FORMATION TOWARD WHOLENESS IN CHRIST

DALLAS WILLARD

Lunch break was over. People often straggle back from conference lunches, but not today. Almost everyone was back in their seats when Dallas stood up to speak. There was expectancy in the room. Dallas had a warmth about him and spoke as to a room full of friends. Each one present seemed to sense *Dallas really wants me to take this into my heart*. His voice was steady and soft.

. . .

Within evangelical circles, the language of spiritual formation has arisen in the last fifteen to twenty years, at most. But within the church as a whole, it is very old language—two thousand years old, practically. Saint John Cassian has a book of spiritual formation, called *Institutes*, dating from the 400s. When you read it in our context today, however, unless you have a peculiar background, most of it doesn't fit—it's just too monastic.

Institutes was written at a time when the church had accepted that there are two different ways of Christian life. You find this laid out and detailed in other early writers, such as Eusebius. The one way, the way of perfection, was for people who stepped out of ordinary life and engaged all of their time in religious activities of one sort or another. The other way f life was for people who do what normal people do, who have children and run farms and businesses and participate in the military. They come to the people leading the life of perfection to help them carry on special days. You don't have to think very deeply until you recognize that this is a pattern that still exists and is quite strong, in fact even in Protestant and evangelical circles: There is an expectation that ministers will lead a different kind of existence than ordinary folk.

This expectation bleeds out into a number of distinctions in contemporary understandings of the Christian life, one of which is a distinction between being a Christian and being a disciple. Now that distinction we must talk about at some length, because it has led to a circumstance where people who sincerely identify with the church don't lead their life outside the church in a distinctively Christlike way. They don't know how to approach it *because* they don't know how to fit vocation into Christianity as they've come to understand it. So their ordinary life is led outside of what they understand to be their devotion to God. Very often the Scriptures they might read in church or at home, the prayers they might offer, and their relationships have little to no bearing on their character.

So we need to consider how distinctions like this one between "being a Christian" and "being a disciple" have raised a barrier to a pervasive, intensive concentration on spiritual maturity—and with it, emotional maturity. Now I remind you: Emotional maturity means that your life is not governed by your feelings or your desires or your emotions. Those are all okay in their place, but their place is not to govern life. Emotional maturity is a characteristic or condition of people who are able to do what is good regardless of how they feel, or what they want, or their emotional engagements of various kinds. I wish we had time to go over the distinctions between desire and emotion and feeling, because if we are going to walk the path of emotional maturity, we have to be able to identify those and to know what to do about them so we can choose what is good, regardless of how we feel or what our emotions and our desires are.

Spiritual formation is a process—not an outcome. There is an outcome, but formation itself is a process, that of taking on a certain character for your whole life. As such, spiritual formation doesn't *have* to be Christian. In fact, everyone gets a spiritual formation. It begins when a child is quite young, and they pick up on the feelings and emotions and ideas and thoughts and beliefs of their parents and other more mature around them. These elements coalesce to determine how they sta... act. Sometimes, there are profoundly difficult physical conditions that go into this and other variables which we might not understand. Medical and scientific people work very hard on trying to understand these conditions. But there's also what you might think of as a natural process: A character begins to manifest itself in children fairly early. The feelings and the emotions that inform their character are matched to reactions and thoughts about how they respond to them.

Most people don't have a consistent character because their models for character were inconsistent: They take a part of their character from this person, another part from that person. There are periods, for example, when young people reject what had been modeled for them earlier and begin to take on the characteristics of some influential new person in their life—maybe a peer or a teacher, maybe a person in the public arts, music— all the media that are constantly pounding them.

But Christian spiritual formation is a process of taking on the character of Christ. That means the person begins to think with—to have beliefs and images and ways of interpreting things that are characteristic of—Christ. This process begins at what we call "the birth from above"—the impartation or implantation of a new life in the person. The record of history and the Scriptures testify that salvation is best thought of as having a new kind of life.

A New Kind of Life

I hate to become too philosophical, but when we talk about life from above, new birth, and all of that, we need to try to mean something by our words. I define life as self-initiating, self-sustaining, self-directing activity of a specific kind. The child who has a goldfish knows when their fish is upside-down floating around, it's no longer self-initiating. It's quit. The child has come to know about death and life.

But life comes in particular forms; a cabbage has a certain kind of life, a fish has a certain kind of life, dogs and horses and so on—each has a certain kind of life. And each human being has a certain kind of life based on a certain range of abilities. When that *new* life comes into them, it comes with new abilities born of the new activities going on in them.

The activity of the new kind of life that we mean by the "birth from above" is reliance upon Christ and God for everything—the restoration of the relationship to God intended for us in the first place and that alone enables us to fulfill our nature. To "seek first the Kingdom of God and His kind of righteousness" is the natural response to the new life that has come to you. Paul says in 1 Corinthians 12:3, "If you believe that Jesus is Lord, that is because of the Spirit that has moved in you."[1] You actually believe that.

Believing that Jesus is Lord is a tremendous shift from not believing that Jesus is Lord. We are actively misled about its significance by the fact that people so often profess Jesus as Lord and yet seem no different from their previous life or from the life of nonbelievers around them. But to actually believe Jesus is Lord reorients your whole life. To believe something is to be ready to act as if it were true.

Now, that has to be worked out. It doesn't all come in a lump. But when we have that elemental Kingdom life implanted in us, we are drawn forth by our vision of Christ the Redeemer and what life in the Kingdom of God is like with Him, and we increasingly grow in our likeness to Him by changing all of those dimensions that I mentioned. That's where the change happens: The will now is turned toward God. The mind is now focused on God. The feelings respond to that new focus, which then orients our body and our social context. All these variables are progressive—they take time. Such an all-encompassing reorientation doesn't happen overnight. The battle, if you like, has just begun at the new birth.

As with natural birth, a lot of your development in the Kingdom life depends on how you were nourished before the birth. That turns out to be extremely important for those of us who want to be teachers and leaders: What are we providing to people as they are coming *toward* Christ? How are we teaching them? We can teach them in such a way that at birth into the new life from above, their old life is over. But spiritual formation is the development of a kind of life that is imparted through the birth from above and yields not a life that is over but a life that is beginning.

What Are Disciples?

So now let's think a moment about disciples. The word *Christian* occurs three times in the New Testament. It is introduced in connection with disciples of Jesus who can no longer be thought of as a Jewish sect. You'll hear various explanations of what the word *Christian* means, but basically, it was introduced once there were followers of Christ who were no longer Jewish. At this point, the movement of Christianity began to sweep out into the Gentile world.

So "Christian" was a designator, a way of classification that differentiated followers of Jesus from Judaism. What about "disciples"? In the New Testament context, "disciples" was a designation for people who were physically present with Jesus while He was here on earth. To be a disciple was to have been *with* Him, learning to be like Him. That's the foundation of discipleship: To be with someone, learning to be like that person.

For Jesus, to disciple someone was to teach that person how to live their life in the Kingdom of God. Remember, the Kingdom of God is God in action. So to say "Seek first the Kingdom of God" is to invite someone to be caught up in the action of God and the kind of righteousness that comes with that. That's a major point that we have to hold on to: The basic idea of being a disciple, in the New Testament, is being with Jesus, learning to be like Him.

Of course, after Jesus' death, "with Him" takes a different form. But the meaning of *disciple* is still the same. The disciple is someone now who is with Jesus, still, learning to be like Him. That's a status. *Disciple* is a status; *spiritual formation* is a process.

Spiritual formation, in the Christian sense, is the process of transformation that occurs to the disciple. Such transformation involves emotional and spiritual maturity. And if we are not disciples, we won't move forward in that process. You cannot experience spiritual formation—transformation into the likeness of Christ—without being a disciple of Christ.

So now you see the seriousness of accepting a form of Christianity that does not involve being a disciple. If you ask Christians generally, "Are you a disciple?" you get a lot of different responses. The general assumption that will emerge is that you don't have to be a disciple to be a Christian. You can't overestimate the importance of that for how our churches work and what we might undertake.

As important as churches are—and I don't think there is any substitute for the church as Jesus conceived of it—churches have the challenge of being populated by both disciples and Christians, and in some cases, by all

Christians and no disciples. It depends on what is being taught. If someone is brought into a fellowship of Christians without any reference to discipleship, then any introduction to discipleship will come as a surprise. Whether or not you have to be a disciple to be a Christian is at the heart of our problem with spiritual and emotional maturity—in the churches generally, and in Christian leadership particularly.

Generally, people do not believe that discipleship is required for salvation. The picture of salvation that now emerges does not involve spiritual formation that yields maturity. It's wonderful if it happens, and of course the New Testament is full of spiritual formation. But it's not thought of as essential to the Christian life. That's what we're up against.

When spiritual formation is not considered essential, then it's not made central to what we do with folks who are called Christians. And as a result, they don't grow in the characteristics of Christ. They may look at the parts of the Scripture that talk about these kinds of things with admiration but not hopefulness. They really don't know what to do about the Sermon on the Mount, for example. They hear these things like "Turn the other cheek," "Don't curse those who curse you," and so on, and they don't know what to do about it, because it's not thought of as part of salvation.

Consider the following diagram.

WHERE ACTION COMES FROM

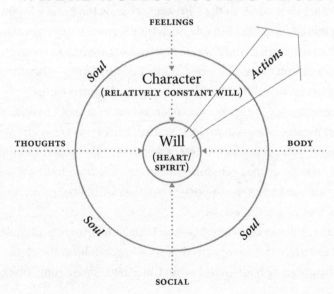

If a disciple of Jesus is defined as one who is "learning from Jesus how to lead my life as He would lead my life if He were I," we have to ask ourselves, *Is that me?* Then we have to answer honestly in terms of what is happening in our life. And *then* we have to ask, *Have I chosen that? And if I have chosen it, what am I doing to carry through with it?*

If a disciple of Jesus is learning from Jesus how to live, what am I learning from Him now? What have I learned from Him in the past? How does that whole progression look? As a disciple, my consciously chosen aim is to learn the life of Jesus, and I am constantly arranging and rearranging my affairs to realize this goal.

Consider prayer as an example. The big issue I'm working on currently is trying to learn from Jesus what He said about prayer. This is just mind-blowing stuff. There are areas in the Gospels—and elsewhere for that matter—that paint such a picture of what can be accomplished with prayer that you almost want to stay away from it. John 14 is full of that; Jesus is trying to explain to His disciples, "I'm leaving you, but I'll still be with you and you can work in the same power that I work in." He makes these statements: "If you ask anything in my name, I will do it, that the Father may be glorified in the Son."[2] I look at that and I say, *I must have a lot to learn about asking in His name because I don't think that I can preach and teach what I do about Jesus and the gospel of the Kingdom unless I know a lot more about it than I do now.* So I'm constantly trying to learn what that means. I try to put it in practice and understand where somehow I got it wrong or why I occasionally get it right.

I just use that as an illustration of what being a disciple of Jesus means in my case now. Most of the folks in our congregations have never been invited to become a disciple. We don't do discipleship evangelism. We do Christian evangelism, but perhaps we should have some occasions when in an appropriate way, we invite people to decide to be disciples of Jesus. Of course, we'd be immediately confronted with the issue of a two-tiered citizenship: "Oh, you're a disciple? I'm just a Christian." How to go about doing that would be a matter of great difficulty. But until we start calling people into discipleship (as opposed to inviting them to be Christians), we don't have a basis for talking about emotional maturity as a variable of our Christlikeness.

Now, I will often have people say to me, "Do you mean that if I'm not a disciple, I won't go to heaven?" One of my favorite questions to help them is: "Do you think you're going to like heaven if you get there? And if so, why would you like it?" The enjoyment of heaven will have something to do with our spiritual and emotional maturity. And most people haven't considered what makes heaven desirable beyond a superficial image of "the great Marriott in the sky."

The VIM Model

In my book *Renovation of the Heart*, I lay out the structure of spiritual development, and I use this little diagram—"VIM"—to help us get hold of that structure. The first part is "Vision," which means *What is the good that is set before us when we think of maturity?*

There's a wonderful preacher up in Canada that I heard some time ago who said when he got saved, he thought he got three things: He got (1) a certificate that said he's in, (2) a ticket that said we'll take you there when the time is right, and (3) a catalog, in which he could place orders by praying. I thought how striking that was and how similar to what the vision is for many people. It's a negative one—I'm going to the place that doesn't require air conditioning. Heaven as it really is doesn't make a lot of sense to people, and it won't make a lot of sense except when understood in continuity with life experienced now, because in fact heaven *is* a continuation of life now.

See, eternal life is not something that you get after you are dead. Eternal life is a way of living—now, even as we are alive. Sometimes I think it would help us if instead of talking about eternal life, we talked about eternal living. Eternal living is a matter of living a life so intertwined with the life of God Himself that your life is a part of God's life. Consider John 17:3: Eternal Life is knowing God, the only true God, and Jesus Christ whom He has sent. The knowing Jesus describes here is not cognitive (knowing what the answers are). Knowledge, biblically and in life generally, is a matter of interactive relationship.

For example, if you would like someone to repair your automobile, you don't turn to someone who has read a lot of books about automobiles. You want someone who has had some interactive relationship with automobiles. And when we ask a person, "Do you know such and such?" we are not surprised to hear an answer like "Well, I've met him, but I don't know him." Eternal living is this kind of knowing, an interactive relationship. I am living eternally now. That is why Jesus says, "Those who keep my word will never experience or see death."[3] Why? Because the life they are living now simply continues. And again, consider John 11 at the tomb of Lazarus when Jesus is talking with Martha about resurrection and so on, and He says, "Those that believe in Me, though they were dead, yet shall they live. And he that believeth in Me that is living shall never die."[4] It wasn't death He was talking about—He's talking about life.

That's the vision, that's the *V* in the VIM. The *I* is *Intention* or *Decision*. You have to support the vision. If I have a vision of life in the Kingdom of God now, I am in a position to grow into spiritual maturity and emotional maturity. And I can make a decision to be His disciple because of the clarity of the vision.

I have in one of my rooms some instruments of physical exercise. I don't have a vision for it, frankly. I need to have the vision for it, but I don't. So those instruments go unused. If my doctor told me, "You're going to be dead if you don't do this," I might gain a vision for these instruments. But insofar as the vision is not there, neither is the intention.

At USC we have millions of dollars spent on language training, but almost no one who goes through the program and gets the credits learns the language. Those who do—the students who wind up in places like Paris or Madrid—tend to learn the language because they have the vision. We have the means of language learning, but most of the students don't have the intention to learn, because they don't have the vision.

Do you see the connection there? You can find the means (*M*) for becoming Christlike if you have the settled intention based upon a clear vision. Means are never the problem. But neither are they ever the solution. We have a terrible tendency to think the means are the solution. No, no, no.

All over this world, there are people who speak English better than I do. They don't have better means at their disposal than I do; in many cases, they have no means at all. But they have the intention, and they have a vision. Because of that, whatever comes to hand they use as means to learn English.

As we are becoming disciples, there are three things that we are learning. These are not actually separable in life, but I separate them out just for the purpose of discussion.

DO WHAT JESUS TAUGHT

The first thing is learning to do what Jesus taught. Jesus said, "Bless those who curse you."[5] Don't curse them; bless them and pray for them. Now, how would I learn to do that? As a disciple of Jesus, I have to learn how to do that. This is the part that is most missing from our existing programs and strategies for growth: teaching people how to do what He said. Of course, we have to pursue this growth in His company. That's why in the great commission it says, "Baptize them in the name of the Father, Son and Holy Spirit."[6] That means surround them in the Trinitarian reality, which would be our disciples gathering in the name of Jesus. Jesus said, "Where two or three are gathered in My name, I'm in the midst" and unfortunately we normally quote that only when two or three are all who show up, as if that's the consolation prize.[7] But what He's talking about is any gathering in His name—on His behalf and for His purposes. In such a context, we are in Jesus' company, primed to pursue the growth He intends for us. Our dimensions of personality have been changed, and out of that comes conformity to what Jesus said.

Now, there is a difference between wanting to do what Jesus said and wanting to *try* to do what He said. This difference creates a deadly environment of legalism, and it has happened over and over again in the history of the church. The path of discipleship doesn't emphasize *behavior*; it emphasizes the *sources* of behavior. Spiritual formation in Christ occurs not in a mechanical way, not in an entirely predictable way, but in a certain way that will be adapted to the individual.

You will notice in the teachings of the New Testament—from Jesus, Paul, and the others—you don't get a list of things to do. Of course, you get some things like "put off the old person and put on the new," but you're not told how to do that.[8] We have to resist the tendency to say, "Well, if you do 1, 2, and 3, you'll have put off the old person and put on the new." That won't work. We have to present Christ and His teaching in a way that the heart is drawn to Christ, with others. The path of discipleship is always communal, with a result of our hearts and minds becoming more like His. As we stay with Him, and with others who are following the same path, it soon becomes impossible for our mind to think things that it used to think, for our will to consider doing things it used to consider. They simply become out of the question.

LEARN TO HANDLE DAILY LIFE

This process of disciple making involves people learning to do what Jesus did and taught, learning to handle the ordinary events of daily life within the principles and power of God's rule. Discipleship takes hold at a place of business, during a committee meeting, in the midst of a fund-raising project, at the seat of government. Discipleship is not for the church; the church is for discipleship. And discipleship is for the world.

If discipleship is for the world, then the primary place of discipleship is at work, because that's where we spend most of our time, and that is where the need is the greatest. When you look at all the difficulties we face in our world and ask yourself, *What would it be like if those places were inhabited by disciples of Jesus who are doing their work to the glory of God in the power of His name?*, the answers immediately present themselves: We wouldn't be in this financial crisis if the people running the financial world were disciples of Jesus. Our families, our schools, and all areas of organization depend upon people who are actively learning how to live in the Kingdom of God as He would live in their world. What would Jesus do if His job was my job or your job? That's what's interesting, and that's how we learn to live our life.

ACT IN JESUS' POWER

Now, you can't do the things He said without learning to act in God's power—that's indispensable. And you can't handle the ordinary events of life without accessing His power; they are too challenging, there's too much evil in the world. We ourselves are not well enough put together mentally and emotionally to make this work. We have to learn to act counting on the power of God to act with us. We learn to stop trusting ourselves and what we manage and manipulate, and we learn to trust God.

The primary barrier to this kind of life remains the dominance of a gospel or a vision that has no connection with spiritual transformation and emotional maturity. This is a heavy topic, and I'm sorry to have to address it. But we have to ask ourselves, What is our message? What is our gospel? And I have to ask myself: *Does the gospel I profess have a natural tendency to produce disciples of Jesus? What is the connection between the gospel I preach and emotional and spiritual maturity?* Now each of you, as I do, will have to ask that question and try to answer it honestly. I would have to say that the reason why we do not see a steady progression toward emotional and spiritual maturity among people who self-identify as Christians is because the message they have heard has no clear connection to maturity.

Three Gospels

We have three gospels that are commonly preached. One has to do *only* with forgiveness of sins. Your sins will be forgiven, and you will be in heaven in the afterlife if you believe that Jesus suffered for your sins. Now, you can't leave that out in my opinion. But is forgiveness of sins the gospel, or is it something that naturally goes along *with* the gospel? If forgiveness of sins is the whole gospel, what connection does it have to emotional maturity? I'm afraid we have to say none. Now, does it work that way for some people? It certainly does. History is, of course, full of people who have been so burdened with guilt that when they were presented with a gospel of forgiveness of sins, they went on to give their whole lives to God. But the question is whether such a gospel produces that result *regularly* in people, and particularly when the gospel is *reduced* to the forgiveness of sins. I don't think so. And that's not a theoretical claim: Watch how it actually works in real life—and there's little connection to character transformation.

The second gospel commonly preached is that Jesus died to liberate the oppressed, and you can stand with Him in that battle. I see a large segment of self-identifying Christians believe that liberation from oppression is the sum total of the gospel message. Was Jesus in favor of liberation from oppression? You bet He was. And arguably, from a human point of view, He got killed for that very reason. So liberation from oppression is important. But does it have a *natural tendency* to regularly produce character transformation? I think the answer again is, "No, it doesn't." Again, I encourage you to look at people who believe this gospel and see if it does, because we want to be true to the facts; we want to be empirically careful on how we handle this.

Finally, the third gospel message commonly preached is "Take care of your church, and it will take care of you." It's surprising how common this is, actually. It's not widely recognized, but I'm talking about how the gospel comes over to people. Sometimes it's communicated to people an emphasis on correct doctrine: "If you accept the doctrine we're teaching, participate in it, then we're going to take care of you with God." Is it important to take care of your church? You better believe it is. But that is not the fullness of the gospel by any means.

Gospel of Grace

Let's look at a fourth gospel presentation as an alternative to these three: Put your confidence in Jesus, and live every aspect of your life with Him as His disciple now in the present Kingdom of God. I'm suggesting that salvation is participating in the life which Jesus is now living on earth. Listen to these words from Colossians 3: "If you have been raised up in the new life with Christ, set your mind on things above, where Christ is seated at the right hand of God. Set your affections on things above, not on things on the earth. For you are dead and your life is hid with Christ in God."[9] Now, we need to think about what that means. According to Paul, your life is hid with Christ in God. You have an eternal life that is a part of the eternal life of Christ that is part of the eternal life of God.

Salvation in this gospel is participating in the life which Jesus is now living on earth. Of course, that involves forgiveness from sin, and liberation of the oppressed, and faithful church membership, and correct doctrine, and heaven afterward. But the key question is: What is primary to our life in Christ? Grace. If we had never sinned we would still need grace, because grace is for life, not just for forgiveness.

As a disciple, I am learning how to lead a life of grace in everything that I do. Now, that is going to remove the sources of emotional immaturity; anger, contempt, all of the things that people are troubled by—and trouble others with—are now dealt with by the kind of life they are living with Jesus in the Kingdom of God. Is there room for improvement? Always, always. But simply living as a disciple of Jesus and watching the process of spiritual formation remove the sources of immaturity that curse human life generates a lot of improvement by itself. You think you can't live without anger? You can, and your life will be a lot better for it. You think you can't live without anger, without cultivated lust, or the other sins Jesus touches on in the Sermon on the Mount? Good news: You *can* live without those things, and your life will be a lot better for it. But you have to learn them through life in the Kingdom of God.

Now, for such a gospel, what does heaven beyond this earth look like? My vision of heaven is your best day on earth. I mean, it'll be better than that, but that's a way of getting after it. I don't think heaven is going to be very different from the life we experience now, except the absence of evil and the expansion of our powers—and, of course, we will have the benefit of the whole community of God through the ages that will be engaged in ruling and reigning with Him over creation. I think that the aim of God in all of human history has been to prepare a community for that purpose—and one in which He dwells. He is preparing a living temple in which He will dwell forever. It is God's desire to be with His people, and that is what comes down through the ages as you look into the past.

The Resurrection is precisely the emergence of this kind of life in us. Our conversion is the transfer of everything we do into this new life. So we are counting on the presence of Resurrection life to pick up everything that we do and make it a part of what God is doing. Look at Philippians 3:10-11: Paul makes his goal, "That I may know Him and the power of His resurrection and the fellowship of His sufferings . . . that I may attain to the resurrection from the dead." This is what we do with our lives: We try to take everything we do into that realm of Resurrection life. We are moved out of the kind of competition and envy and often brutal behavior that goes on when we only have this life to look at. And we look at our lives in terms of the life which Jesus is now living and the eternity that it represents.

It is absolutely essential, and the main part of preaching the gospel, to present the goodness of Christ and the world that God has intended and that is held out in front of us as this Resurrection life. I don't think you can make a clear intention to be a disciple without it because Jesus laid down some pretty stiff conditions. He said, "Unless you hate your mother and father and your own self also, you can't be my disciple."[10] He wasn't saying, "I won't let you." He was saying you just can't do it. You will not be able to enter into the reality of the Resurrection life if you are clinging to the values and priorities of the life of this world. So it's really crucial how we present the vision of the Kingdom of God. I like to say you make a disciple by ravishing people with the vision of life in the Kingdom of God. I don't know how else you would do it.

• • •

Before we hear Dallas's fourth and final lecture, we will consider how attachment love deepens what it means to be disciples. Dallas has said that salvation means we receive new life from above. Does this new life grow from a new and remarkable attachment? Does this new attachment include a people as well as the living God? We'll find out in the next chapter.

7

TRANSFORMED BY LOVING ATTACHMENT

JIM WILDER

Dallas makes a distinction between two different forms of spiritual life. *Christians* have beliefs *about* God but are mostly unchanged by their faith. *Disciples* have lives *with* God and become increasingly mature. Dallas says that to be a disciple is "to have been *with* Him, learning to be like Him. That's the foundation of discipleship: To be with someone, learning to be like that person." What Dallas has had in mind, beginning with "the Kingdom of God is here," aims entirely at developing *life with God*.[1]

What creates the difference between a *Christian* and a *disciple*? Why do some people not become *disciples* or live life *with* God? Dallas has a mental model that explains the difference and provides a solution based on the spiritual disciplines. He says, "In my book *Renovation of the Heart*, I lay out the structure of spiritual development, and I use this little diagram—VIM— to help us get hold of that structure."

V = Vision
I = Intention
M = Means

The neuroscience of attachment suggests some modification of the VIM model. Attachment love (called *hesed* and *agape* in Scripture) empowers discipleship through active force created by attachments. To provide a structure for our study, we will compare the VIM model with the neurotheological Life Model that developed in the counseling center where Jane Willard and I worked. Counseling is the practical work of helping *Christians* become *disciples*.

In the counseling office, we observed that the human will was rarely in charge of much and could be quite ineffective. Spiritual disciplines worked better for some people than others. The active presence of Jesus in the minds of those who loved Him, however, produced dramatic healing and growth—particularly for those who had loving relationships in their lives. We organized what we were learning and called this framework the "Life Model." Dallas placed his endorsement on the first published copy of the Life Model, saying it was "the best model I have seen for bringing Christ to the center of counseling and restoring the disintegrating community fabric within Christian churches."[2]

The neurotheological elements of Life Model extended what is possible under the VIM model. Most American Christians have little awareness of how often they revert to more truth, better choices (using my will) and the limitations this approach to Christianity creates. What is the alternative?

Spiritual Maturity

The Life Model proposes that human maturity is the responsibility of humans. We need to grow emotional maturity with one another. Normal human maturity requires a multigenerational community, where the relational-brain skills needed to be fully human are practiced and passed from generation to generation. Normal human maturity requires two elements; redeemed (spiritual) maturity requires a third element.

Human maturity, as necessary as it is, falls short of developing full maturity that matches God's design for us. Spiritual maturity adds God's redemption to produce what no human community can achieve alone. This redemptive element comes from an interactive life of loving attachment with God. The three elements needed for full (spiritual) maturity are

1. multigenerational community;
2. interactive (Immanuel) life with God; and
3. relational-brain skills needed to be fully human.

A multigenerational community is where we acquire human role models. "Knowledge, biblically and in life generally, is a matter of interactive relationship," Dallas stated. The church is a central multigenerational community. Yet the church must be more than human community. Dallas says, "When that *new* life comes . . . , it comes with new abilities born of the new activities going on in them."

How could these three elements of spiritual maturity be practiced? The Heart and Soul Conference became the first public forum where the VIM and the Life Models were compared as ways to grow spiritual, yet human, maturity. Our central goal was to produce disciples who were alive with the character of Christ.

When you take a moment to reflect, you will notice that *life with God* is at the center of both the VIM and the Life Model. Life *with* God is not one of the three letters of VIM, but it is Dallas's objective for VIM, nonetheless. He wants us to begin a life with God immediately upon salvation.

Christians *and* Disciples

Before we compare models any further, we need to be clear about the talk we have just heard. Why does Dallas start by contrasting *Christians* and *disciples*? Dallas intends two things based on his VIM model. First, he wishes to correct the prevailing understanding of life with God—that the Christian life is simply securing a ticket to heaven. His corrected vision becomes one of life *with* Jesus that begins now at salvation, not when we reach heaven. One could feel the conference audience wanting to cheer!

Second, Dallas wants to create intention (*I*). We will need intention (focused attention) on life *with* Jesus so we will understand the means (*M*) in his next and final talk. Intention is where the VIM model struggles. Dallas must use "thinking *about* God" methods to try to achieve "life *with* God" results. The VIM model has ideas (slow conscious thoughts) as its tools. Dallas says, "The will now is turned toward God. The mind is now focused on God. The feelings respond to that new focus, which then orients our body and our social context."

Dallas is convinced that the "*with*-God-life" must and does begin at salvation, not in heaven. He knows that *Christians* have lots of beliefs and show little change of character. We can now ask, "Could part of why we have Christians who aren't experiencing life with God be caused by emphasizing beliefs as the means of transformation?"

Perhaps you have already noticed how Dallas explains the transformation process. "Christian spiritual formation is a process of taking on the character of Christ. That means a person begins to think with—to have beliefs and images and ways of interpreting things that were characteristic of—Christ." He states that we "think . . . have beliefs and images and ways of interpreting things" like the person we have as a model.

Does Attachment Shape Beliefs, or Do Beliefs Create Attachment?

Are intention and focus the best way to learn and transform character? Does God expect to produce attachment love and activate the most powerful force in the human mind or direct our wills to make feeble redirections of our conscious attention? Are *disciples* restricted to slow-track, focused-thought methods? Fast-track processes control character formation in the brain. Do *disciples* use the same mutual-mind skills with Jesus that we use with other humans?

The Life Model expects that we can share mutual-mind states with God and people. For example, I can sense when God wants me to stop what I am doing and pay attention to what is distressing my wife. Christlike character begins with attachment love, develops through mutual-mind states, and ultimately, creates a people with a shared sense of identity—in real time. These relational-brain skills in the fast track direct our lives. Life *with* others allows the brain to become human and regulate feelings, desires, impulses, and emotions. Mutual mind with God replaces the predatory reactions that emerge toward anyone who is not "my people" with gentle, protective responses.

Our conclusion hinges on the *I* in Dallas's VIM model. Whether our intention (*I*) to live life with God comes *mostly* from a focused decision by the will (with very little power) or *mostly*[3] from a loving attachment (the most powerful force in the human brain) makes a very large difference when selecting the means (*M*) of discipleship.

Before we hear Dallas's final lecture about the means (*M*), we should focus our attention on whether Scripture gives any strategic importance to attachment love. We should also understand how attachment love transforms character. Understanding attachment love will allow us to listen to Dallas with discernment. Keep in mind that we are not discarding options. We are examining which intention (*I*) works better for making *disciples* out of *Christians*.

Life with *Jesus*

If life *with* Jesus begins at salvation and thinking *with* another begins with attachment, then salvation must involve the creation of a new attachment with Jesus.

Relational-brain skills, a pillar of the Life Model, are the activities of a smoothly running fast track in the brain. Relational-brain skills contain all the functions needed to think *with* God, not simply *about* God.

In the brain, the basis for learning to be like someone is a loving attachment. Attachment leads to mutual mind. Mutual mind creates identity and character. Identity develops into a "people." Thus, attachment creates a people who are alike in significant ways. Dallas says, "A disciple is someone now who is with Jesus, still, learning to be like Him." He adds, "The heart is drawn to Christ, with others. The path of discipleship is always communal, with a result of our hearts and minds becoming more like His." The process Dallas highlights suggests that attachments will form our character.

The Heart and Soul Conference was the beginning of this conversation, not the culmination of it. My year of study with Dallas around neurotheology never materialized. It is you who must now consider this "soteriology of attachment," as Dallas named it. Could loving attachments be what Paul called "a still more excellent way"?[4]

If there was ever any doubt that Dallas saw loving God as the primary purpose of disciples, those who lined up to speak with Dallas had the clarification in their hands. NavPress released the tenth-anniversary edition of Dallas's *Renovation of the Heart* in time for this Heart and Soul

Conference. Dallas signed a stack of books in advance of the conference, writing "Mark 12:29-33" below his name. This passage is the story where Jesus is asked, "Which is the greatest commandment?"

> "The most important one," answered Jesus, "is this: 'Hear, O Israel: The Lord our God, the Lord is one. Love the Lord your God with all your heart and with all your soul and with all your mind and with all your strength.' The second is this: 'Love your neighbor as yourself.' There is no commandment greater than these."
>
> "Well said, teacher," the man replied. "You are right in saying that God is one and there is no other but him. To love him with all your heart, with all your understanding and with all your strength, and to love your neighbor as yourself is more important than all burnt offerings and sacrifices."[5]

If God Works through Attachment Love, What Should We Expect?

Our most obvious expectation, if God works through attachment love, would be clear messages from God to us that we are to love God. We should expect that such love should involve our entire selves, all the time, and go to the deepest parts of us—our hearts.

If God worked through attachment love, we would expect to hear that the love of God goes beyond our conscious understanding, cannot be broken by anything good or bad, and is immensely powerful in ways we cannot comprehend. God's attachment love to us would be kind, enduring, gracious, and would delight over us. This attachment love would be reciprocal. God would expect us to return the same hesed, attachment love.

We know loving God is commanded in the Old Testament and by the law of love in the New Testament. Still, we may not be certain whether "attachment bonds" are what God has in mind when love is mentioned. I propose that we apply a series of tests to Scripture that will show us whether God is talking about attachment love. First, God should say directly that we should attach to God. Second, God should use the processes that form healthy attachments in the brain rather than avoid them. Third, the words in Scripture that describe the nature of God's relationship with His people should make sense if we substitute the word *attachment*. Fourth, attachment systems should affect our relationship to God. Fiftl expectations about the character and identity changes in disciples should match the effects of attachments. More tests could be devised, but we shall start with these five.

Test One: What Does God Say about Attachment?

Attachment or *bonding* is language that comes from gluing things together. What glues a duckling to its mother or a baby to a family is what we mean by attachment. The Hebrew of the Old Testament provides us with the word *dabeq* (קָבַד), which means cling, adhere to, follow closely, join, stick or stay with. Dabeq means attach. Let's consider some occurrences:

- "But you who *held fast* to the LORD your God are alive today, every one of you" (Deuteronomy 4:4).

- "You shall fear the LORD your God; you shall serve Him, and to Him you shall *hold fast*, and take oaths in His name" (Deuteronomy 10:20, NKJV).

- "If you carefully keep all these commandments which I command you to do—to love the LORD your God, to walk in all His ways, and to *hold fast* to Him . . ." (Deuteronomy 11:22, NKJV).

- "You shall walk after the LORD your God and fear Him, and keep His commandments and obey His voice; you shall serve Him and *hold fast* to Him" (Deuteronomy 13:4, NKJV).

- ". . . that you may love the LORD your God, that you may obey His voice, and that you may *cling* to Him, for He is your life and the length of your days" (Deuteronomy 30:20, NKJV).

- "Take careful heed to do the commandment and the law which Moses the servant of the LORD commanded you, to love the LORD your God, to walk in all His ways, to keep His commandments, to *hold fast* to Him, and to serve Him with all your heart and with all your soul" (Joshua 22:5, NKJV).

There is little doubt that the law of Moses commands us to glue ourselves to God. This attachment covers the entire length of our lives. Attachment is intimately tied to obeying God and having godly character. Attachment includes all our heart and soul and is essential to life with God.

Is attachment to God the same attachment that connects us with people we love? The same word, *dabeq*, is used for people and for God without distinction. Let's consider a few instances.

- "They lifted up their voices and wept again; and Orpah kissed her mother-in-law, but Ruth *clung* to her" (Ruth 1:14).

- "My soul *follows close* behind You; Your right hand upholds me" (Psalm 63:8, NKJV).

- "I *cling* to Your testimonies; O LORD, do not put me to shame!" (Psalm 119:31).

- "There is a friend who *sticks closer* than a brother" (Proverbs 18:24).

Based on these texts, it would be very peculiar to think that God does not mean for us to be attached to Him with the same attachment love that made Ruth follow her mother-in-law, the same attachment that connects brothers and best friends.

What, then, of the New Testament Greek words? Does the New Testament expect that we will attach with God? Two words will help us. The first word is κολλάω (*kollao*), which comes from *kolla*, the word for glue.

- "Let love be without hypocrisy. Abhor what is evil; *cling* to what is good" (Romans 12:9).

- "He who is *joined* to the Lord is one spirit with Him" (1 Corinthians 6:17, NKJV).

We who are glued to God (attached) are one spirit with God. That is good glue! Paul gives us a description of this glue:

Who shall separate us from the love of Christ? Shall tribulation, or distress, or persecution, or famine, or nakedness, or peril, or sword? As it is written:

> "For Your sake we are killed all day long;
> We are accounted as sheep for the slaughter."

Yet in all these things we are more than conquerors through Him who loved us. For I am persuaded that neither death nor life, nor angels nor principalities nor powers, nor things present nor things to come, nor height nor depth, nor any other created thing, shall be able to separate us from the love of God which is in Christ Jesus our Lord.[6]

A second word points to an attachment that cannot be separated. The word, προσμενω (*prosmeno*), means to remain with and hold fast—to stay attached. Here are some examples:

- "When he came and had seen the grace of God, he was glad, and encouraged them all that with purpose of heart they should *continue* with the Lord" (Acts 11:23, NKJV).

- "I feel compassion for the people because they have *remained* with Me now three days and have nothing to eat" (Mark 8:2).

The passage from Mark suggests that Jesus and the crowd were developing an attachment and that Jesus wanted to be the One to feed them. In chapter 5, I mentioned that we attach to the one who feeds us. With this in mind, we should consider the characteristics that form strong attachment bonds.

Test Two: Does God Use the Processes That Form Healthy Attachment Bonds?

If we take the characteristics that form strong and healthy attachments from the brain science of Dr. Allan Schore[7] and compare them with what

God does, we should find the following characteristics of healthy bonds. Healthy bonds

1. connect us to the source of life (i.e., food and drink);
2. form unique attachments with no substitutions—one mother or baby (loved one) cannot be exchanged for another;
3. see the other as special and mine (grace);
4. build through joy with someone who is delighted to be with us;
5. provide both joy and rest (peace);
6. develop mutual mind;
7. grow stronger by moving both closer and farther apart;
8. grow stronger by sharing both positive and negative emotions;
9. help all parties feel stable and act like themselves;
10. provide both freedom and connection;
11. stretch limits and capacities slightly to promote growth; and
12. create an enduring people (i.e., families, tribes, and nations).

Let us run what we know about the Bible through the grid of attachments. Each of these twelve points could be a book.

1. Source of life. Jesus says that our first birth was to a human mother and our second birth brings new life. We are to attach to this new life as children whom Peter later calls "babies."[8] God (Jesus) says that He is the Source of Life, our food and our drink. We are fed by milk, bread, wine, and every word that comes from God.

2. No substitutions. God wants to be recognized. God expects our attachment to be unique to God. We should not mistake anyone else for our God. Like a loved mother or father, no one else will substitute.[9] We should know His voice.

3. Mine and special. God sees us as special and calls us His. The ancient term for showing someone they are special is to extend "grace" to them.[10] When we are given special favor without earning it, we receive grace as a free gift but not without reciprocity. Grace is always given with the expectation of grateful attachment by the recipient. Are we to experience God as special, unique, and ours? The "special" in a bond is different from the special of "that is really nice" because bonds are possessive. God is possessive. The very wonderful other (who receives grace) is mine.

4. Built by relational joy. Life with God is built on joy. Jesus says that He has taught disciples so that His joy would be in them and their joy would be the biggest joy possible.[11] Isn't the *with-God life* joyful exactly because God is with us and that gives us joy?

5. Provides joy and rest. God repeatedly offers us peace and rest. There are too many offers of joy, peace, and rest in the Bible to consider them all! The wicked strive, but the righteous receive joy from God.[12] The Son of God said, "Come to me, and I will give you rest."[13]

6. Mutual mind. Dallas has already made all the points we need to hear about thinking *with* God. Can we expand the concept of thinking beyond conscious-speed thoughts (in the slow track) to mutual-mind thinking in the fast track? Let us consider what Paul says:

> For by grace you have been saved through faith; and that not of yourselves, it is the gift of God; not as a result of works, so that no one may boast. For we are His *workmanship* [ποίημα; poiēma], created in Christ Jesus for good works, which God prepared beforehand so that we would walk in them.[14]

We are God's craftsmanship of a special sort who are designed to do what God prepared ahead of time. We can be quite sure that doing what we were designed to do equals spiritual and emotional maturity. But this design is called *poiēma*—that is, "poetry." Hebrew poetry is a rhyming of thoughts rather than sounds. One example of rhyming thoughts is:

> Great is the LORD and greatly to be praised;
> He is to be feared above all gods.[15]

Suppose our thoughts are to rhyme God's thoughts—not worded the same way but with the same theme. When we think God's thoughts in the conscious, slow track, it takes great effort, effort that does not change our character very much. Through attachment, our thinking can become mutual mind in the master fast track; mutual-mind thoughts change our character, identity, and spontaneous responses. By thinking *with* God rather than *about* God, we do what God would have us do: the works God prepared for us ahead of time.

7. *Strengthened by moving both closer and apart.* Just as we learn to walk by a process of holding a hand and letting it go, we develop character through alternating times of being close with times of doing things on our own. Didn't Jesus call disciples and then send them out, meet with them then go to the mountain, send them in a boat then follow them, spend time on earth then go to prepare a place where we cannot yet go?

8. *Handles both pleasant and unpleasant experiences relationally.* God is with us during both joyful and difficult times. We notice that Jesus began His ministry by building joyful times, healing people and feeding crowds. The test of attachment came when He spoke of picking up our crosses together. The strength of attachments began showing at that point. Have we seen our character change by experiencing Jesus' presence in hard times?

9. *Helps us stably be ourselves.* The strength of attachments directly ties to the strength of our identities in our brain. The more secure our attachments ("Nothing can break our relationship"), the less our character changes under pressure from feelings, emotions, desires, relationships, threats, or world cultures. God (and our own experience) predicts that stable Christlike character is the sign of those who deeply love God. Developing a stable self has been a major focus in these talks by Dallas.

10. *We feel both connected and free.* Bonds that provide both freedom and connection might be one of the hardest to describe, but we know when we experience them. Are we remembered when we are out of sight? Can we be curious, explore, develop, grow, change, make mistakes, fail, have a will of our own, and even go fully "prodigal" and return to find the attachment from God is still there? Do we act more like the people we were created to be the deeper our attachment love with God grows?

11. *Stretches us to grow.* God is steadily stretching us to more trust, clearer faith, more character, harder tasks, better understanding, responsibility for more people, and facing bigger problems. Do we find similar stretching in the lives of all the major figures in Scripture?

12. *Creates an identity group (people).* The characteristics of the bonding process in the brain create a group identity. How many stories can you remember from Scripture where God is creating a people? God spends time creating couples, parents, families, clans, tribes, and nations. God expects His disciples to be a family of love and attachment. Peter said, "For

you once were not a people, but now you are the people of God; you had not received mercy, but now you have received mercy."[16]

If you are thinking like I am thinking (a sort of mutual mind about attachment), we can reflect on our lives and see that our best relationships and best times with God match the twelve characteristics of attachment formation. Nothing in the conscious, slow track of the brain has the twelve characteristics of an attachment bond. Our best character formation has been through healthy bonds—even when we had no conscious idea how attachments worked.

Test Three: Do the Words Translated "Love" Mean Attachment?

Does hesed mean attachment? Hesed is often rendered as *lovingkindness* in English. Attachment love is both loving and kind. Attachment love is merciful (as hesed is also translated). Hesed matches the twelve characteristics of a healthy bond. If we read the nearly 250 passages that use hesed, the meaning remains clear when translated as *attachment*. Many of these passages refer to relationships between families, relatives, friends, and kings across generations. Hesed is invoked to remind readers that they have a committed relationship of kindness and good intent. Rahab the harlot tells the spies, "Now therefore, please swear to me by the LORD, since I have *dealt kindly* [hesed—attached / made you my people] with you, that you also will *deal kindly* [hesed—attach / make us your people] with my father's household, and give me a pledge of truth, and spare my father and my mother and my brothers and my sisters, with all who belong to them, and deliver our lives from death."[17]

Healthy attachments improve character. Proverbs equates hesed with loyalty, saying, "Many a man proclaims his own loyalty, but who can find a *trustworthy* [hesed] man?"[18] If we render hesed as *lovingly attached*, we have the meaning of loyalty intended by the passage.

The Psalms are full of praise to a hesed God. God's hesed gets people out of every possible problem. What sort of character explains God's continuing care? The answer is God's hesed.

Attachment is meant for life-giving purposes. When we receive life, we become like the source of that life. Yet attachment can also be used wrongly. When we see hesed used to describe incest, we may be shocked. "If there is a man who takes his sister, his father's daughter or his mother's daughter, so that he sees her nakedness and she sees his nakedness, it is a *disgrace* [hesed]."[19] Translating hesed as "a permanent attachment" makes sense in this passage. We are not to make attachments that produce a permanent attachment that is simply wrong. Unholy hesed (violating attachment) creates deep attachment wounds. We see evil entering hesed when parents abandon families, relatives molest children, children kill their parents, and one partner murders another. When death takes over our hesed attachments, it produces the character of the devil himself. Unhealthy attachments take our character in the wrong direction. Since we don't want the devil's own attachments, our life must be lived with righteous attachment to the people God places in our lives. God does not leave the enormous power of hesed to the devil and not use attachments Himself.

Does the Greek word *agape* mean attachment? We have seen that the Hebrew word *hesed* (attachment) fits the ways God relates to human persons. The New Testament was written in Greek, and Greek words were needed for Hebrew concepts. If God's love is attachment love, then agape (Greek) is our word for attachment love.

Hebrew uses the w ord *aheb* (אָהֵב) most often for love. The New Testament translates aheb as *agapaō* (verb form of agape) when quoting "love your neighbor as yourself."[20]

God says through the prophet Hosea, "For I desire *mercy* [hesed] and not sacrifice, and the knowledge of God more than burnt offerings."[21] When the scribe for Mark 12:33 (the passage Dallas wrote next to his autograph) said, "Agape is much more [to God] than all burnt offerings and sacrifices," he has used agape to express the hesed in Hosea.

Agape combines the meaning of aheb and hesed. Micah uses aheb and hesed together when he says, "He has told you, O man, what is good; and what does the LORD require of you but to do justice, to *love* [aheb] *kindness* [hesed], and to walk humbly with your God?"[22] Loving attachment (aheb hesed) is agape. This relational love is the central requirement for spiritual formation and godly character.

Test Four: Do Human Attachment Systems Affect Our Relationship to God?

The attachment system in the fast track is subject to damage from abuses like unholy hesed and neglect left behind by a low-joy life that lacks agape. Attachment and attachment damage are some of the most extensively studied topics across human cultures. If God uses the attachment system in the brain, then our spiritual life should have the following characteristics:

- People with damaged human attachments should have difficulty understanding God's love of and special delight in them.
- Repairing normal human attachments should improve the ability to attach with God.
- God should say that our attachments to mother, father, family, tribe, and all else should be something we count as small compared to our attachments to new life and God.
- Communities who practice good human attachments should emerge from people who experience attachment with God.
- People and groups who hated or avoided one another should become family.
- God would expect anyone with an attachment to Himself to exhibit the same attachment to all God's family.
- Those attached to God will offer attachments to their enemies because God offers attachment.

Attachment damage explains the problems that the staff and I were puzzling over in the counseling office. When people's normal human attachments improved, they were better able to connect with God. When people's attachments with God improved, they were better able to regulate emotions, connect with others, and resolve trauma. I cannot recall any instance when someone formed a better attachment with God and then their emotional and relational life became worse. Increased peace was the consistent outcome.

Seeing that a sense of shalom peacefulness accompanies improved attachments with God and people revealed a useful compass for healing and guidance. Were we losing peace? We were headed the wrong way. Were we gaining peace? God must be near. Trauma memories were not peaceful. Resolved memories were peaceful. We began studying ways to increase peace. Simple ways to share this peace soon followed, which became known as "Immanuel healing" or the "Immanuel lifestyle."[23] Immanuel means "God with us." The word is now used for the different ways in which we can enter a mutual-mind state with God and become aware of God's attachment to us.

Immanuel prayer and the Immanuel lifestyle involve activating our relational attachment to God through gratitude and remembering what God has done for us. There are many styles and methods of strengthening our attachment with God, but they all lead to a heightened sense of God's presence. Once aware of God's presence, we ask to share God's view of things that take away our peace. What God shows us lets us have mutual mind with God and share God's peace. This way we know that God is with us.

TRAUMA RECOVERY AND ATTACHMENT REPAIR

Dr. Karl Lehman and his wife, Charlotte, who were presenters at Heart and Soul, have many videos documenting case studies where healing attachments improved people's connection to God.[24] Better attachments with God healed all kinds of issues, from phobias to dissociative disorders. Attachment to God resolved many kinds of disorders and distortions of relationships. With each healing, the fast track in people's brains ran more smoothly so they connected with God more consistently. False beliefs about God "spontaneously" resolved to the truth once the attachment was corrected. Once people experienced God's love, they no longer believed God was distant, uncaring, or cruel. Challenging false beliefs had no similar impact on attachment. Arguing with clients that God loved them did not produce any sustained sense of God's hesed presence. Karl's books, websites, and videos provide abundant examples of the central role of attachment to a properly running fast track and connection to God.

Physical brain damage from drugs, accidents, strokes, and disease can influence character by disrupting the attachment-based fast track in the brain. Karl and I understood the issues caused by direct physical and chemical damage. Karl found that the impact of organic and genetic brain damage could be reduced by improving attachment with God and God's people.

Trauma recovery was a key problem that Karl and I explored together. We found that when we helped people start from a secure-attachment state with either God or people, traumas resolved about six times faster. Helping people stay connected to God during recovery became our main priority. Karl has made the biggest contribution by helping those who experience (falsely) that God is the source of their trauma. Just thinking about God shuts down their fast track and triggers an "enemy-mode" reaction. As we would expect, if attachment love is God's transformation plan, those who go into trauma reactions at the thought of God are really stuck. Feeling "God is my enemy" is not corrected by pointing out right beliefs about God. In such cases, a significant attachment to God's people often makes the difference.

Karl's wife, Charlotte, named the process of establishing attachment through God's constant presence (hesed) with us "Immanuel healing prayer." Since then, Immanuel prayer, Immanuel journaling, Immanuel lifestyle, and Immanuel healing have all developed as different ways to spread attachment with God to every moment of the day and to the darkest places in life.

ADDICTION RECOVERY AND ATTACHMENT REPAIR

Addictions develop when we replace painful, failed attachments to people with attachments to whatever gives us our "buzz." Ed and Maritza Khouri, presenters at Heart and Soul, developed attachment-based recovery that takes the Higher Power of Alcoholics Anonymous a step deeper.[25] Darrell Brazzell uses Immanuel healing prayer to repair attachments with God and people to resolve sexual addictions and pornography. Darrell helps people enter a mutual-mind state with God, so they can share God's mind about whatever has addicted them.[26]

ATTACHMENT REPAIR AND RELATIONSHIPS

The range of applications for attachment-based discipleship is very broad. Chris and Jen Coursey, who led Heart and Soul, use attachment-based relational skills to restore identity, marriages, families, and church fellowship.[27] Dr. Marcus Warner, who coauthored *The 4 Habits of Joy-Filled Marriages* with Chris, also finds attachment is key to such widely different topics as resolving demonic issues and developing church leadership.[28] Missionaries find that the process of evangelism involves helping people begin an attachment process with the God who introduces Himself. Instead of slow-track persuasion about beliefs, why not help people experience a mutual mind with God and discover God's hesed nature for themselves?

Disrupted attachments and a lack of hesed/agape relational skills (in the fast track of the brain) explain what blocks the mutual-mind states that could transform our character into Christlikeness. This explanation answers the issues that troubled the staff when we attempted to apply Dallas's teaching in the counseling office. It appears that God wants clear, shared attachment love, the most powerful motivator the body possesses, for creating and correcting human character.

Test Five: Do God's Expectations for Disciples Match the Effects of Loving Attachments?

Attachment (hesed) is the one force or process that determines our identity before we can think consciously. The human brain develops or changes character through attachment bonds. Attachment bonds are a compelling force. Paul says:

> For the *love* [agape, or attachment love] of Christ controls us,
> having concluded this, that one died for all, therefore all died;
> and He died for all, so that they who live might no longer live for
> themselves, but for Him who died and rose again on their behalf.
> Therefore from now on we recognize no one according to the
> flesh; even though we have known Christ according to the flesh,
> yet now we know Him in this way no longer.[29]

Having become attached to God in Christ, we see through the Spirit of Jesus in our hearts. This spiritual sight is not reserved for Jesus alone but applies to everyone. Hesed is the strongest force the human brain knows—more important than our own life and existence. Should we consider this force as we consider spiritual formation and developing the character of Christ? If this is the force Jesus uses, then we should. The attachment love of Christ will compel us. We will be transformed by who we love. Our character will be changed through loving attachments. We will see others as God sees them in real time. This is the intention toward love—even love of enemies—that Dallas established as a mark of spiritual maturity.

CHANGING OUR CHARACTER (FOR THE ADULT BRAIN) REQUIRES AN IDENTITY GROUP

We have one more major characteristic of attachment to consider. The twelfth characteristic of attachment bonds was the creation of an identity group—a people. We need to ask whether the expectations God has for disciples matches the very peculiar needs of the brain's attachment system for a group identity after age twelve.

The brain has a very distinct group-identity development pattern that is genetically built into each human brain. During infancy and childhood, the brain works hard to learn how to be a human person. Creating a human person who can survive is top priority. At puberty, the brain goes through a major change. Many systems are weakened by pro-grammed brain-cell death (apoptosis). From age fourteen on, our brain begins to consider the survival of "my people" more important than "my survival." Character moves from being something I develop individu-ally to "acting like 'my people.'" You may have noticed this change in adolescents.

If apoptosis takes place at puberty, then we should expect that God will employ group identity for people over age twelve. We should be told to practice Christlike character with each other as adults. Because we are learning character rather than receiving imparted character, we expect admonitions and are patient with learners. More experienced group members should be teachers and demonstrate better character than learn-ers. We should be encouraged to test character and follow good examples. The Bible should provide case studies with good and bad examples.

Most importantly, Jesus should be a clear model. Jesus should correct and develop character in a group more often than one-on-one. An identity group should develop as the result of Jesus' efforts. Jesus should consider the group to be learners—called disciples at the time.

Neurologically, we would expect God to develop character by encour-aging spiritual practices that involve both (a) God guiding our thoughts and (b) practicing character with people. Spiritual-formation methods that are "brain friendly" include activities that help us share the mind of God and activities that share God's mind with other people. God would change our reality through mutual mind with us. Character building would be strengthened through practice with our people.

We particularly need a visible people when we are too upset to do mutual mind with God. When we are really upset, it is harder to notice that God is with us. We begin to feel that whoever upset us is an enemy. We need people around us who understand that "we are people who love our enemies" to help us when we cannot do so alone.

My prayer partner Gary and I both experienced times of conflict with our wives, times when God seemed to be gone. At those moments, our wives felt like our enemies. We each could lament but could not seem to hear God's thoughts. Our minds were not in a relational mode. We felt all alone.

When I was in no mood to love my "enemies," Gary would say, "I am rejoicing for you, brother!" He did not rejoice that I was suffering. He rejoiced that God was with me. I could not tell that God was there. He could. Gary would say, "Two are better than one because they have a good return for their labor. For if either of them falls, the one will lift up his companion. But woe to the one who falls when there is not another to lift him up. . . . A cord of three strands is not quickly torn apart."[30] Gary wore a wedding band made of three strands twisted together to remember this truth. In Gary's times of suffering, when he felt alone and like God had lost His hesed, I returned the favor: "I am rejoicing for you, brother!" We truly became like brothers.[31]

The Greek word *koinónia* (κοινωνία) speaks of shared relational resources we could call partnership. Having the mind of Christ in an active sense—for life in real time, seeing reality, bringing healing, and finding guidance—requires koinónia. Practicing our new self in Christ requires feedback from others who can see what God sees and have mercy for our learning process.[32] After age twelve, the brain absorbs such feedback only from "my people." Attachment is required. "My people" feel (as I do) that the survival of our people is more important than mine. Others matter more than ourselves, not because we do not matter but simply because that is how our brain values our people.

Disciples Are the People of God

Does God consider us a people? Do we have a strong enough attachment to God and to one another to be a people? After Peter betrayed Jesus, Jesus asked him, "Do you love me?" Are we attached? Are we at least friends? And how shall we stay attached? We shall feed sheep and lambs together.[33]

Beliefs and conscious, focused attention will not create a people in the human brain. Sure, we can talk about concepts, but our spontaneous responses will be entirely unchanged. Willful attention changes our strategies but cannot create a "people" directly.

The VIM model has Vision, Intention, and Means. Dallas has shared a vision for a life with God powered by grace and advanced by intention (*I*)—the focused attention of the will (heart/spirit) in conjunction with the mind, soul, body, and relationships. The Life Model proposes that attachment love provides a more compelling intention (*I*) for transformation. In fact, intention becomes the wrong word for the *I* in VIM. I suggest "impetus," so we stay with the letter *I*. Neurotheology, the science of spiritual maturity, proposes that a new attachment with God begins new life, one with Jesus in our hearts. From this love attachment, we are moved and motivated to live the vision—becoming like Jesus.

In his final lecture, Dallas will tie spiritual disciplines into his VIM model of transformation. Willful, focused attention is a weak force and there are many things it cannot do directly; conscious thought and attention will create our strategies. The right strategy will take us places that simple choices cannot.

Exercise: Nine Minutes with God

This exercise has three parts, each three minutes.

Take a deep breath and let it out slowly.

1. Bring to mind a time you were aware God was with you. If one does not come to mind, ask God to help you remember. Pick a word or phrase to describe God's presence.

2. Ask God to help you remember a time when God was with you but you were not aware of it at the time.

3. Notice what changes as you become aware of God's presence. Pick a word or phrase to describe what changed as you become aware. (Finding a word can be surprisingly hard to do.)

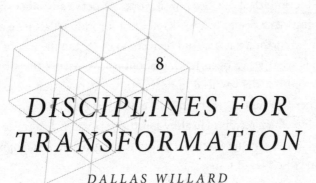

8

DISCIPLINES FOR TRANSFORMATION

DALLAS WILLARD

Our Thursday with Dallas at Heart and Soul is going very quickly. Chris Coursey (who, together with his wife, Jen, coordinated the conference) recalls, "People were hungry to connect with Dallas. There was an expectation by those who came that this was a historic moment. Something that needed to come together was coming together in their presence. Nothing like this had happened before." Let us listen once again.

· · ·

We have been trying to make clear what constitutes spiritual and emotional maturity. Simply put, emotional maturity is the ability to direct feelings, and desires, and emotions into the service of the good. A person who can do that will not be dominated by emotions like a child, for example, who has to have what they want.

You can't count on having emotional maturity without *spiritual* maturity. If you have spiritual maturity, you *will* be emotionally mature. So if we're concerned about emotional maturity, then we will work on spiritual maturity.

People who aren't Christians don't know how to do this. And you may regard that statement as pure arrogance on the part of a Christian, but please put it to the empirical test. See how it works. Observe any other spirituality that interests you. See how it works not just for individuals here and there but for a group, for a nation. And then compare that to the way of Christ.

This is what we've been talking about as we discuss the structure of the self. And it's why we need to deal with the barrier that we experience in churches that do not teach a gospel and salvation that naturally include discipleship which results in healthy spiritual formation, leading to spiritual maturity, leading to emotional security. So let's give people an opportunity to become disciples of Jesus.

The primary field for discipleship evangelism is the American church. It's in the church that you find the people who hunger for the kind of maturity that we're talking about—not just for themselves but for their loved ones and their community. Many of them see that it's the only hope of the world, even if it's just to get people to stop killing one another.

The place that the world can find that hope is in Christian churches, where we as leaders have a responsibility to address the world with the message and person of Jesus Christ.

Now if you've got something else that offers hope for the world, please let me know. Seriously. Look at the glimmers of hope that are offered from every source, including our educational system in this country, which now declares itself to be secular. What's your hope? What can you offer the world that might allow some possibility of redemption?

Just think for a moment. What is the hope that is offered outside of Christ in today's world? Perhaps it's the return on your investment, or practical knowledge for current circumstances, or just learning to tolerate everything so we can all get along. But what would those messages do for the issue of character formation?

If we want to open up to people the possibility of living as disciples of Jesus in the Kingdom of God, then our churches should be centers focused on that—practical leadership, and example and instructions as to how we could change in the ways that we live, so that our character and our relationship to others would be as presented in the teachings of Christ and His people. How could we do that?

Many people in and around the church visible today are struggling intensely against the pervasive and dominant condition of *untransformed professing Christians*. Today we've looked at ways of approaching that problem, and there are some churches that have done studies on what happens to church members if we just do what we've been doing. One such study found clear evidence that people who involve themselves in church work and stayed with the routine church advice did not grow. We need to consider this: What are the ways that we advise people to engage themselves with the church, and with the Christian cause, or the gospel of Christ? What do we tell people?

Read your Bible and pray every day.
Go to church.
Stop sinning.

These are good statements. Now we ask: Does this do the job? Does this accomplish what we would like to see in Christians? We have to be very practical and empirical and honest in our appraisal.

Transformation into Christlikeness

The Life Model and similar programs are searching for ways in which genuine transformation into Christlikeness, and the emotional and spiritual healing and maturity it brings, can become the routine business of Christian groups and congregations. Once we accept an understanding of the "good news" and of salvation that secures life "from above" in the Kingdom of God with Jesus Christ now, we see many things that can be done to move transformation of individuals and communities forward into a life without the agony and destructiveness of human lostness. In fact, many such things have been known to the church for ages. Ministries of various kinds are effective, as are therapy, rearranging the circumstances of life, education, or direct action in the healing of paralyzing wounds ("healing of the memories," etc.). The Life Model developed by Jim and his associates shows great promise of transformation processes that could be at home in many social contexts, including the local congregation.

But to the extent we revisit how our local congregations come together in community to represent a transformed humanity, we are faced with the problem of what to do with our traditions. And currently, our traditions—including our doctrinal statements—keep us from working together. We need a united front, one which prioritizes transformation as inherent to the gospel, with spiritual and emotional maturity as the metric of success. This is, as we've argued, to prioritize discipleship to Christ over the other priorities in our ecclesiologies. And I would suggest that the true ecumenicism is discipleship to Christ—that churches should focus on discipleship instead of the doctrinal issues that probably gave rise to their particular brand of Christianity. That's huge—truly huge.

Well-meaning people have problems with thinking of people in other denominations or congregations as sharing a basic identity in Christ. Moreover, if you have people who are pursuing discipleship to Christ and they begin to be obedient people in their community, they are going to stand out. You can't hide this. That's why Jesus said, "A city set on a hill cannot be hid."[1] You don't have to advertise it any more than a light has to say, "I'm shining." It just shines.

Of course, we are raised in traditions and we know the goodness of traditions both generally and in the particulars. But our traditions can take on a priority that sets us against one another. I know when I was a young person, it was hard for some denominations to think that the others might really be Christians. That wasn't all that long ago. There is something of that institutional bias that still remains, and we have to overcome it.

I'm suggesting that the way to overcome it is to base our identity in Christian discipleship—being formed in the character of Christ. And then let that go out from our groups and individuals into our communities. Again, discipleship is not for the churches. The churches are for discipleship. And discipleship is for the world.

Spiritual Disciplines

So now, we come to the idea of spiritual disciplines that make the spiritual formation of the disciple a reality. I'm not just talking about obedience to laws. I'm talking about having a different quality to life that affects our ability to have hope and love for those around us. I'm talking about the internal condition of the follower of Christ, in relation to faith, hope, and love—the central realities of the life of a disciple.

Let's look at hope as an example. The Christian, and especially a Christian leader, should be the most happy and hopeful person in the community. What people live for and how they successfully manage life's problems come to a head here, so this is vital. What are people basing their hopes in? If they are not able to believe that they are unceasing spiritual beings with an eternal destiny in God's great universe, understanding that their life now is a time of training to live in the power of God, then what's the point of prayer?

If you look at the teaching and practice of prayer in the New Testament and through the ages, you will see that it is a way of taking on an eternal life or eternal living. I think of it as a power-sharing device for a world of recovering sinners. Consequently, prayer not only gives hope, it transforms personal relationships. When people engage in prayer seriously—when they learn a life of prayer, not just an occasional send up—and especially as they learn how to pray together, they become more hopeful about their lives. Their prayer habit and the hope that undergirds it gives them a basis for the anticipation of good. Hope is the joyous anticipation of what is good. Prayer thus reinforces hope, helping people to be happy and content no matter what is going on around them.

Where does anger come from? Anger comes from the frustration of will. When your will is frustrated, anger is a natural response. Of course, there's nothing wrong with anger in itself, but you have to be very careful with it. If you become governed by it, it will lead you into doing what is wrong. Anger, in this instance, is very closely matched with contempt, which involves regarding someone as lesser than you.

How does one withdraw from feelings of contempt? How do you, "in your anger . . . not sin"?[2] It could only be if you have resigned your will to God. The person who has thus surrendered their anger to God discovers that if you stand up for what is good without anger, you will be much more effective, because anger that degrades into contempt invites a contemptuous response.

Total surrender to God enables you to have a different presence in the world, one that is redemptive in far-reaching ways. It presents an alternative form of life and enables people to see the reality of the Kingdom of God through discipleship to Christ in real life. Total surrender to God consistently yields an attractive spiritual and emotional maturity.

Now the spiritual disciplines are practices that we use to deal with the habits, if you wish, of wrongdoing that are imbedded in our lives when we come to know Christ. For example, it takes discipline to overcome the presence of anger and contempt in human life. Basically, discipline is a voluntary activity in your power that makes possible for you something you cannot achieve by direct effort. As they began in church history, the classic disciplines of spiritual formation were simply following Christ into His practices. Jesus Himself spent a lot of time doing things that, especially for his followers, were disciplines. He spent a lot of time in solitude and silence. He obviously studied the Scripture a lot. He worshiped, He had fellowship, and so on. All these things count as disciplines. They are activities within your power you yourselves can do to enable you to do what you can't otherwise do by direct effort. Churches need to be centers where people are practicing these things that will enable them to take on the character of Christ and become lights in a darkened world.[3]

INDIRECTION

Spiritual formation, then, may be thought of as an act of indirection. Think of a person who is practicing to play a musical instrument or to sing or to master a sport. They don't do the disciplines of those activities for their own sake. The person learning a musical instrument runs scales not because they long to play a scale beautifully. But they know that if they run the scales, they will be better equipped to read and perform a beautiful piece of music. The principle is true in almost every human activity worth engaging in. Conversation, saving money, losing weight—all have that familiar order of indirection. You do things that you wouldn't do just for their own sake because you desire the outcome that doing these things makes possible. That is the basic idea of indirection.

STRIVING VERSUS PRACTICE

Without engaging in the disciplines, our desired outcomes are sources of striving, of frustration. They certainly aren't likely to yield something beautiful. Without engaging in the disciplines of piano practice, I might be able to strike every note in Beethoven's "Moonlight Sonata," but I guarantee you I couldn't do it when it needs to be done and as it needs to be done. And in general, human life is like that. We need to do things when they need to be done, and as they need to be done. A timely word, for example, or an act of grace. Consider Paul's instruction to "let your speech be always with grace, seasoned with salt": The readiness implied in that instruction involves preparation, practice—the outcome is necessarily arrived at indirectly.[4]

"Yes, let's talk about grace," you might say. "Isn't the natural effort you're advocating for at odds with the grace of God that saves us?" The fact that in the spiritual life, we are dealing with grace and not just natural effort, does not change reality: Even though grace is involved, we still have to do things that have an indirect consequence. Grace does not mean that we don't have to do anything, or that whatever we do will bring the desired result. That isn't grace. Grace has to do with God acting in our lives in ways that enable us to do what we can't accomplish on our own. That is very similar to what I've just said about disciplines. With both—grace and discipline—there is something being brought about in and through us indirectly, not merely by our own efforts.

Grace is meant to be a part of human life. We would still need God's grace even if we had never sinned. God created human beings to accomplish things that are not in our natural power. That's the basic principle of human life.

So grace is God acting in our lives to accomplish what we cannot accomplish by our own abilities. When we practice spiritual disciplines, we tie in with the presence of grace. That's why some people have called spiritual disciplines "means of grace" or "means to grace."

Now, you might ask, "Why would God set up human life in such a way that disciplines are necessary for transformation?" And the answer is, I believe, that He has made it possible for us to determine, to some significant degree, what kind of person we will become. Consider speaking French or playing the piano. We determine to a very significant degree whether we will be the kind of person who speaks French or plays the piano, based on our decision to engage in disciplines that make doing so possible. Similarly, we determine, to a very significant degree, whether we will be the kind of person who loves their neighbor, or who loves their enemy, or who blesses those who curse them. It's all the same story. What kind of person do you want to become? What activities put you on track to become that kind of person?

Now, many people are really stymied at this point because they think that if you take action, then it's no longer grace. Often, however, we see that the people who know the most about grace, who have been inspired the most by grace, are the people who work the hardest at living as though Jesus is living their life in them. Grace is not opposed to action; it's opposed to *earning*. That's an *attitude*, not an action. Disciplines are actions not that earn us reward but that make possible the life we want.

Normally, in the Scriptures, grace is contrasted with flesh because flesh stands for natural abilities, which you *can* accomplish on your own. Hagar and Abraham were able to produce a child on their own; Sarah and Abraham were not. So their having Isaac was a result of God's action on their behalf. Now, Abraham and Sarah still had to *do* something for Isaac to be born, of course. But what they did was not in itself enabling them to produce a child. Isaac, the child of promise, was produced by the action of God *with* the participation of Sarah and Abraham. That's the mark of grace. And the idea of spiritual discipline includes it.

A DISCIPLINE IS NOT A RIGHTEOUS DEED

Always remember a discipline is not a righteous deed, even though some activities that are disciplines are in other capacities righteous—deeds we are commanded to do. Prayer, for example, is in some ways an act of righteousness; it is also a spiritual discipline through which God forms us. Fasting, by contrast, is a discipline through which God forms us but is not itself inherently righteous. Many of the disciplines are like that. Some disciplines (I call them disciplines of abstinence—solitude, silence, fasting, frugality, and so on) are made to *empty* us, to make a place in our life for other kinds of activities that would otherwise be crowded out. Such disciplines are not righteous; they are more accurately considered *wise*. They are good means to a good end.

That's the basic nature of disciplines. Even prayer, for example, has a tremendous disciplinary effect in that it enables you to do what you cannot do by mere effort. For example, you may not be able to love your enemy unless you pray for them or serve them. But if you do pray for them or serve them, you will find that doing so has an amazing effect on those people who have hurt you and wanted to see you damaged in other ways. It changes our whole attitude toward them.

Do you see the indirection there? That's a discipline.

Disciplines in Communal Life

In my book *The Spirit of the Disciplines*, I delineate the disciplines of abstinence and the disciplines of engagement.[5]

DISCIPLINES OF ABSTINENCE
- Solitude
- Silence
- Fasting
- Frugality
- Chastity
- Secrecy
- Sacrifice

DISCIPLINES OF ENGAGEMENT
- Study
- Worship
- Celebration
- Service
- Prayer
- Fellowship
- Confession
- Submission

What I'm coming up on rapidly is the idea that in our church services—in our leadership roles—we should help people learn to practice disciplines.

Solitude, for example—simply the practice of being alone for lengthy periods of time, and doing nothing—proves to have a great effect in diminishing hurry and anxiety, anger and contempt. It lessens busyness and loneliness in our lives. It enables us to see ourselves, our lives, and other people much more clearly. The entanglements of life are broken for a time and we find that the world really does not rest upon our shoulders. Solitude and silence establish in us a conscious awareness of the sufficiency of God alone. That's the principle of Sabbath.

We have a hard time hearing an invitation to solitude—to doing nothing. How could doing nothing be a discipline? What power would such a discipline afford us?

The main thing that solitude does is to take us out of the ordinary connections of life that keep us so engaged that we don't have the opportunity, the strength, or the time to do the things that we feel we ought to do. The pulls and the pushes of ordinary life can obsess you to the point that the very things that you feel like you should do, you wind up not doing. One of the best teachings on the function of solitude is in connection with Galatians 5:24: They that are in Christ have "crucified the flesh."[6] Remember that "flesh" refers to natural abilities—good in themselves, but they cannot rule your life. Think about what Paul is saying here: These good, natural abilities have been crucified. "With the affections and lusts thereof," he continues. Many people experience the practice of solitude as a crucifixion, and that's because that's exactly what it is: In solitude, you take the ordinary experience of life (and your ordinary ways of engaging life) and wrest yourself from them.

The effect of solitude is that you are released from the things *in* life that preoccupy you and make you live in your natural abilities. The kind of release that comes from that is something that one has to experience in order to know the reality of it. Most disciplines are like that. If you just talk to people about them, they can't really discuss it in the abstract. You have to practice solitude in order to know its benefits.

Solitude is not righteous. You don't become more righteous because you have gone into solitude. But you may come out of solitude with abilities that you did not have *before* you went into it. For example, you stop being busy. Busyness is a badge of recognition in our society, but there is a saying that is attributed to C. S. Lewis: "Only lazy people are busy." Normally, we think of busy people as non-lazy. But Lewis suggests that becoming busy is easy—it's the natural way of the world. To exclude busyness from your life requires strength, and awareness, and strategy. You have to make plans. If you don't make plans, other people will make plans for you.

The theology of this runs pretty deep. For example, if we have too much to do, that's because probably we didn't make decisions. Why didn't we make decisions? That gets into the deeper levels of our faith, because we may have thought that the solution to our problems is to work harder—in other words, to rely more and more on our natural abilities. Do you believe that God gives people too much to do? Would you entertain the proposi-tion that the solution to busyness might be to work less? That's going to test your faith. But it also gives you a chance to make decisions about what you may be caught up in: decisions about what is significant and what is insignificant. It gives you a chance to look at your activities and evaluate them in terms of what they produce in your life, as well as their impact on those around you. Solitude helps you see more clearly.

Another thing solitude does is to help you be quiet. Quietness is an essential condition of the spiritual life; it represents a peace that our bodies and our souls hunger for. Silence, then, is a discipline that helps us access quiet when quietness is appropriate. What do you experience when you go into real silence? It's possible to even forget what that's like. You might need a cork-lined room or something of that sort to get it. (Interestingly enough, natural sounds—gentle winds, birds, running water, that sort of thing—don't seem to disturb us.)

There's another dimension of silence that has to do with not speak-ing. That's actually more important than the absence of ambient noise. James, you may recall, says anyone who cannot offend by speaking is a perfect person.[7] And we need to at least reflect on that. What does he have in mind? It takes a certain kind of character to control your tongue in a way that it doesn't do harm. Such a person is rarely tempted to jump in and straighten people out. Moreover, given that so much of what we do in speaking is to correct the image we think other people may have of us, to be able to *not* engage in image management is a sign of great faith. To resign your image to God and let Him take control of it, so you don't need to manage it, is a great step forward in spiritual life. This putting God in charge of how people think about us is a major part of what happens as we practice silence. When you are silent, you resign yourself to God, stepping out of control of others, which, of course, has implications for things like loving your neighbor.

There is a quotation that I like very much from a woman in Japan who was learning to practice disciplines. I tell her story in *The Spirit of the Disciplines*. She says,

The more I practice this discipline [of solitude and silence],
the more I appreciate the strength of silence. The less I become

skeptical and judgmental, the more I learn to accept the things I didn't like about others.

Imagine that effect. She goes on:

> The less I talk, the fuller are words spoken at an appropriate time. The more I value others, the more I serve them in small ways, the more I enjoy and celebrate my life. The more I celebrate, the more I realize that God has been giving me wonderful things in my life, the less I worry about my future. I will accept and enjoy what God is continuously giving to me. I think I am beginning to really enjoy God.[8]

That last line is especially significant: The enjoyment of God is foundational to the transformation of character. The enjoyment of God is a primary part of what is required if we are going to be emotionally mature people.

Other disciplines are really important—not because they are righteous but because they are wise. Secrecy, for example: There is nothing wrong with your good deeds being known by others, but there is a great temptation in each of us, given how the world works, to do good deeds for the sake of them being known. Jesus addresses this very complexity in Matthew 6 alongside prayer and fasting. Secrecy allows us to live before the audience of One; it helps us off-load the burden of approval and disapproval of people. Of course, approval and disapproval are important currencies in our world, and we have to deal with them. But practicing doing good things without it being known who did them helps us not to give people's approvals and disapprovals too much hold over our lives. We come to prioritize God's approval.

Fasting is similarly important. Fasting aligns us with God's action because fasting is a way of taking in substance from God and His Word that actually nourishes our bodies. Fasting is an affirmation of the reality of the Kingdom of God. Fasting involves a learning process, of course: You have to think about fasting when you do it, in the same way that you think about praying when you pray. But just as you want to get beyond the point of wondering as you pray if you're going to get an answer, you must learn to get your focus off fasting as you fast.

To the unexperienced, fasting sounds like a miserable experience, but those who have practiced fasting find that inherent in the practice is the lesson for how to be strong and cheerful when you're not getting what you want. That's the indirection inherent in fasting: By denying yourself food for a period of time, you grow in the capacity to be strong and sweet even when you don't get what you want.

You can see how that would cut to the root of most emotionally immature behavior and open the way to the realization of spiritual maturity we're describing here. The old saints used to say that if you practice well, then everything else will fall into place. Your will will have been trained in a certain way where not getting what you want doesn't lead to anger, disappointment, or attacking people. Fasting is a way of saying that God will meet your needs. The teaching of Psalm 23:1 is proven in the experience of fasting: "The LORD is my shepherd, I shall not want."

Scripture memory is the way, to use modern language, you reprogram your thinking. As you pursue memorization of Scripture, your mind is reformed. If I were pastoring or leading a church or a group, I would try to make sure that there was an operative Scripture-memory program working in that group. Everyone can memorize. And when you memorize Scripture, you take the Living Word of God into your system, into your body, and that will make it run on the right tracks of the Kingdom of Heaven.

Now, you probably can't do Scripture memory well without a lot of the other disciplines. As a practice, it requires time, for example. You have to devote time to it. Other disciplines also help make Scripture memory possible in different ways. In order for Scripture memorization to happen, you'll probably need to be leading a certain kind of life first. If you do, however, then the effects will be that your life will run progressively according to what is said in the Scripture.

The Disciplined Life

Disciplines are not like muscle exercises, where if you do certain ones, you get certain muscles. Disciplines are ways of learning our dependence upon God. And so one of the things that we're aiming at is humility— humbleness of mind. Humbleness of mind is the recognition of our dependence upon God and on others. All of the advance we make in the practice of disciplines is due to the divine assistance that we call *grace*. This humbleness of mind keeps us from looking at ourselves as spiritual "musclemen" and taking pride in how advanced we are over others. The discipline of service, for example, can help us stay in the place of humility, especially if we are serving people who don't seem to have the attributes that we would regard as indicating advanced spiritual condition. So service to the poor, and to the people we disagree with, and so on, helps us retain a proper understanding of who we are in relation to others.

Now, a disciplined life is not the same for everyone, so we can't measure our practice of disciplines by how other people do it. You may not need what someone else needs. Disciplines are like medicine: You take what will help, and you don't take what won't help. Ideally, you would come to the place where you didn't need them, because your soul, your body, your mind have been attuned over time to what is good, so you simply act accordingly. That is the condition you want to be in. If you are thinking about disciplines or if you are trying to lead others into them, think of a configuration of disciplines that would be suited to their needs rather than a list. Look at their lives and serve them by suggesting what they might do to meet the needs they might have. It will be most helpful if you have first come out of the misunderstanding of disciplines as acts of righteousness. They are means of grace, intended for our well-being and spiritual and emotional maturity. This exercise of configuration is a matter of wisdom, not a program for righteousness.

As such, the configuration of disciplines needs to be done in the context of a community. You need friends who themselves are living a disciplined life with whom you can share and discuss what's happening. Even solitude has a communal quality. The people early in Christian history who went into solitude misjudged it, so it quickly shifted from an individualized monasticism to a community monasticism. Community is essential because love is essential. Everything is directed toward love.

We can take *that* to our communities. We can help people who are having trouble with their desires and their emotions by directing them into the way of life in the Kingdom of God that will help them see the good, that keeps feelings, desires, and emotions in their proper place.

• • •

With those words, Dallas went to sit down but was quickly taken to a room to rest. That night, there was a banquet to honor his life and contributions to Christians everywhere who wished to live life with God. In the next chapter, we will consider what Dallas has said about spiritual disciplines in the light of attachment love.

THE SCIENCE OF SPIRITUAL MATURITY

JIM WILDER

Dallas was clearly tired after speaking all day. After this fourth talk, Dallas went with Jane to rest. The banquet we had arranged in his honor would start in two hours. He wanted to keep pace with his speaking and writing commitments, but he was forced to withdraw from many of them due to his health. Our plan to work on a book together was not to be.

One of the most formative thinkers in recent Christian history, Dallas left a clear message that spiritual maturity includes all the lesser areas of maturity that we call emotional and relational maturity. Disciples cannot claim spiritual maturity without emotional maturity.

Dallas left us the VIM model for spiritual maturity—Vision, Intention, and Means. He told us that new life in Christ begins immediately at salvation and that character should start changing then, as well. This alone challenges Christians to move beyond "I'm going to heaven; how about you?" We are not simply despicable sinners waiting for the upgrade we don't deserve once we reach heaven. New life starts now! New life produces relational maturity as part of spiritual wholeness.

Spiritual Maturity Includes All of Emotional Maturity

Dallas said, "Community is essential because love is essential. Everything is directed toward love." What if everything is directed *from* love, as well—as the Life Model suggests? Dallas declared the Life Model the best model he had seen for developing mature Christian communities. The fabric of a mature Christian community includes a harmony of all that is spiritual, emotional, and social about human persons. Let's examine how complete maturity develops when we combine the VIM and Life Models.

"How sacred are your cows?" my friend and fellow Heart and Soul presenter Ed Khouri asks when it's time to examine practices that have helped us. Can that which is good be improved? Dallas was prepared to change what he taught if he found a more excellent way. Let's see if attachment love provides a more excellent way. By examining the Intention (*I*)—or Impetus—and means (*M*) of Christlikeness, we support the vision (*V*) Dallas gave the church.

VISION

When Dallas speaks of vision (*V*), he is not giving a vision but rather naming an active element in transformation. Here is a summary of the characteristics of vision that can guide Christians into a with-God life:

1. Our churches should be centers focused on practical leadership, examples, and instructions about how to change how we live, so that our character and our relationships would be models of what is presented in the teachings of Christ and His people.

2. We should reorder what we do as people gathered in Christ in a way that would lead more consistently toward transformation.

3. The primary field for discipleship evangelism is the American church. Discipleship is the only hope of the world, even if it's just to get people to stop killing one another.

4. We need a united front, one which prioritizes transformation as inherent to the gospel, with spiritual and emotional maturity as the metric of success.

5. You can't count on having emotional maturity without *spiritual* maturity. If you are spiritually mature, you *will* be emotionally mature. So if you're concerned about emotional maturity, then you'll work on spiritual maturity.[1]

6. Simply put, emotional maturity is the ability to direct feelings, desires, and emotions into the service of the good.

7. We have the responsibility of addressing the world with the message and person of Jesus Christ.

INTENTION

For Dallas, intention (I) came from the mind and the will/heart/spirit. We have examined how Greek and medieval models of human persons based on "faculties" led to the intellect and will becoming central. But attachment is the most powerful impetus in the human brain. In Scripture, the words *agape* and *hesed* clearly include attachment love. Attachment love directly changes character. Attachment allows us to think with another and thus become like them. As I left Dallas's house the last time, his parting thought was "If life with Jesus begins at salvation and attachment is how we think with and become like another, then salvation must create a new attachment with Jesus."

Intention and impetus. We cannot be transformed into Christlike character by bad motives. The impetus (I) of transformation must be righteous. Dallas saw this righteous process starting with true beliefs, which bring the heart (with God's grace and involvement) to make righteous choices and actions. He used this reasoning when he said of hope, "If they are not able to *believe* that they are unceasing spiritual beings with an eternal destiny in God's universe, *understanding* that their life now is a time of training to live in the power of God, then what's the point of prayer?"[2]

A newborn will be transformed by attachment love long before the baby can believe or understand. The need to believe and understand places great constraints on transformation. In addition, the will has very little power for transformation, so the means of transformation must be indirect. Dallas says, "Spiritual formation, then, may be thought of as an act of indirection." He adds, "Basically discipline is a voluntary activity in your power that makes possible for you something you cannot achieve by direct effort." There are, however, things we do directly but we do not do by effort. The fast track in the right brain is full of activities we do directly but not by conscious, willful effort. Loving attachment and mutual mind are only two of them.

The impetus provided by attachment love allows direct access to the most powerful of human motives and the central dynamic of character development and change. The will is still used, as Dallas suggests, for correcting our strategies, but the will is more like the steering wheel; attachment love is the engine. Loving attachment is a direct and energized activity.

Attachment thus provides the means for all maturity. Without attachment love, Saint Paul reminds us, all kinds of gifts, talents, and activities that appear spiritual are nothing—an illusion of spiritual life, but not spiritual maturity. Dallas has asserted that disciples will be emotionally mature if they are spiritually mature. He also suggested that working on spiritual maturity always produces emotional maturity. Because emotional maturity is the lesser category, we can be emotionally mature without being spiritually mature. Dallas told us in his first lecture, "It is not at all uncommon that a church is caught up in tiptoeing around leaders who are babies emotionally." We cannot be spiritually mature without being emotionally and relationally mature. In chapter 10, we will see the different elements needed for emotional and spiritual maturity.

Attachment is the central force in rebuilding character and identity. Out-of-control emotions and desires give evidence of a flaw in our identity. Identity flaws are corrected through attachment. When emotions, desires, and feelings run life, it is much like hemorrhaging. The solution for a hemorrhage is not removing all the blood from the body but rather rebuilding the body so it constrains blood flow to useful purposes. With a well-trained identity in the fast track, emotions do not drag saints into sin.

We return for a moment to the assertion that the Impetus (I) must be righteous to create righteous character. Loving attachment to God and those God places in our lives is righteous. Hesed and agape are the character of God. Loving attachment provides the opportunity to experience mutual mind with God. Attachment love for God is a righteous, powerful motive for our transformation.

Adding the Elements of the Life Model to VIM

The Life Model adds three perspectives to what we have heard from Dallas. Keep in mind that we are adding, not subtracting. What we have learned from Dallas about intention is wisdom. We will go beyond the means (*M*) provided by intention and add the means (*M*) provided by attachment love. The three elements that the Life Model adds are:

1. Multiple causes produce similar symptoms of immaturity but require different solutions.
2. Correcting iniquities (deformities) meets deeper identity needs.
3. Attachment creates stronger options for transformation.

STRONGER OPTIONS

We are so accustomed to thinking only about the conscious mind that we fail to notice other brain activities. Just as Dallas focused his attention after the first lecture while people in line communicated through mutual-mind states, we can miss processes we use constantly. Part of what the Life Model adds is strategic awareness of these stronger processes.

One example of the stronger options provided by attachment involves attention. We begin by comparing the *focused attention* of the will (the slow track in the brain) with *joint-directed attention* in the fast track. This discussion gets a bit technical. Recall that *focused attention* is a characteristic of activities dominated by the left brain. Conscious focus is unable to grasp the big picture of reality but can pick out a detail to study. We risk becoming focused on lesser things and ignoring weighty ones. The fast track considers all the possibilities at once, always looking for what is more important to us and our people. From there, we select what most needs our attention and action. This activity of the right prefrontal cortex provides simultaneous attention to all that matters to us. What matters most to me/us is highlighted during *joint-directed attention*.

Joint-directed attention. Doing what is important without neglecting lesser things requires a wide range of awareness. We need to notice the relative importance of each element and harmonize them all. As a young father, I was occasionally left in charge of the family. Cooking a meal and watching the baby were two of my central tasks. There is no question which was more important. I fell into slow-track, focused attention on one task while I lost track of the other. I would forget to check on the baby while finding ingredients for a recipe. Do you know how far a baby can crawl and what he or she can get into during that time lapse? When my wife returned, I discovered I had missed many tasks. She asked me why I had forgotten to clean the kitchen. And couldn't I have washed a load of baby clothes? Need I say more?

Slow-track, focused attention made me lose sight of reality. Had I used my fast-track identity, feeding the baby, keeping him safe, and cleaning up would have all received attention. Good parents (those using their fast-track identity) notice and value all these things. With the fast track, parents can monitor the home and see what matters at any given moment. But those using the focused, slow track get locked onto a specific job.

Better choices on my part would not have solved the problem. My weakness came from using a slow track to direct my parenting. I had a list and a plan. It took me years to learn about joy, staying mindful in the moment, and discovering how a father builds strong attachments to his wife and children. With a stronger mutual-mind connection to my wife (or Jesus), I would have seen what she would value when she returned home. In the same way, it has also taken practice to stay mindfully present with God as life gets busy. Now, the longing to know that God is with me becomes more frequent as my hesed grows.

Our spiritual life is also subject to our getting locked into details and missing what is important. How often do we lose God's perspective? The Pharisees were taking houses from widows[3] but tithing their mint and dill. Jesus said to them, "You . . . have neglected the weightier provisions of the law: justice and mercy and faithfulness; but these are the things you should have done without neglecting the others."[4] When we use the fast track, we can keep perspective; when we use the slow track, we only measure a tithe of our cumin.

Disciples do not simply determine priorities for themselves. Disciples are guided by God's Spirit. The slow track (focused attention) picks options based on what we think. The fast track (joint-directed attention) allows us to share a mutual mind with God, where God highlights priorities. Joint-directed attention is illustrated in Psalm 123:

To You I lift up my eyes,
O You who are enthroned in the heavens!
Behold, as the eyes of servants look to the hand of their master,
As the eyes of a maid to the hand of her mistress,
So our eyes look to the LORD our God,
Until He is gracious to us.

Be gracious to us, O LORD, be gracious to us,
For we are greatly filled with contempt.
Our soul is greatly filled
With the scoffing of those who are at ease,
And with the contempt of the proud.

Notice that the eyes of the servants are on whatever has the master's attention. I have already said that the slow track cannot grasp reality because it is too focused and the fast track cannot be focused, as it takes in all reality. Suppose that the mutual mind you are following is focusing on a detail? What then? How does the fast track handle that?

Imagine that among your animal friends, you have a dog friend and a monkey friend. While you and your two animal friends are out playing, your attention goes to something interesting. Both dog and monkey are watching your face. Dog will continue looking at you eagerly. Monkey will look to see what has caught your interest. Monkey friend has a prefrontal cortex that does *joint-directed attention*. Dog friend does not; he can only be trained (with some difficulty) to look where you point.

Both animals can develop strong attachments to you. Both can learn mutual mind with you. But only monkey friend can think about things that have your mental attention. His joint-directed attention in the fast track continues to take in the full picture while knowing that some parts are more important than others. We could call that "highlighted attention." The left brain acts more like dog friend when he sees a squirrel. In his focused attention, he forgets the street, cars, training, and mutual desires, and dashes toward it.

Your child or grandchild will change from being like dog friend to being like monkey friend somewhere between six and nine months of age. At that age, the right prefrontal cortex (fast track) is growing and learning to do *joint-directed attention*. The baby begins to show an interest in what you notice. If we enter mutual mind with God's Spirit and are interested in what has God's attention, this highlighted attention would direct our paths. Is there any evidence of this in Scripture?

HOLY SPIRIT

Dallas states, "The Holy Spirit is constantly active in this process, as are all the instrumentalities of the Kingdom of God. So you're not alone in it; this isn't a solitary trip. And indeed, a major part of our process of growth is our relationship to other people." But by what means does the Holy Spirit's activity change character? Does the Spirit guide us by conscious truth, or does God's Spirit shape us to bear fruit through attachment love, joy, peace, and mutual mind with God? If the answer is both, which means has a more powerful effect on character? Let's consider a case study.

A remarkable change in character took place in the upper room after the Holy Spirit came upon the disciples. Soon afterward, Peter and John were on their way to the Temple. They said to the lame man at the gate called Beautiful, "We're out of cash, so how about a miracle?"[5] Was this a case of joint-directed attention? Were Peter and John now thinking *with* God rather than *about* God? Thinking *with* God while seeing the lame man would reveal what God wanted to do. The disciples only needed to make the announcement. We are not told whether Peter and John had been thinking *about* God by meditating on Jesus' teaching about healing. If meditating on Jesus' sayings was the central point of this text, we would have been told so. No, the disciples were on their ordinary walk to the Temple when what God wanted to do was highlighted in their minds. Haven't most of us considered praying for a sick person and thought, *I wish I knew what God wants to do*?

The Immanuel lifestyle is nothing other than increasingly sharing mutual-mind states with God. When we notice we have lost our peace, mutual mind with God restores us. When we are troubled about the past, thinking about it *with* God restores our joy. When we see others as enemies, mutual mind with God gives us hesed. Brother Lawrence's *The Practice of the Presence of God* has the same goal of an Immanuel lifestyle but with slightly different methods.[6] We seek what is obvious to spiritual eyes but hidden to natural eyes.

Thinking with God (in this case, about a lame man who wanted money) led to a test of character. Peter and John immediately become enemies to the priests, the captain of the Temple guard, and the Sadducees. The conflict between the Sanhedrin and the disciples is a classic moment between those who think *about* God and those who think *with* God. The next day, in front of enemies (the Sanhedrin), Peter provides strong evidence of his character change. Peter is filled with the Holy Spirit in front of the Sanhedrin[7] and begins speaking for God. At the gate called Beautiful, Peter was already thinking *with* God.

Does thinking *with* God explain the character transformation that we see after Pentecost? The disciples had been living *with* Jesus for years, but the Spirit added something new. We want to see Christians experience the kind of change that happened after the Holy Spirit's arrival. How we explain the change dictates our disciple-making strategies. Is this a story about power, or is it more than that?

Displaying the Holy Spirit's power by giving gifts and performing signs, wonders, baptism, indwelling, anointing, revelation, and other miracles does not sound at all like attachment. Paul needed to make it clear to the Corinthians that power and gifting are without value if we lack loving attachment to God and others. There is a synergy between what the Holy Spirit does and attachment love. As we come to understand more of how God has created us, how Jesus saves us, and how the Holy Spirit works in us, we can improve our discipleship strategies. Keep in mind that what is changing are our explanations and strategies. God has been using attachment, the fast track, and mutual-mind abilities all along.

Deeper Needs

We have seen how the Life Model adds stronger options by changing our impetus from willful intention to loving attachment. Attachment reaches our deepest needs. The core of these deeper needs revolves around incomplete identities. Both individuals and groups can have incompletely formed identities. We may lack essential abilities needed for maturity. Once we accept that emotional maturity is part of spiritual maturity, we need all the abilities that produce complete maturity.

Jesus had a complete human identity. We read in Luke 2:52 that Jesus grew in wisdom, stature, and favor "with God and men." The sense given by this passage is that Jesus became fully human. Jesus had no deformities (iniquities) of character. His life demonstrates all the identity and relational skills needed to be a human person. Jesus practiced the spiritual disciplines that prevent striving. He did not rely on human strength and ability.

Jesus completed His identity as a child. Most of us have not completed ours. Identity and relational skills are both learned. Holes in our identity must be filled for us to become mature.

Identity requires a great deal of training from those who have skill and practice being human. Acquiring identity skills can be compared to learning to read the Scriptures in English, Greek, Hebrew, and Aramaic. Nothing about these tasks is righteous, but without learning from those who know, even God's Word remains beyond our comprehension. Likewise, we do not know how to be human without learning from someone. The brain relies on attachment with those who have people skills to build and correct our identities. A good deal of practice must follow.

I interviewed pastor and counselor John Loppnow about his passion to be a disciple of Jesus. His story can help us understand how relational solutions build identity. John discovered Richard Foster and the spiritual disciplines while he was still in high school. John soon found Dallas Willard's work and loved it. During seminary, John drove across Los Angeles to hear Dallas teach at the Valley Vineyard. Simultaneously, John completed a three-year spiritual-direction program. Following seminary, John spent five years under the spiritual direction of Jan Johnson, a speaker at Heart and Soul who coauthored books with Dallas and became president of Dallas Willard Ministries.

John saw fruit from practicing spiritual disciplines. Scripture meditation kept him anchored and gave the fastest transformation of any discipline. Fasting helped John become sweeter when he did not get what he wanted. Silence plus solitude helped him quiet and break free from relying on people's opinions about him.

John also trained in the relational skills of the Life Model. He was one of my coauthors for *Joyful Journey*, a book about the relational skill of mutual mind with God.[8] By now, John was approaching twenty years of experience with the spiritual disciplines he loves. Because John has experienced both fast- and slow-track training, he can tell us where each practice has helped him.

Like all of us, John had some missing relational skills that led to gaps in his identity. Spiritual disciplines were making very slow progress toward building what was missing. John has told me:

> The road map of maturity and the associated skills brought me great understanding and freedom as a pastor and Christian leader. Relational skills helped me grasp where I was and which specific next steps would be wisest for me to take. This has been tremendously helpful. Instead of ramping up more spiritual disciplines (which I love) and hoping that a day retreat, fasting, memorization, or serving would help me have better relationships, I can now identify what I am missing and practice the missing piece. I am building my identity as the person Jesus created me to be.[9]

Dallas tells us, "Disciplines are not like muscle exercises, where if you do certain ones, you strengthen certain muscles. Disciplines are ways we learn of our dependence on God." Relational skills, on the other hand, are very much like muscle exercises. Doing many repetitions builds strong neural pathways, along with capacities, endurance, and skill. Relational exercises are very specific; one exercise will not build other relational skills. For example, quieting practices do not build mutual mind.

We should not be surprised that relational skills had a more direct and powerful impact on John's relationships. John says, "While spiritual disciplines indirectly supported my marriage, my marriage was deeply transformed by relationship-skill training. Relationship-skill training is much faster at helping individuals and couples get traction."

Before we begin thinking that relational skills are only human interactions, we need to remember that mutual-mind states with God are also a relational skill for the fast track in the brain. Practicing mutual mind with both Jesus and people became important for John. His wife, Sungshim, reports the results she has witnessed:

I have seen John engage in different spiritual disciplines like silence, solitude, and fasting. He desired to remain sweet and kind when he did not get what he wanted. I witnessed a subtle yet positive impact from his engaging in spiritual disciplines. I saw a change in John's inner person; he seemed less reactive and defensive.

Once John began practicing relational skills—such as having a mutual mind with God and working on holes on his maturity—I witnessed measurable changes in his daily interaction with me, our children, and others. He clearly became bolder, and his true colors and flavor blossomed. John had always longed for a strong identity yet did not attain one easily. Developing a mutual mind with God (plus a road map to maturity) freed him from fear. John developed a new freedom and power! Practicing mutual mind with God and sharing (as a couple) the peace we gained has been the best thing for our marriage.

Becoming disciples involves growing in human identity. Again, we must ask, "Does Scripture speak of this?" The answers come from (1) understanding how the brain transmits character from generation to generation and (2) studying how the Bible speaks of deformed and missing character (called iniquity). To become mature, we need to learn and exercise our missing capacities. We will first examine how character is formed, so we can understand how it becomes deformed.

How Character Is Transmitted

A brief introduction to how character is transmitted from generation to generation will help us understand how easily the process can leave holes in character and maturity. Any holes in one generation will be passed to the next. Holes in maturity are cumulative: We cannot pass on what we have not received. The solution for missing skills is exchanging missing relational skills with other members of our people who have the skills we lack. This process only works when there is (1) attachment love, (2) a people, and (3) a model for human persons that is greater (more complete) than anything we know from our human family. Could this be a partial model for making disciples?

ATTACHMENT

Attachment begins with grace—being the sparkle of joy in someone's eye. Joy is relational. Someone is very glad to be with me. Joy is a high-energy state and must alternate with quiet rest. Energy from joy must be limited to the abilities of the weaker member of the bond, so the stronger member doesn't overwhelm the weaker.

Attachment begins long before birth and continues developing across our entire life. Attachment is exclusive. Although we may have many attachments, one attachment cannot be exchanged for another. Attachment links us to the flow of life; it grows identity and builds resilience, and it governs what gets our attention and forms our thoughts. Attachment is the strongest force in the human brain.

Dallas tied spiritual formation to the science of attachment without knowing it. He quoted a woman who said, "I think I am beginning to really enjoy God," adding, "That last line is especially significant: The enjoyment of God is foundational to transformation of character. The enjoyment of God is a primary part of what is required if we are going to be emotionally mature people."

Joy is personal and is often exchanged face-to-face. By activating the mirror neurons in each brain, the two faces come to know one another and build a bond and shared identity we call character. Father Richard Rohr says:

> So many Christian mystics talk about seeing the divine face or falling in love with the face of Jesus. I think that's why St. Clare (1194–1253) used the word "mirroring" so often in her writings. We are mirrored not by concepts, but by faces delighting in us— giving us the face we can't give to ourselves. It is "the face of the other" that finally creates us and, I am sorry to say, also destroys us. It is the gaze that does us in!
>
> Now surely you see why a positive and loving God-image is absolutely necessary for creating happy and healthy people. Without it, we will continue to create lots of *mean* Christians who have no way out of their hall of negative mirrors.[10]

CRITICAL PERIODS

The brain develops in stages. Stages include critical periods when essential abilities are growing. Later in life, these abilities grow very slowly or not at all. Passing character from one generation to another requires face-to-face times when development is greatest—at critical periods. My sons were born while I was in graduate school and working full time. I was generally home while they were asleep. There was little overlap between my brain and theirs during many critical periods. As a result, they copied little to none of my relational abilities but copied anyone who was present that had a bond with them.

ACQUISITION

Very specific conditions are needed to acquire relational-brain skills. The same conditions are not needed to use relational-brain skills. Acquiring skills requires interaction with a better-trained brain. Identity and character-building, relational skills are almost entirely nonverbal and are learned in the first two years of life. When missing skills are remediated, the process is still nonverbal, based on attachment, and requires real joy *but* needs much more practice because the brain is no longer in the critical-growth phase.

PRACTICE

Once acquired, relational-brain skills require repeated practice to become ingrained, trained habits. Habits can run through the brain up to two hundred times faster than new activities. Practice takes time. Practice is done best with peers who are about as bad or as good with the skill as we are. Remedial skills take much more practice than those acquired during critical periods from primary bonds.

CAPACITY

Maturing involves using relational skills under increasingly complex and difficult conditions. Children barely take care of themselves. Parents must manage marriage, work, school, community, church, friends, family, aging parents, and many other things. Mature parents should not lose their peace or relational ability under increasing demands. Joyful relational capacity comes from intense and repeated joy practice. As joy capacity builds from good experiences, we withstand higher levels of distress and fatigue, thus becoming less likely to lose control of emotions, desires, and feelings. We become much harder to traumatize.

FULL SET

Jesus had a full set of relational-brain skills. For example, He flew into a rage, and in His anger, healed a man's withered hand—a physical defor- mity (or iniquity, as I will explain shortly).[11] Jesus showed no change in character when He was angry. As we shall see in a moment, anger is one of six unpleasant emotions hardwired into the brain. If we can use all six emotions to improve our relationships, we will not change character when we feel angry, ashamed, hopeless, or some other feeling. A full set of human emotional skills produces a consistent life. Most people fall into sudden immaturity precisely when they need a skill they neither possess nor know exists.

Because most people have not heard of relational-brain skills, these skills often go unnoticed. Relational-brain skills are frequently illustrated in the Bible[12] and are a serious component of fellowship experiences.[13] Relational- brain skills are needed by godly leaders[14] and healthy marriages.[15]

WHAT "MY PEOPLE" DO

The culmination of fast-track processing is knowing how "my people" would act under these conditions. How "my people" act is the reference for our first reaction—our response before we are consciously aware of what is happening. As we continue to experience new circumstances, our people must supply more answers. How "my people" act is a mental file that never stops growing.

Transformation comes through replacing an old "how 'my people' act" file with a new people and their file. After age fourteen, the survival of *my people* becomes more important to the brain than our own life. Transforming character therefore depends on becoming attached by love, joy, and peace to a new people. Dallas acknowledges this group-identity influence when he says, "The configuration of disciplines needs to be done in the context of a community. You need friends who themselves are living a disciplined life with whom you can share and discuss what's happening. Even solitude has a communal quality."

INCREASING COMPLEXITY AND DIFFICULTY

As mentioned in the "capacity" section, maturity requires mastery of identity expression (staying relational) under increasingly difficult circumstances. Life becomes more complex as we grow. We acquire responsibility for more people. Suffering becomes one of the complexities of life at some point. Suffering and enemies test our character and maturity. We will always have a breaking point. Pain, drugs, poison, fatigue, starvation, lack of rest, dementia, and other factors limit how much the brain can take. Our faith does *not* rest on how well our brain will run; it is not based on how well we hold on to God. Our attachment comes from God's hesed and how well God holds on to us. Years of practicing mutual mind with God does pay off through learned capacity to know God's presence in whatever state we find ourselves.

HEALING

When our fast-track system has been badly trained, has missing functions, or has been traumatized, we develop deformities/iniquities (again, see below) that need healing and training. A deformed identity may break down for almost no external reason or may run persistently in the wrong way. Healing and deliverance may be needed before we can form new attachments, learn relational skills, and develop the character of disciples.

REMEDIATION

Joyful attachments to a people who practice mutual mind with God allow a new identity to grow. People who have a vision for who God is creating in others provide the vision (*V*) for transformation. Each disciple needs this vision to remediate iniquities. Remediation—that is, growing whatever has been missing in our identity so that we display the character of Christ—requires much practice. Paul reminds us to remind those who have forgotten, encourage those who are tired, carry some of the load for the weak, and be very patient with them all.[16]

Iniquities

God spoke to Moses about the three ways people stop being what God designed us to be. "Then the LORD passed by in front of him and proclaimed, 'The LORD, the LORD God, compassionate and gracious, slow to anger, and abounding in lovingkindness and truth; who keeps lovingkindness for thousands, who forgives iniquity, transgression and sin; yet He will by no means leave the guilty unpunished, visiting the iniquity of fathers on the children and on the grandchildren to the third and fourth generations.'"[17]

Scripture, particularly in Hebrew, introduces us to the concept that people can be deformed. That we have developed differently from what God intended is seen everywhere in the Bible. The concept of deformity is expressed by the word *iniquity*. Consider a tree in my yard that was bent into a loop as a little sapling. The tree is now at least thirty years old. Its trunk goes up about a foot, loops down and then goes up like any normal tree. Once grown into a shape it was not intended to have, the tree trunk cannot be changed. This shape is an iniquity.

1. Iniquity is deformed growth—in particular, both character and identity.
2. Transgression is not doing what we should and could do.
3. Sin is falling short of what we aimed to do.

Here is a place where reliance on the will (voluntarism) has made understanding iniquity almost impossible for Western Christians. If we cannot see, it may be because we won't look (choice) or because our eyes are deformed or missing—an iniquity. We think of both iniquity and sin in terms of choices and the will. Sin is a "bad" choice, so we must make better choices. Disease and deformity is not a choice, so how can we choose a different way? We hear that Jesus "healed diseases" because iniquity includes the blind, deaf, crippled, and paralyzed. Because of Western assumptions and language, translators have translated these physical deformities as "diseases." We think of Jesus, therefore, as healing diseases but not restoring deformities. The idea that these deformities are iniquities never crosses our minds. But Jesus used physical deformities to make his point about deformities of the soul.

Jesus made the point that iniquities are more difficult to correct than sin is to forgive. He said, "Which is easier, to say to the paralytic, 'Your sins are forgiven'; or to say, 'Get up, and pick up your pallet and walk'? But so that you may know that the Son of Man has authority on earth to forgive sins'—He said to the paralytic, 'I say to you, get up, pick up your pallet and go home.'"[18] By doing the harder activity (heal iniquity), he showed he could do the easier one (forgive sin).

When Jesus called the Pharisees "blind guides," he was calling out an iniquity of character.[19] Discipleship must also deal with iniquities of character to produce the character of Christ. Let us return to Peter and John as they encounter an iniquity (paralysis) by the gate called Beautiful. The disciples, in mutual mind with God, responded with God's response. Disciples have authority to address iniquities.

Disciples have their own iniquities. Because we need to have our iniquities corrected, we need spiritual practices Jesus did not need. Jesus had no iniquities. Iniquities of character must be healed. Identity must be completed and trained for new character to grow. Healing and attachment love will be needed.

Effort

Dallas said that grace is not opposed to effort. We do well to remember that it requires effort to grow missing bits of our identities as individuals as well as groups. We must be retrained. We neither want to make excuses for our iniquities nor pass them on to others. Training requires practice and effort. Our fast track must exercise a new identity that rebuilds the attachment system. The strongest impetus for retraining is our attachment love to God and others.

Multiple Causes

In addition to stronger options to meet deep identity needs, the Life Model reveals multiple causes for the symptoms of immaturity. Attachment and relational skills provide unexpected solutions for problems we generally attribute to other causes.

ANGER

The ability to use anger (or other unpleasant emotions) to improve relationships is a basic relational-brain skill. Most people lack this skill. Dallas seemed unfamiliar with this relational-brain skill when he said, "If you stand up for what is good without anger, you will be much more effective, because anger that degrades into contempt invites a contemptuous response." Anger that degrades to contempt is evidence that a relational-brain skill is missing. One solution is to avoid anger; a second option is to learn the relational-brain skill that makes anger helpful.

There are multiple forms of anger in the nervous system—hot anger, cold anger, right-brain anger, and left-brain anger. These multiple causes for anger may be as unfamiliar to the reader as they were to Dallas, who addressed slow-track, left-brain anger when he said, "Anger comes from the frustration of will. When your will is frustrated, anger is a natural response." Anger comes in response to our thinking and frustration. Spontaneous anger is in the fast-track system.

Fast-track anger is a modified fear response to a threat. When we should run away (we see a snake), we call it fear. When the threat must be stopped (someone is attacking our child), the same adrenaline rush becomes hot anger.

UNPLEASANT EMOTIONS

There are, in fact, six unpleasant emotions wired into the brain's fast track that must be individually trained how to be relational. The six emotions are anger, fear, sadness, shame, disgust, and hopelessness. These emotions in the fast track are not premeditated. None come as a response to our thoughts. All six emotional responses are there before we start thinking consciously.[20]

John Loppnow describes learning emotional maturity with the six unpleasant emotions this way, "Remaining relational while experiencing six upsetting emotions was central and vital to my character being transformed. I learned there is a good 'myself' that I can become. I discovered it is worth my attention and energy to become that person. Now I value acting like my true self." Our true self will always be Christlike as when Jesus healed the man with the withered hand.

We may have some doubts that all six emotions are designed to improve relationships. Let's examine the skills involved. Most of us have learned to get closer to someone who is sad. We see someone's tears and want to comfort them. When we see someone feeling afraid we want to be protective. Raising a baby, doing medical work, or farming helps us build relationships while cleaning up disgusting messes. Most of us can imagine using sadness, fear, and disgust to improve relationships.

The relational-brain skills that go with anger, shame, and hopelessness are similar but much less common. Sometimes a whole culture lacks one or more of these skills. A good way to know what skills are missing is watching what unpleasant emotions are used for motivation. Some people avoid shame and others avoid anger. When people work to avoid one of these six feelings, it is because they lack the brain skill needed to use that emotion to improve relationships. Teaching specific missing skills is part of the means (*M*) of discipleship to correct a specific iniquity.

(Note: If you are missing the skill of using anger—or any of the six—to build better relationships, then what I am saying makes little sense. Our brain cannot see how a missing skill would work or why we would want it. This is the nature of any gaps in our relational-brain skills—we don't see the gap and it does not make sense to seek the skill. We avoid that feeling and use it as unpleasant motivation for ourselves and others instead.)

TROUBLE QUIETING

Quieting is a relational-brain skill that releases serotonin on demand. Serotonin quiets the brain from all sorts of arousal states. The ability to self-quiet is the strongest predictor of mental health for a lifetime. Dallas mentions quieting while speaking of the disciplines of abstinence. He says, "Some disciplines (I call the disciplines of abstinence—solitude, silence, fasting, frugality, and so on) are made to *empty* us, to make a place in our life for other activities that would otherwise be crowded out. Such disciplines are not righteous; they are more accurately considered *wise*." When the conscious mind is driving us to constant activity, the indirection from disciplines of abstinence will reduce our striving. Dallas then says about solitude, "Another thing solitude does is to help you be quiet. Quietness is an essential condition of the spiritual life; it represents a peace that our bodies and our souls hunger for." He also says, "You have to practice solitude in order to know its benefits. Solitude is not righteous."

Once again, differences between the fast and slow tracks create different means of quieting. The nervous system has multiple quieting systems.[21] The fast track[22] controls the neurochemicals needed for rest. The slow track has strategies for quieting but lacks direct means. We need both quieting abilities and strategies. We need relational (attachment-based) neurochemical abilities to quiet emotions, feelings, and desires.

We need the strategies to stop striving. Disciples with emotional and spiritual maturity need to learn both.

Means

The means (*M*) of transformation are wise but not righteous. Dallas has told us, "Always remember a discipline is not a righteous deed, even though some activities that are disciplines are in other capacities righteous." We want to do every righteous thing, but the means of discipleship are supplemental, and we must be careful not to make them sacred.

Once more, John Loppnow directs us to an important difference in means (*M*) between the fast and slow tracks. John loves books. The slow track can easily acquire ideas from books. John points out:

> The spiritual disciplines have a much longer history, depth, and breadth of writers that I as a reader can draw from when I desire to learn more. Spiritual disciplines have a common, understood language for people who are part of the church. Relational skills have a shorter history. They have brain science to support them and draw my attention integrating relational-brain science and theology.

Relational skills are not acquired through reading. Let me give you an example. The relational fast track can speed or slow our heart rate to match the energy level of our partner in a mutual-mind state. Now you have read about the skill, yet you are likely unsure if you have the skill. Reading about the skill will not help you change your heart rate. You can tell others about the skill, but you cannot train them to have this ability through anything you read. Yet a baby could acquire this skill by the time he or she learns to talk if attached (by mutual mind) to a bigger brain with the skill. If our means of transformation are to succeed, then we must train the brain the way it learns.

FOUR CATEGORIES OF MEANS

Transformation begins with love instead of ending there. The fast track is needed to complete the development of character and correct deformed character directly. Iniquities (deformities) of character require direct solutions. We still need the corrections provided by spiritual disciplines, and we will soon see why.

We can roughly divide our expanded means into four categories: (1) Some people with fairly complete identities are striving to do too much. Spiritual disciplines will reduce striving. (2) Some people lack the relational skills needed to have full human identity. Relational training based on attachment will replace their striving with relationships. (3) Some people are striving to compensate for deformed identities and need healing and relational training. (4) Some people feel hopeless because they see so little progress. They have just stopped because their spiritual life is not working. They need their intention upgraded to attachment love.

STRIVING

Dallas has made the point that grace is not opposed to effort. He also points out that the disciplines help us control our effort. "Without engaging in the disciplines, our desired outcomes are sources of striving, of frustration." Striving is exactly what is best corrected by spiritual disciplines. Striving is not a righteous motive. Yet, immaturity causes a different sort of striving.

Consider an expert swimmer who tries swimming across the ocean, becomes tired and cold, and starts thrashing. We would advise the swimmer to cease striving. If we saw someone who could not swim thrashing in the water, the problem is different. Both make an intense effort. The expert swimmer strives doing too much with the skills he or she has. The drowning person strives exactly because skills are missing. The answer is not to stop striving but to acquire skill. The need to acquire identity and character precedes the need to manage them.

With or without relational skills, there will be striving. When we simply need to stop striving, we need disciplines to create enough space to redirect our attention. When what we need are the basic elements of a human person, then training is needed. Perhaps this distinction is the very reason many people experience meager growth in relational maturity using only spiritual disciplines.

IS MORE OR LESS EFFORT NEEDED?

Compensating for the lack of an unknown relational or spiritual skill is a common source of striving. We have all observed how people who lack a normal human ability compensate with another. People without hands play guitar with their toes. My parents taught a blind student in Bible school. He could tell the denomination of bills by touch. Try as I might, I could never feel the difference between one note and another. His hearing was also well developed. Sometimes his acute hearing made it hard for him to sleep.

We overdevelop some abilities when we lack others, and that leads to striving. A common example is how hard people work to avoid upsetting others. Entire families and churches guide their lives and make great efforts to avoid upsetting certain individuals. Being sensitive to others morphs into what Dallas called "tiptoeing around leaders who are babies emotionally."

Dallas knows that the solution must fit the need. For example, he says, "Disciplines are like medicine: You take what will help, and you don't take what won't help." We are considering a wider list of solutions, but applications are still selective. Is it time to learn and practice the relational skills Jesus developed when he was younger? A complete set of relational-identity skills still cannot replace dependence on God. Is it time to practice the reliance on God that Jesus developed when he was older?

Learning neither relational skills nor spiritual disciplines is righteous. Neither one is the place we start. We start with attachment love. Salvation brings attachment to God as members of a new family. A living identity moves into the fast track of our brain, creating Christlike character. All our moral choices and first reactions begin resembling our new people—let us hope they are disciples of Jesus.

Relational Iniquities Are Increasing

Numerous factors are increasing the extent of relational iniquities across the globe. Many of these changes are spelled out in *Joy Starts Here*,[23] a book I wrote with several friends. Some of the causes will help us understand why attachment and relational identities must be part of our spiritual formation.

Traumas continue creating iniquity. War, AIDS, famine, genocide, revolution, drugs, and other tragedies continue to disrupt cultures. The numbers of those who are impacted continue growing. Weapons of mass destruction are technical rather than requiring the joint social effort that was needed for the huge armies of the past. Very few cultures have the social cohesion to maintain huge armies, but anyone with money can buy some rather nasty technology. A very small cluster of people can terrorize large groups.

People travel more easily and often move frequently and far. How often has someone moving in or out changed your community? Few people live where anyone can tell them what their great-grandparents were like. Group identities break easily and have much less time to form. Relational interactions that form character receive less time and attention as families decreasingly work, eat, or live together.

Communication and connections with the world now provide a huge array of possible identity groups. The problem for our character is that diversity will not replace relational practice. Belonging to everyone does not provide enough practice to belong to anyone. Knowing that there are a thousand musical styles will not help us play one song well. Saying we will play every instrument in the world does no good if we cannot play the first instrument. Lack of relational practice becomes acute after the twelve-year-old's apoptotic period when the brain must grow a group identity. This missing or defective group identity becomes the basis for adult character iniquity. The most common symptom is addiction.

The most extensive and insidious problem in developing identity and character is that character skills require attachment and direct, in-person practice time. Attachments without time together are shallow at best. Older people with relational skills have less and less face-to-face practice with infants, children, and adolescents. The average child spends several hours a day in front of a screen. Although a child may have hundreds of social-media "friends," none of those count for developing character. The fast track of the brain is not activated by screens. Screens run too slowly for the fast track.

It is simply not possible for every generation to figure out these relational skills for themselves during the critical periods of development. Strong character requires transmission of identity and relationship during the critical periods, when the next generation grows them quickly. Lack of attachment and relational-skill practice creates people who are as delicate as snowflakes when things go slightly wrong. Their engagement with the world looks more and more depressed and distracted. Thousands of hours playing games where one wins by making others lose does not correct our predatory tendencies. The sense of being a people weakens. Being able to live with one's basic self and relate to the opposite sex becomes confusing. Development lags for those who must figure out everything for themselves. People mature later and later.

These are the issues of our time. They are modifications of issues that have always existed, but the scale and pattern are new. Problems accumulate from generation to generation because we pass on only the character we have. Skills will not be passed on without attachment. Skills will not be learned while we or they are watching a screen, away at school or work, in a retirement home, loaded on drugs, or living in a different town. Christlike character will not be passed on if we were never disciples.

The Problem with Corrections

We will find no new ingredients for Christian life. Neurotheology provides no solutions for creating Christian character that are not historically Christian. Yet, just as the messages to the churches in the book of Revelation were tailored to each congregation, we must match current solutions with current needs. What needs emphasis and what constitutes the next step varies by situation. Wouldn't mutual mind with God be rather helpful guidance about what we need now? We need an Immanuel lifestyle with relational joy and hesed attachments for our transformation into disciples.

Examining Christian practices based on how the brain creates human identity and character reveals that Christians are not very attached to God or one another. We already know that a loving attachment to God and others is good doctrine. Disciples need more practice with relational maturity.

Sometimes a correction is no longer needed because culture has changed. One of the volunteers at Heart and Soul came from a tradition that does not wear jewelry. Not wearing wedding rings was a correction for people who found their value in wealth. Not wearing rings became a statement of Christian values. The volunteer's children lived in a generation where couples live together but do not marry. Her children wanted wedding rings as a statement of Christian values.

Corrections for errors of the past tend to become the sacred cows of the future. Our practice gets cluttered with solutions to problems that no longer need the same attention. Every generation discovers overcorrections from previous generations that produced unintended deformities in character.

These corrections are the means (M) that, as Dallas told us, are not righteous and are to be selected according to wisdom so they will fit the need.

The correction we need at this moment emphasizes disciples grown through attachment love. We must return to our first love as the world enters a global meltdown of relational skills. Hate will rise, and so will opportunities to love our enemies. We will need to be disciples. We will examine what a church designed to create disciples might practice in our next and final chapter.

Exercise: Nine Minutes of VIM

This exercise has three parts, each three minutes.

Take a deep breath, and let it out slowly.

1. *Vision*: How would you state your vision at this point? Text your vision to someone, giving an invitation to discuss what you are thinking.

2. *Impetus*: Of the people you know, who has a strong sense of hesed attachment with God? Send them an invitation, asking to hear more about how they experience God's attachment love (perhaps at a meal or small group).

3. *Means*: Which of the means you have heard here makes the least sense to you? Do a quick online search about the topic, as it might be your blind spot.

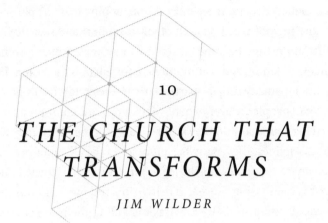

10

THE CHURCH THAT
TRANSFORMS

JIM WILDER

The American church does well promoting a vision. Churches proclaim their vision through websites, videos, podcasts, local media, social media, brochures, signage, visitation, greeters, and the carefully chosen names for their coffee bars. Church vision usually includes a mission and doctrinal statement. Church leadership gathers at many levels to clarify, strategize, and make their vision known. Most Sundays, in most pulpits, a vision is outlined, supported, proclaimed, and applied.

We kill the church when we make Christianity about fulfilling a vision. When a church, staff, program, or outreach is forced to service a vision, striving is about to begin. Joy and peace levels fall—casualties of striving to fulfill visions. The impetus of attachment love gives way to burnout. People who question the vision risk being downgraded as Christians. Justifications begin to multiply—both for visions and for having enough to do. Justifications come with a great deal of "Christianeze"—pious language intended to make supporting (or avoiding) the vision a righteous act. This is striving.

I regularly visit a mission organization I will call Vision Force because it is built around a vision. The vision is wonderful and true. Staff members commit their lives to fulfill this vision. Staff burnout is high. As members burn out, leaders promote more vision, hoping to boost participation. Leaders and members call on each other to support and sacrifice for their vision. Relationships become strained, sometimes broken. Sometimes, attachments to family and community are forfeited to the vision. Personal and spiritual maturity drops—particularly in the children—as hurts accumulate. Tired people are everywhere. Members of the community often tire from striving—and how do they strive? They fast, they pray, they work the spiritual disciplines, they study Scripture and take all-night prayer vigils, but somewhere along the line, the joy is gone. Vision has turned into striving. What is their vision, we ask? Their vision and motivation is to spread God's love. A vision in their slow track is killing them to get results but moments of real attachment with God sustain them in the fast track.

Striving Is Failure

Striving is what we do when a good idea is not working well enough. Striving always supports some vision. Striving is almost always the godchild of the conscious slow track in the brain. Striving is evidence we are overly focused. Bible study, memorization, prayer, church participation, small groups, church growth, outreach, relational skills, and any other good thing you can imagine can produce striving if this vision becomes central. Even spiritual disciplines can become striving when disciplines are considered righteous acts rather than a means. Means, as Dallas has said, are not righteous acts, even when they are righteous in other contexts.

We have commented that the spiritual disciplines help us stop striving, and yet we have now reached the conclusion that spiritual disciplines can also become striving. How is this so? The answer comes from this observation: Pushing for results with solutions that do not work *well enough* creates striving. Striving is the sign that our will is overheating. David Takle, a presenter at Heart and Soul, has described striving using a boating metaphor: We are rowing rather than sailing with the wind of the Spirit.[1]

There are basically two errors that lead to striving. The first error is trying to correct an iniquity (deformity) with the indirection of spiritual disciplines. Direct relational-skill training is needed. We need a more complete self. Start with attachment, lead into mutual mind, provide healing, and build group identity to correct iniquity. Skill training requires lots of practice. If we start with spiritual disciplines instead, the disciplines will be difficult, hardly touching our character. We will strive to control feelings, emotions, and desires rather than become spiritually mature.

The second error goes the opposite direction. We try to be bigger than we really are and do more than we can do. We strive to do God's work and serve our vision. This second error comes from an inflated sense of ourselves. We work harder when what we need is to back off and allow God to work. Now we need disciplines of indirection to help us become smaller.

The Vision Force mission I visit regularly desires strong attachments with God. When they do experience hesed with God, their joy, peace, and love for external enemies grows. Yet, conflicts and hurts emerge within teams. There are casualties.

Members dig into their pain and call on the Holy Spirit for healing with some success—but not enough success. Before long, striving sets in—striving to be healed, to find the source of their pain, and to practice spiritual disciplines.

The mission vision is strong on love for God and for outsiders. Yet, building hesed relational skills and loving attachments in their group identity has proved inadequate. Building a lasting group identity would take them away from their vision to reach the world. The mission vision is focused like a flashlight on people who do not know God. Vision thus becomes a destructive master. Serving the vision gains the world by trading their souls for results. They call this "burning out for Jesus." At the same moment, their vision points toward attachment love with God, who sustains them. Members who arrived without a complete set of human relational skills are left in a painfully unrelenting spot with feelings, emotions, and desires that get out of control. Members strive, collapse, or leave.

When relationships break down, spiritual means are used for solutions instead of relational means. When they become angry, they might fast and pray but still be unable to use anger relationally to produce better attachment with their team or family. Spiritual disciplines are expected to replace relational skills. The result is striving. Striving springs from overlooking the iniquities (missing brain skills) the participants bring with them. Attachment-based skills with God's people are not part of their vision.

Striving and Spinning

Striving, overheating while trying to make the wrong solution work, is common, but it's not the only church problem. Churches often do little more than keep their doors open. They are like a gym with no weights or a motor, spinning endlessly without a load. Churches that spin are very happy with their own vision. Every meeting celebrates how much they like their views. Spinning churches are doing what they intend to do. Their means are tried and true. Some hand out tracts, wear old-style clothes, promote pacifism, get blessed by the Spirit, give exegetical sermons, support food banks, observe holy days, visit the inner cities, worship for hours, paint over graffiti, or any number of things. Spinning happily in their practices, they do not overheat. Many churches close as spinners go from gray to white hair.

Spinning churches age but do not produce disciples. One can be a pacifist, evangelize heathens, and worship and feed the hungry while "the people we help" never become "my people." There is no load on our character. By contrast, attaching to our enemies with love reveals our hidden character flaws. Staying in a comfort zone results in overlooking our own iniquities. Our children and grandchildren are led to believe these iniquities are Christian character. "That is how Christians are!" our children think and tell their friends.

Churches who make disciples must neither strive nor spin. Actively practicing spontaneous, loving attachment to our enemies will keep us on the right track. We are training character in the fast track. Only a mutual mind with Jesus provides spontaneous, loving attachment to "horrid people."

How does attachment love become spontaneous? We have all encountered a horrid little child in a store or restaurant. Nothing would please us more than having that child removed. While we are still appalled by this little monster, we see the parents or grandparents spontaneously accepting the child as their very own. There is not even a question whether the child belongs with them, will eat with them, and will go home with them. The family is attached, even if they are upset.

Jesus sees God's children in horrid people. When we have a mutual mind with God, people acquire value to us. God's children have value in our fast track when we are part of God's people. Even before we are conscious of our feelings, our group identity is at work. When we have the relational skills to use unpleasant emotions to improve relationships, we do not withdraw—we spontaneously attach.

Sustainable Vision

Vision is always corrective. We must be sure we make the right corrections. Vision belongs in our conscious (slow track), where it can direct our priorities back to our first love. A vision of joyful, lovingly hesed disciples sustains us without burnout.

A sustainable church has a vision that builds attachment to God and God's people. Attachment love allows mutual mind with God and creates the kind of people we call disciples. Disciples allow their loving attachment and mutual mind with God to adjust their vision. Awareness of which connections will build strongly hesed character matches the means (M) to the vision (V).

SUSTAINABLE VISION

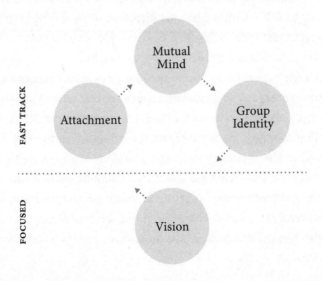

Sustainable Vision for Mature Disciples

Spiritual maturity is the ability to sustain a mutual mind with God and God's people under increasingly difficult conditions. Communities that train spontaneous attachment love for enemies will build maturity. *Enemies* may sound like an extreme term, but our brains often expect that others will not help us. We feel it is all up to us. No one around is on our side. Many school and work days provide enemy-like moments. This "we are not together" feeling grows stronger during hard times like divorces and family or church fights.

When our spiritual family uses these alienated moments to teach attachment love, we will discover our iniquities and weaknesses. We develop relational and spiritual maturity by building mutual mind with God and God's people *while* others feel like enemies. We begin by noticing when we feel alone and hurt. Success will depend on thinking *with* God *while* we are upset.

VIM and Life Model Together

Our revised (hybrid) model for spiritual and relational maturity has Vision (*V*) solidly in the slow track of the conscious mind. Impetus (*I*) flows from the fast track powered by attachment love—the most powerful force in the human heart, soul, and body. The Means (*M*) are divided between the fast and slow tracks.

Whereas our brain processes experience in a clear order and direction, the revised VIM model has no direction of flow. Vision, impetus, and means interact with each other. For example, attachment love creates vision. Vision builds attachment love. Means go either way, as needed. Fast-track style means (*M*) address the iniquities in our identities. Slow-track means correct any overinflated sense of self that tries to do too much. Spiritual disciplines create room for God and reignite our attachment love.

The three ways people depart from their God-given identity are also represented in the revised VIM. Transgressions are corrected through vision, which clarifies what we should and should not do. Means that develop the fast-track mind (attachment, mutual mind, and group identity) will correct iniquities of character. A multitude of sins are covered by our impetus toward attachment love (hesed).[2]

REVISED VIM MODEL

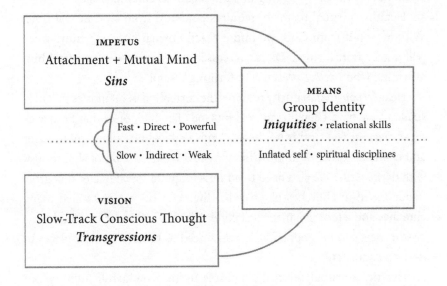

Healthy Spiritual Maturity

Our full salvation begins with God's hesed attachment love. Healthy *spiritual* maturity includes all relational maturity plus the relationship Jesus had with the Father. Our discipleship starts by developing loving attachments. In chapter 7, we considered twelve characteristics of healthy attachments and found them all in God's patterns as described in the Scriptures: God gives us life, allows no one in His place, sees us as special (grace), builds our joy, lets us rest, thinks with us, draws close and moves away, shares good and bad times with us, helps us discover our true selves, gives us freedom but stays hesed, stretches us to grow, and makes us part of God's people. To build disciples, then, churches should devote much of their programming to producing strong hesed. Some creative ways to start are suggested in appendix A.

Healthy spiritual maturity requires us to identify and address our character iniquities by training essential relational skills in hesed relationships. More mature and less mature church members must form lasting hesed attachments. We must be transformed in every generation; otherwise, the church will pass on iniquities and call them "spiritual." See appendix B for relational resources, including Life Model books and materials.

Healthy spiritual maturity requires guidance from God in real time. Without input from God, we might reach normal human maturity but will not be transformed. Dallas agrees; in his *Hearing God*, we find him affirming God's active presence in forming disciples.

Healthy spiritual maturity requires the correction of memories that persuade us we have been abandoned by God. The memories that bother us most make us feel God is not hesed. Unhealed wounds allow evil to fester and character diseases to grow in churches. We need a bit of skill to deal with dark spirits. We also need to address iniquities of character that grow unaddressed in churches like weeds. Character disease has killed many churches and left others in critical condition. The epidemic of church narcissism needs to be stopped.[3] Churches need to become healthy places to develop character.

Healthy spiritual maturity requires us to grow a full identity but remember we are still quite small. When we think we are bigger than we are, we become proud, tired, vulnerable, and self-justified. Spiritual disciplines help us stay small and let God be large. Dallas and friends have provided many resources to avoid spiritual bloating and fatigue.[4]

Healthy spiritual maturity requires exercise. We exercise by actively attaching to our enemies with love. Churches that grow disciples constantly test their attachment skills in moments when people are "not on our side." The church has done most damage exactly at this point as well. When we try to win, we lose. When we learn to attach with love, we mature. We stick with others as God sticks with us.

Summary Statement

Now we have a model for spiritual formation that includes full emotional and relational maturity. We have means to develop the character of Christ to the point that we can spontaneously love our enemies. Our identity and actions derive from ongoing, mutual mind with God in real time. Our character has its iniquities healed and corrected by extensive relational practice with our hesed people. We avoid striving and being "too big" through disciplines of indirection. Life is now driven by the most powerful force in the human brain—attachment love—rather than the feeble, overly focused will. We become a new people who are being saved here on earth by the active presence of God. The example of our Older Brother lives in our hearts by His Spirit.

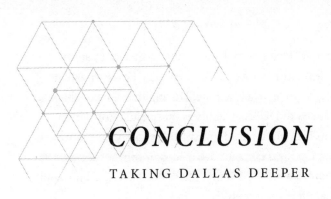

CONCLUSION

TAKING DALLAS DEEPER

Does our revised VIM model work? Our discussion of ideas has been extensive, touching on theology, neuroscience, philosophy, psychology, church history, and culture from the ancient Greeks to twenty-first-century America, when relational-brain skills were first discovered. But what happens when people learn the character of Christ the way the brain learns character? I wanted to know if combining two thousand years of spiritual practices with how the brain learns identity and character helps us become disciples. The lives of people who have been combining spiritual disciplines and relational skills should provide answers. I interviewed twelve of these new disciples to find out. You met John Loppnow in chapter 9 and heard his story; now let's hear from eleven others, beginning with John's wife.

Disciple 2: Sungshim Park Loppnow is married to John and is a coauthor of *Joyful Journey*. Jane Willard is her spiritual director. Sungshim began with spiritual disciplines and was then trained in the Life Model relational skills. She is a counselor and an international speaker. Sungshim says:

> How could I even begin describing the positive impact Dallas
> and his work has had on my life! I discovered Dallas in 1999, as
> an international student entering a foreign land called America.
> Before my exposure to Dallas's teachings, my goal for spiritual
> maturity was meeting all the expectations of the church. I was

pretty good at it. That is why I was sent to America to study further. My immaturity was quickly revealed, however, when life as a foreigner overwhelmed me. During this time of chaos, I was introduced to Dallas's teachings on spiritual formation. His teachings brought a paradigm shift: My focus shifted from "doing" what God wants me to do to "becoming" the kind of person who does what God wants me to do. This saved my soul, for which I am forever grateful!

Although the heavy burden of trying to obey God was dramatically lifted, I found myself still really struggling in relationships, especially marriage and close friendships. That is when I came across Jim Wilder and his teachings on maturity, relationship skills, and Immanuel lifestyle. What was the most helpful from Life Model teaching was that we humans are designed to develop mutual mind with those we love. Until then, I could not bring the peace and calm I gained during disciplines of silence and solitude into my marriage. Mutual mind with God quickly carried shalom to my marriage. I found so much peace in such a short amount of time. I learned and practiced seeing my relational wounds—often caused by marital conflicts—through the eyes of God. The good news did not end there; the peace that I gained from having a mutual mind with God created a safer way to resolve painful moments in our marriage and parenting. This missing ingredient in my spiritual diet (my life as a Christ follower) is what I offer for the world to taste.

Disciple 3: Reverend Michael Sullivant, the CEO of Life Model Works, learned to use spiritual disciplines thoroughly and intelligently through the writings of Dallas Willard and Richard Foster in the early 1990s. He met Dallas personally in 1992. Michael discovered the relational skills and Life Model in 2010. He has spoken in over twenty nations since he began ministry in 1975 and now lives in Kansas City. Michael says:

I eagerly digested Dallas's books and even taught a thirty-hour class on *The Spirit of the Disciplines* in our bustling local church's leadership-training school. Dallas and I saw one another periodically throughout the years and always enjoyed our face-to-face times. I attended the Heart and Soul Conference where Dallas's lectures in this book were delivered. Being in Dallas's presence was a great blessing and was itself transformative.

As a young zealous believer and church leader, I gave myself to practicing the spiritual disciplines regularly. Scripture reading and meditation consistently produced the most transformation within me. Dallas's expanded list of disciplines broadened my spiritual playing field. Spiritual disciplines became foundational to my life with God.

At times, I would still feel an inner pressure to measure achievements and/or justify my spiritual life. A kind of "near perfectionism" regularly beat me up and ate my lunch. I gradually felt an increasing *pressure to perform*. The stages of maturity from a Life Model chart opened my eyes. Now, when an area of immaturity is exposed, I call on the Lord for help and strength while practicing relational skills. I can cast off any shame of immaturity and grow up in God. I find myself free of any pressure to measure my progress or please others. I have found that the relational-brain skills of the Life Model fit very well with my practice of the classical disciplines that Dallas Willard so brilliantly reintroduced to our generation.

I now understand that joy is relational. I can tell when I am not in relational mode. I now see that having my fast track shut down was the source of many unnecessary frustrations and problems in my life and relationships. Staying relational has brought me the most tangible impact of the Life Model as a follower of Jesus. Other people who know me well have told me so! This simple, profound way to increase the joy and resilience that Christians experience has inspired me to take on the challenge of leading the Life Model Works organization to grow relational disciples of Jesus around the world.

Disciple 4: Michel Hendricks has been a pastor, missionary, inventor, and author. He first learned spiritual disciplines and then discovered attachment and relational skills. Michel has been teaching and training for over twenty-five years. He is a former pastor of spiritual formation at Flatirons Community Church in Lafayette, Colorado. Michel has also served in Argentina, Mexico, Kenya, South Sudan, and Uganda. He tells us:

As a pastor of spiritual formation for a large church, I found myself thinking long and hard about Christian growth. How do people change? How is character transformed? How does the character of Jesus get inside me so that it leaks out my pores and becomes my natural way of life? If we take a good, unhurried look at Jesus (what He did and said, how He acted) and then we look at ourselves, the difference can be shocking. I saw my job description as keeping our messy lives on the road to Christian maturity.

I devoured the books of Dallas Willard. He mentored me through his writing, and he often made me feel validated. He would say that a pastor's primary responsibility is forming the image of Christ in the lives of people. Dallas was a realist, though. He warned that the church is largely failing at this task. Other projects, often important and legitimate things, slowly push this primary responsibility off to the side.

Dallas's answer to my big question—how character is transformed—was spiritual disciplines. He saw in them an indirect way to accomplish something we could not do by direct effort. If I'm honest, my experience with teaching and training spiritual disciplines was mixed. Some people were blown away by the changes they saw in their lives. Other people made little movement. It seemed to me that something was missing. There was a variable that I didn't understand.

When I met Jim Wilder and heard about the importance of attachment and joy, the pieces of the puzzle fell into place. God designed our brains to run on joy, almost like fuel. People with low joy and an undeveloped attachment to God had difficulty responding to my training. Spiritual disciplines didn't seem to work. Now, I disciple people by starting with exercises around joy, relational skills, and strengthening their attachment to Jesus. In a relationally joyful environment, the spiritual disciplines flourish. I nurture a group identity that changes character. Group identity was new to me, but the first time I heard Jim explain it, I thought, *I need to redesign everything I have done!* I no longer feel like I am missing an important variable. The Life Model brings it all together in a way I can apply immediately.

Having a relational model of maturity helped me recognize a dangerous spiritual disease that infects churches and has driven many people away from fellowship. This sickness thrives in communities with shallow attachments and weak group identities, often producing spectacular failures of character. Without strong attachments and relational skills, narcissism flourishes—especially in leadership. I am devoting my life to growing relationally healthy disciples of Jesus and making our churches resistant to disorders that develop around weak spiritual character and immaturity.[1]

Disciple 5: Dave Mead serves on the staff of The Navigators—recently as one of its vice presidents—and has been with The Navigators for over thirty-three years. He ministered at Vanderbilt University, the United States Military Academy at West Point, and in France. Dave is a leadership coach and the CEO of WeAlign. Dave diligently practiced spiritual disciplines, but something was missing in his relational maturity. Dave tells us:

I just wish you could connect with me better, relate to me at a deeper level," my wife said, not mad this time but full of heartbreaking sadness. After decades of marriage, we were once again having this weighty conversation. My dismissive attachment style made me want to run and hide, as I had done many times before. This time, however, I found words. "Hon, I love you with every fiber in my body, and I want to be with you in that intimacy." What I didn't say was that I didn't have a clue how to do that. All the Scriptures I had memorized, Bible studies I had attended, and books I had read didn't seem to move me one step farther on the journey of true intimacy.

I grew up in a military family and easily marched into the Army at eighteen. I was taught that emotions get in the way of sound decision-making, and after all, "There's no crying in baseball!" Be cool, calm, collected . . . and unattached. I still considered myself a sensitive guy. I cry at movies and funerals. Still, my wife knew (and had known for a long time) that something was missing. Now I knew.

I prayed and asked questions. Why don't my spiritual disciplines lead to a more intimate, enriched marriage? Why can't I relate more deeply with my wife? Could intimacy also be missing in my relationships with God and my friends?

God answered my prayers in the fall of 2016, when Jim Wilder shared his experiences and the principles of the Life Model with me. I realized that in this imperfect world, my infant brain didn't receive what it needed. As a result, my body grew but the relational part of my brain didn't. An underdeveloped and untrained brain is the hallmark of most evangelical men.

Everything changed twenty years ago, when the neuroscience community discovered that the relational brain grows and can be developed through training, and can literally be rewired to reflect more of God's original design and purpose. Jim introduced me to several relational-brain skills and techniques: how to quiet myself, share joy, ensure my relational circuits are on, and create appreciation and deep gratitude. A few months later, my wife and I went to a five-day THRIVE seminar, where these skills (and others) were practiced within a community of like-minded believers of Jesus. At this gathering, everything connected! It was like the amazing day my dad brought home our first color television. That box showed a brilliant blue sky and lush green grass! I was fascinated—like I felt now. I walked into the seminar with a black-and-white relational screen that suddenly switched to color!

It's been two years since that experience, and the color only gets deeper and richer. As I mentor and coach others, I pass on these same relational-brain skills and share integrated stories. I continue to see dramatic life changes within my friends. Simple, intentional brain skills bring profound character change. Just ask my wife. She now has the husband she's long desired. I'm delighted to be with her: fully present, engaged, and filled with joy!

Disciple 6: Ed Khouri is a pastoral counselor with forty years' experience. He is an author, a teacher trainer, and an international speaker. His work in addiction recovery has impacted more than sixty nations. Ed began with spiritual disciplines. Now, he tells us that attachment with both God and others is central to every good thing he has learned or teaches. He says:

> I was at Heart and Soul. I'll never forget having lunch with Dallas, Jane, Jim, and my wife, Maritza.
>
> Much of Dallas's writing, especially in *Divine Conspiracy*, comes from Dallas's deep attachment with Jesus. He seems to describe the disciplines as the means to grow that attachment. That didn't work for me. I would get stuck while doing the things I'd been taught would grow a relationship with God. Disciplines and disciplined quiet times were, unfortunately, often mechanical and morphed into performance without me recognizing it. I was relational to a degree, but not enough.
>
> I had difficulty teaching others to be disciples of Jesus after their recovery. I taught them the disciplines once they got over the pain of addiction and trauma. Somehow, spiritual disciplines lacked the same relational flavor as recovery work. The turning point for me was experiencing and practicing the relational skills. I began to recognize that God shared both joy and quiet with me—and synchronized with my energy level. I also discovered mutual mind, which suddenly made a lot of Scripture make sense to me in new ways.
>
> Aside from the difference this all made in my relationship with Maritza, it has revolutionized my relationship with God. Joyful attachment allowed me to connect with Him as an actual being, and that changed everything for me. Now, I write books about grace-based attachments with God and others as our primary GPS for life.

Disciple 7: Marilyn Grant is a member of the Madonna House Catholic Community located in Combermere, Ontario, Canada. She has served with her community in a variety of mission houses, loving the poor, since

1987. Marilyn's community diligently practices spiritual disciplines and works in low-joy environments around the globe. She tells us:

> For several years, I worked as a Christian counselor, listening and praying with members of my community and others who came for healing. During that time, I came to know the Life Model work of Jim Wilder and, through him, some of the teaching of Dallas Willard.
>
> Although listening and praying with others could be very satisfying, I noticed that unless a person had a strong attachment to Jesus, little healing and change was manifested in their lives. In my own life, I thought I had a strong attachment to Jesus, but my relationships with others were at times fraught with fear and ambivalence. Although I enjoyed many friendships, I felt separated and isolated even in the midst of a community gathering. I did not know how to make connections and be part of the group. I didn't know much joy or know how to return to joy after misunderstandings, despite a strong spiritual life supported and fostered by the community disciplines.
>
> Learning about the Life Model and attachment to Jesus made a big difference in my life in major ways. Recognizing when I am struggling with disorganized attachment and low joy leads me to Immanuel prayer, helps me find joy again and develop healthier relationships. I find great joy watching another's eyes light up when they realize the importance of developing joy to resolve traumas and relationship problems. It gives me great joy when I see healing and maturity growth in others.
>
> I continue to learn new skills as I read and practice what Jim Wilder and the Life Model team has given. Although I never knew Dallas Willard personally, I know that what he formed and taught Jim is bearing fruit for many others, certainly for members of my community throughout the world.

So far, we have heard from experienced church leaders, pastors, missionaries, and counselors who represent conservative, evangelical, Pentecostal, and Catholic traditions from North America, South America, and Asia.

These serious disciples nevertheless struggled with maturity, relationships, marriages, and character issues. Adding relational-brain skills to their spiritual disciplines furthered their growth and relationships.

I wanted to hear how relational discipleship changed ministry models, so I asked Ken Smith and other innovative leaders how they combined spiritual disciplines with relational attachment in their ministries. I wanted people who had been trained in brain skills for my interviews. Yet, if God was behind hesed relationships, then God should show that disciples were learning attachment-based skills outside of formal training with no theory at all. Here is what I found.

Disciple 8: Kenneth Smith is a bi-vocational ministry leader from Philadelphia who worked in Asia for fifteen years. He has been applying what he has learned from Dallas Willard and the Life Model to ministry and business for two decades.

> At the end of seven years of ministry in Asia, I was struggling with ministry and family life. Day to day, I anticipated good would prevail, but those around me anticipated bad things. Nothing I tried seemed to help. A light went on for me while reading Erikson's stages of maturity. The very first stage develops trust, and the result is hopefulness. Trust and belief in the Bible go together for me, so I began noticing passages where God was drawing us into a deeper relationship with Him. When I attended the first few THRIVE events (relational-skills training), I really started understanding how relationships develop trust. Trust builds when others continue loving us (in every situation) and help us return to joy when we are distressed. I started using vocabulary like *secure attachment*, *building joy*, and *returning to joy* from distressing emotions.

> About the same time, I worked through *The Divine Conspiracy* by Dallas Willard. His handling of the Sermon on the Mount challenged me greatly. I saw how the Sermon fit maturity stages. Being a blessing came before dealing with anger, and anger was resolved before the harder things later in the Sermon. I made a chart that lined up the Sermon on the Mount, Willard, Erikson, and the Life Model.

I made it a point to practice the easy stuff first (like being a blessing and encouraging others), which helped me notice quickly when relationships got disconnected. My discoveries didn't suddenly make me or the people around me different, but it gave me a road map. I was pursuing joy in relationships—especially with God. As I saw the impact of building skills (like returning to joy) in my life, I began sharing skills with others. I saw Christian leaders transformed from denying they ever got upset to eagerly telling stories of being angry because Jesus was teaching them to improve relationships in those situations.

I helped a man start a men's ministry. Each meeting started with something we each appreciated from the last week. Next came the stories of when we lost the appreciation and peace that comes from God during the week. We helped each other reconnect to God in some pretty heavy situations—marriage, kids, jobs, even death of loved ones. The men's group was filled with stories of reconnecting to God from our distress. Little did they know they were telling stories of repentance and returning to joy. By the time we opened our Bibles, our hearts were listening. Noticing a loss of peace and reconnecting with God took less and less time, both inside and outside of the group. The more we stopped to appreciate and listen to God, the more He changed what was in our hearts.

I discovered all kinds of ways my heart wasn't connected to God and His people at my job. I served in a nonprofit organization where a dear Christian brother was the executive director. Cancer took his life too soon. In the ensuing years, God tested my attachment love for community through some opposition. *The Pandora Problem* by Jim Wilder really helped me see that dealing with oppositional leaders needed to be done from our group identity, not as isolated individuals. Learning loving ways to give a good shame message is very similar to how the Christian leaders I mentioned earlier learned to use anger to improve relationships. Reminding each other about who we are and what it is like us to do was much more fruitful than grumbling and inciting each other. Living in a community means we need to speak plainly to others about what pleases and displeases us and God. We think with God and discover what God knows is important.

I have been dialoging with Jim Wilder about teaching the next generation to be disciples and learning to love our enemies. Building a healthy group identity and passing a healthy group identity to the next generation requires grace and staying connected to Him.

Disciple 9: Misa Garavaglia has been a transformation coach for ten years. She trained as a spiritual director and now trains Immanuel prayer facilitators, and leads THRIVE events and retreats on relational skills. Misa is preparing for ordination as an Anglican deacon. She practices mutual mind with God and others by doing Immanuel journaling with a close friend regularly. Misa recovered from severe abuse and describes her growth and healing as very "layered." Healing, spiritual disciplines, fellowship, mutual mind with God, and other relational skills work together like a stairway, with one step leading to the next. Different parts of her life sometimes seem to be on different steps.

Misa's spiritual maturity began growing at salvation. God created a miraculous attachment with her immediately. She tells us:

From the moment I was saved at age fourteen, I found myself in God's arms, sitting on His lap. He created an attachment of love I had never known. My youth group helped me learn about prayer and Bible study. When I was fifteen, I met Mimi in church camp. Mimi saw me though God's eyes and taught me to journal my thoughts and record God's thoughts toward me. She saw what she called a "very special fire" in my soul and told me to tend it carefully. God showed me that one day, I would bring God's church closer to Him.

I have had the same spiritual director for thirteen years. She personifies joyful relational skills, but she does not know she has them. I have learned from her how to be a spiritually mature person. Together with spiritual practice, relational skills help me learn to love my enemies. The Life Model pulls it all together for me.

Disciple 10: John W. Messer is a pastor, pharmacist, life coach, and counselor from Littleton, Colorado, whose spiritual journey began with the spiritual disciplines and moved toward relational attachments. He says:

I have conservative roots and graduated from Denver Seminary, so spiritual disciplines have been the dominant focus of my training and education. Richard Foster was a strong, clear contributor. Dallas's *Renovation of the Heart* significantly impacted my life. I taught the book in church. What it means to be a person and his accurate descriptions of the Bible's teaching about our different dimensions (heart, will, spirit, mind, soul, etc.) empowered Christlikeness and measurable growth over time. Dallas's teaching has been hugely satisfying.

Yet the Life Model fits far more powerfully and effectively for me as I watch transformations in myself and small groups. I have longed for an adjustment from Dallas's use of the will and his VIM model to something with greater emphasis on the relational-attachment realm of people's lives.

Ohhh my! How the concept of having a mutual mind not only with Christian brothers and sisters but also with God has been life transforming! Jesus, Father, and Spirit want to and are capable of bringing communication into my mind of what God Himself is thinking and feeling. Thinking *with* God is incredibly freeing and challenging at the same time. I can have the mind of Christ. This frees me from concern about making the "right" decision on my own.

That Jesus wants a hesed connection with me as an individual person (contrasted with a God who only speaks through Scripture to Christians in a church) was very transforming. This attachment is somewhat difficult to fully grasp; it's still a growth area for me. Immanuel prayer and journaling helps me believe, feel, and know that I, John, am a unique creation. Jesus wants to communicate with me, answering my questions and bringing guidance to my life. The peace and joy in my heart make life much more experientially rewarding in every way.

Disciple 11: Reverend Esther Wakeman, PhD, is a missionary teaching pastoral care and counseling to seminarians at McGilvary College of Divinity at Payap University (Chiang Mai, Thailand). Esther trained in clinical psychology and is ordained as a Presbyterian minister. She is currently leading a large, collaborative research project on "good persons" stimulated by Dallas Willard's *The Disappearance of Moral Knowledge* with the Association of Christian Universities and Colleges in Asia. Esther teaches Dallas's VIM model, integrated with the Life Model and incorporating the gifts of the Spirit that Pentecostal churches use.

Esther says she has not been particularly diligent practicing spiritual disciplines. Although she has training in the Life Model relational skills, she has not worked hard in a disciplined way on those either. She began learning joyful relational skills from villagers in northern Thailand, where she raised her babies while doing missionary work. Her life shows us that understanding models and working hard at relational skills or spiritual disciplines is not the essence of maturity. God guided Esther through a vision and her community before she encountered the VIM and Life Models. Mutual mind with God and community have healed her attachments and supported her growth. She tells us:

> At age forty, during my "midlife crisis," I began learning how to have an interactive relationship with God, through the writing of Leanne Payne in *Listening Prayer*. I had been praying for healing for many months. At a conference for missionaries, I had a profound experience, a vision I guess, of God's presence at my birth—He was brooding over the room—God was real and awake and delighted that I was being born. This was the most real thing I have ever experienced—more real than physical reality. It made God real to me. Perhaps it created the foundation for a learned secure attachment that began to form between me and God. I'd grown up in conservative evangelicalism, been baptized in the Holy Spirit, and been in therapy for years while studying to be a clinical psychologist, but this was a real God revealing His real and healing presence to the depths of my being. It became the pivot point for the rest of my life.

I've not been particularly disciplined in practicing either the spiritual disciplines or relational skills but rising every morning to spend time with the Lord by reading Scripture with a listening ear and writing out our conversation has been the mainstay of my life, and from the beginning, I've felt that God wakes me up. After learning Immanuel Journaling at a THRIVE training event, I adapted it to become the pattern for my morning conversation with the Lord. The conversation continues through the day. I've been trying to practice the presence of Christ moment by moment ever since I was introduced to Brother Lawrence and Frank Laubach by Leanne Payne. Willard also notes them as good examples of how to live in constant fellowship with the Lord. I remember Him when I see beautiful flowers and enjoy thanking Him for gifts of beauty. Remembering that God is glad to be with me and responds to my weakness tenderly has significantly strengthened a more secure attachment with the Lord.

Another hugely important part of my journey has been prayer partners—women with whom I can be real, seeking to grow into maturity in Christ together. Payne notes this as crucial for growth. I asked God to provide such people for me. For the past twenty years, I've met weekly with a small group of women to talk about life and pray for each other. This discipline of real fellowship and prayer has held me, challenged me, comforted me, and I think it is helping to shape my identity as a beloved daughter of God, and one of His beloved people—who can be honest about our weaknesses and find God's loving provisions of joy, forgiveness, guidance, purpose, and growth.

Disciple 12: Betsy Stalcup is the executive director of Healing Center International in Reston, Virginia. Betsy has a PhD in science from Stanford and has been involved in healing prayer for more than thirty-two years. Her mission is making joyful relationships with people and God a reality. Betsy found that healing and attachment love go together. She says:

I emerged from childhood with a mixed-up attachment style. I was highly educated and a leader. I knew how to behave, but I was always on edge, watchful. During my years of performing, I practiced spiritual disciplines without much tangible benefit. In 2009, an intern told me about the Life Model, which teaches relational skills as well as spiritual disciplines. It is all about the relationship with Jesus but could also be considered a spiritual discipline. Learning mutual mind with Jesus through Immanuel prayer in 2011 was—and continues to be—key. Spiritual disciplines became a way to make space to interact with God rather than something to check off my "good Christian" list.

As I learned to interact with Jesus, who looked at me with delight, I began to attach to him securely. Many memories rose to the surface, memories that were hard to understand in the light of our new loving attachment. My biggest reaction was thinking, *If He let me suffer like that as a child, how can I trust that He won't allow something just as horrible to happen to me again?*

God told me He was putting me in "trust training." As I talked to the Lord about what I was experiencing, He attuned to me. I was not alone. He was with me in my struggles, felt what I felt, comforted me, and brought shalom. As I experienced this over and over, my heart began to trust. I saw that He was not watching me suffer from a distance. My buried pain surfaced so He could heal me. I began to see my suffering with new eyes. I formed a secure attachment to God that has stabilized my life and brought me peace and purpose in the midst of trial.

Every one of these twelve modern disciples I interviewed reported a surge of growth, wisdom, and maturity when they discovered a relational Christianity based on hesed attachment. Jesus was invited to their fast track to use the most powerful force in their human brain through His Spirit. Emotionally mature disciples were building joyful identities, families, churches, and communities using relational-brain skills they can teach to others. These disciples help others share a mutual mind with God.

We become spiritually mature by letting God and God's people into the fast track in our brain through attachment love. Attachment love empowers the changes in character that the New Testament church experienced. The science of spiritual maturity helps us learn the character of Christ so that it shows through our relationships—even with enemies. The two greatest commandments really work!

What Sticks

As we come to the end of our day with Dallas Willard, it is time to see what sticks with us. Most books naturally end with slow-track conclusions and challenge us to make better plans or choices. This book has led to the (slow-track) conclusion that saving attachment with God opens the way to a transforming mutual mind with God. We have yet to help you (the reader) experience a mutual-mind moment with God. How about a fast-track book ending this time?

Unlike the nine-minute exercises at the end of other chapters, I cannot promise this exercise will be so fast, nor will everyone succeed on the first attempt. Fear and spiritual abuse in the name of Christ can make this a slow process for some. Pastors in particular can feel pressured when it comes to God's thoughts. It is common for pastors and leaders to experience people's expectations for them to answer for God. We are not after such a difficult goal here. We are seeking God's help in noticing what we should notice in our own thoughts.

As we think with God, let's notice where God is guiding our attention. Sometimes, God draws attention to us, our circumstances, our character, or our relationships; other times, God draws our attention to Himself. In this exercise, we will ask God what He is showing us in *Renovated* (this book). What God wants you to notice concludes this book.

Exercise: Mutual Mind (Fast Track) with God

I have provided a structure in this exercise that can guide you if you would like help entering a mutual mind with God. Start by activating your attachment to God: Remember anything about God that makes you thankful. You can remember good gifts or the times that God felt close to you.

To be sure that our fast track is running smoothly, check how thankfulness feels in our bodies. When the fast track is running correctly, we can remember memories, feel gratitude, and notice how our bodies feel at the same time. This is a test for the aware but unfocused mindfulness of the fast track.

We will need to stay thankful for at least two minutes to allow brain chemicals to stabilize.

[Observe two minutes of thankfulness.]

In this thankful and mindful state, we invite God to think with us. To help us become aware of the big picture and let God highlight the relative importance of things we are thinking, we ask God, *What do You want me to know now?* In this case, we can ask, *What do You want me to know about love attachments with You and others?*

[Make notes of what is in your mind.]

What comes to mind will be a mixture of your thinking and God's. After you have written down what you noticed, read it aloud and look for "God content" that feels peaceful and true.

[Read your notes to another disciple.]

When you have reached a state of shalom (your mind and God's mind feel in harmony), read what you have written to another disciple. Don't try to explain what you wrote, as explanations rarely have God content. By reading your thoughts in the community of other disciples, you will gain clarity about what God wants you to notice.

[Repeat as needed.]

Additional Help through an Example

I did the exercise myself and wrote down what I thought God wanted me to know about salvation as a hesed attachment to God—the topic that Dallas first proposed to me. As I wrote, I could not tell if the thoughts were God's or mine. They look a bit like both. As you read, notice for yourself any "God content."

After two minutes of thankfulness that I could feel in my body, I asked, *God, what do You want me to know about salvation and attachment, now that I am finished writing a book about it?* A stream of ideas came to mind. I wrote:

> Think about evil and attachment. What are the besetting sins? Are they not all connected to attachment gone wrong? Addictions stick with us strongly. Addictions develop when the brain's attachment system is taken over by chemicals, experiences, and things rather than hesed people. Addictions are tenacious exactly because they come from attachment.
>
> Sexually predatory sins are also attachment gone wrong. Rather than attach to people in ways that last our whole lives, we attach to our sexual feelings. The extent to which sexual abuse and exploitation has destroyed the church will never even be estimated on earth. This, too, is attachment gone wrong. Did you think it was a sex drive causing trouble? No, the sex drive is not nearly as strong as attachment. When sex is substituted for attachment, the combined power will destroy all life in its path. Think of the price we pay in sicknesses and abortions alone. This is attachment (hesed) gone very wrong.
>
> Hesed attachment goes wrong in incest, as we have already noted. Crimes of passion are almost always tied to attachment or attachment pain. How many people (mostly women) are killed by some attachment-deranged partner? It is rare to read of a shooting or killing that is not done by someone who can neither sustain attachments nor let partners leave alive. This is attachment gone wrong.
>
> Gangs, organized crime, drug lords, cults, warlords, blood oaths, affairs, divorces, and the endless human misery they cause leave an endless cycle of bad and broken attachments. Slavery, human trafficking, gang violence, serial killing, starvation, and crime would end if people had normal human attachments to one another. This, too, is attachment gone wrong.
>
> Greed is attachment gone wrong. Jesus said, "No one can serve two masters; for either he will hate the one and love [*agapaō*] the

other, or he will be devoted [ἀντέχομαι; to adhere, attach, cling to] to one and despise the other. You cannot serve God and wealth."[2] Saint Paul named attachment to money as the root of all sorts of evil: "But those who want to get rich fall into temptation and a snare and many foolish and harmful desires which plunge men into ruin and destruction. For the love of money is a root of all sorts of evil, and some by longing for it have wandered away from the faith and pierced themselves with many griefs."[3] The author of Ecclesiastes said, "He who loves money will not be satisfied with money, nor he who loves abundance with its income. This too is vanity."[4] Attachment to money makes money into the source of life—but instead, this attachment becomes the source of death. Crime, wars, economic exploitation, poverty, genocide, environmental destruction, much disease, and sexual exploitation are all the result of greed. Greed is attachment gone wrong.

Attachment is pivotal to character development. Hesed with bad company grows bad character, while hesed with upright company grows good character. Pain that sticks with us comes from broken attachments. Attachment sticks. Death, abandonment, neglect, betrayal, conflict, and the social problems associated with them derive from attachment gone wrong.

All evil is rooted in attachment gone wrong. Human troubles started when Eve liked the fruit a higher being offered. Adam failed to say, "Honey, this god is not the one who feeds us." The god started a discussion about whether we would surely die, distracting them from the true source of life. We attach to the ones who feed us. A wrong attachment killed us.

Could salvation be attachment gone right? Attachment forms around the source of life. Family, friends, babies, intimacy, and all we treasure come from attachments gone right. Godly, hesed attachment sticks with us. I thank God for my food each day. Jesus is the Bread of Life, the well that always flows, the One who will not let go of me, the eyes that are always on me, and the attachment that lasts. Yes, by this attachment love that has gone right, I am being pulled free from all the attachments gone wrong. I am saved that I may also learn attachment love.

APPENDIX A

IDEAS FOR HESED ATTACHMENT AT CHURCH

Building Hesed

In chapter 7, we listed twelve characteristics of hesed attachment. Wouldn't it be fun to focus on one of the twelve characteristics each month of the year? Every year, the church could work through the list and develop traditions. By adding complementary spiritual-formation practices, the church could have a varied "diet" of ways to become disciples. Consider this appendix an idea starter that can take you beyond the content of this book. You will likely need many of the resources in appendix B. Few churches are prepared to grow emotionally and spiritually mature disciples. Because building hesed is not part of most standard church services, these suggestions may not fit church routines. Adapt suggestions or change routines as needed.

This imaginary yearly cycle aims to help people become *disciples.* Let's consider ways to introduce hesed each month. These suggestions start in August, when most schools start, but you can begin anytime.

HESED CHARACTERISTIC OF THE MONTH

AUGUST
Connect us to the source of life (as through food and drink)

- Take the children to see a garden, orchard, or farm. See how God feeds us.

- Have everyone bring and share one "food from God" they enjoy. Say something like "This is from God to your mouth." Thank God for giving such life-giving food. Stop to notice God's response in your mind. Tell the person who fed you (on God's behalf) what came to mind.

- Engage the discipline of fasting and be fed by God directly.

SEPTEMBER

Allow no substitutions—every attachment is unique to one being

- Create a spiritual family tree for your church. Does your church trace to Zwingli, Luther, Saint Peter, Wesley? How did your faith family reach your town, and how has it grown relationally? We are tracing the faith family and how it has changed lives. List a unique gift God placed in each person on the tree.

- Provide opportunities for each church participant to create their personal spiritual family tree. Tell a three-minute story about someone in your spiritual ancestry and what makes them unique. (It is hard to tell a three-minute story, but it encourages the storyteller to focus on what is important.) Send notes of thanks and affirmation to everyone in your tree who is still alive.

- Who is God adding to your spiritual family right now? Have a church party to welcome new family members from this last year.

- Engage the discipline of silence. While any discipline (act of indirection) would work, silence is a good contrast to creating a spiritual family tree that traces what people have been saying and doing.

OCTOBER

See the other as special and mine (grace)

- After a time of thanksgiving and praise to God, have people tell one another what God finds special about them. Write each characteristic on a name tag and stick it on them.

- In small groups of three to five people, listen for what God wants to grow in each member of the group. Commit to praying for that blessing to grow.

- Engage the discipline of worship.

NOVEMBER

Build through joy with someone who is delighted to be with us

- Sing to one another. Sing songs like "The Servant Song" or "I Love You with the Love of the Lord."[1] Have everyone share their face with Jesus, and then use their face to bless every other person present.

- Thank three people who have contributed to your spiritual maturity and tell them how you have grown as a result of their help.

- Engage the discipline of celebration.

DECEMBER

Provide both relational joy and rest (peace)

- Have the children create artwork, videos, songs, and pictures of relational joy. (Start in November or earlier.) Put this art on the church website and social media. Display relational-joy pictures during services. Arrange for every business in town (that will participate) to have a contest for pictures of relational joy, and display entries and winners in the workplaces.

- Notice who is getting tired at church and work as a group to give them a time of rest.

- Engage the discipline of service.

JANUARY

Develop mutual mind

- Create mutual mind with God from reading Scripture.

- Gather in groups of about five people. Give each group something to write on.

- Read a passage of Scripture aloud once and only once.

- Have each group recreate that passage from memory and write it down.

- Next, have each group answer the question, "What was God thinking when God inspired this passage?" When they have written down the answer, have each group share their answer with the full group.

- Now ask, "What would be different if I thought that way?" Share answers in small groups. Pray for each other to think more like God thinks.

- Engage the discipline of Scripture meditation.

FEBRUARY
Grow stronger by moving closer and farther apart

- Have everyone go on a small "mission trip" outside their usual comfort zone this month. When you come back together, have everyone tell what they saw God doing. Have "my people" pray about the outcome.

- Repeat the "trip" a second and third time. Three practice times helps the brain learn something new.

- Engage the discipline of solitude.

MARCH
Grow stronger by sharing both positive and negative emotions

- Learn to "rejoice with those who rejoice, and weep with those who weep."[2]

  Do a survey of your group, asking, "Which of the six unpleasant emotions do you use to build closer relationships?" The emotions are sadness, fear, shame, disgust, anger, and hopelessness. Note: These emotions are hardwired in the brain and are essential to fellowship. If you are uncertain, you might consult *Relational Skills in the Bible* (Brown and Coursey) or *Transforming Fellowship* (Coursey) in appendix B.

  On a name tag have people write any of the six emotions they use to improve attachments.

Gather in groups of five or so and tell an example of as many good expressions of the six emotions as are represented in the group. Focus on Jesus' presence in the emotion, the joy that results from using the emotion for better relationships, and how you would do it better next time.

- Play the "God be praised! and Lord, have mercy!" game together. The leader makes a list of matching items—one joyful and the other distressing. Have the congregation respond together when hearing the pairs read:

We have met our missionary budget—*God be praised!*

But only 23 percent of our church is giving—*Lord, have mercy!*

Deacon Bob is home from the hospital after his heart attack—*God be praised!*

But he has many weeks of recovery ahead—*Lord, have mercy!*

Start with lighthearted idea-pairs and then move to concerns about the church and community.

End with a thanksgiving-and-intercession prayer time of thinking with God.

- In triads, share a high point and low point from your week.

- Engage in the discipline of confession for the times you didn't use unpleasant emotions to build better relationships but acted from iniquity instead.

APRIL
Help all parties feel stable and act like themselves

- One relational-brain skill is identifying the main pain of our heart's identity. What is it that upsets us the same way it upsets Jesus? The life of Christ in us feels pain when the world violates that characteristic. Kind people are bothered by meanness. Gentle people are bothered by roughness. Thoughtful people are bothered by harshness. Generous people are bothered by greed. Hesed people love those who do not deserve it, but it hurts.

- Spiritual attacks hurt us most when what we value is despised, mislabeled, and misunderstood. Sooner or later, we will try not to care about whatever is most Christlike in us. We are tired of being hurt in that same spot over and over.

  Help every participant identify the characteristic of Jesus in them that gets hurt most often.

  Write that characteristic on a name tag, ask others about theirs, explain your own, then pray for one another.

  Make a church map of attributes of Christ that need care and nurture.

- Engage the discipline of fellowship.

MAY
Provide both freedom and connection

- Use the theme of "nesting" to inspire art and creativity from the youth—much like relational joy in December. This is a good way to reach both the community and the next generation with a message about freedom, connection, and joy. Songs, stories, videos, pictures, and creativity around nurturing new life fit this spring season.

- May is usually the time for graduations and weddings. This lends itself naturally to providing freedom and connection. Share stories with each other of ways that others blessed you with freedom and connection during times of transition and growth. List your opportunities ahead and ways you can use them to offer both freedom and connection in spite of the challenges. How can the church community support these efforts practically?

- Engage the discipline of chastity (without which, building hesed attachment becomes a disaster).

JUNE
Stretch limits and capacities slightly to promote growth

- The Life Model provides a grid for the stages of maturity listed in Scripture: unborn, infant, child, adult, parent, and elder. Each stage has needs and tasks. Most people are in either infant or child maturity, regardless of their age. Most people are behind on their maturity because they had no maturity map, important maturity needs were not met, and they were injured in some way that blocked development.

Review where people are now, what they need to learn next, and what mature person has the skill. (See the Healthy Spiritual Maturity resources in appendix B for more.)

Identify which maturity skill needs more practice. What skills need practice with peers?

What skill does each person have to train the "next generation" (even when that person might be older than they are)?

Make personal commitments to receive, practice, and give maturity skills. (See lifemodelworks.org if you need maturity-map resources.)

- Engage the discipline of frugality. Keep in mind, as Dallas has mentioned, that all spiritual disciplines should be chosen by the needs of the moment. Spiritual disciplines have no value in themselves. Select your disciplines accordingly.

JULY
Create an enduring people (i.e., families, tribes, and nations)

- Every family of faith is in danger of being the last generation unless they actively engage in loving their enemies.

Help your church identify who feels like your "enemies" and what makes you want to withdraw or attack.

Spend time together in mutual mind with God and with each other to see personal (family), church, community, and cultural "enemies" as God sees them.

Have each member of your church community make a step that you support together to make a personal attachment to an "enemy." This can be an act of repentance, forgiveness, or friendship.

- Have children and youth carry out a "growing hesed" summer project and make a documentary to be shown at the end of summer. Growing hesed can also be an art and creative project showing the redemptive value of breaking down barriers with joy.

- Engage the discipline of sacrifice.

Discipleship Evangelism

Dallas told us the church should build around practices that produce disciples. He adds, "Churches need to be centers where people are practicing these things that will enable them to take on the character of Christ." We have tended to create church patterns that are low on hesed—attachment love. Many of these cultural patterns in churches feel "properly Christian" but reflect cultural needs and patterns that no longer exist. We need creative ways to grow our attachment impetus because attachment is personal and must fit each specific relationship. Yet in all relationships, we must create hesed, develop mutual mind with God and God's people, and grow a group identity. Our personal and group identities must not grow rigid, so we practice spiritual disciplines. Our means of discipleship training nurture our full brain, heart, and soul.

Vision Changing

Discipleship evangelism will require a change in vision for the church. We are all familiar with what happens if leaders attempt to change vision without helping people own that vision as their own. Pushing a vision is a large mistake. The vision of discipleship evangelism emerges from discovering who we are as a people. We are becoming a people who live in joy and peace through ongoing mutual mind with God. We think *with* God to such an extent that we spontaneously love our enemies with hesed, attachment love. We avoid striving—expecting too much from ourselves and compensating for our deformities of character (iniquities). We help one another become relationally and spiritually mature. Churches are very good at creative ways to express their vision once the vision expresses their identity.

APPENDIX B

RELATIONAL RESOURCES

MUTUAL MIND WITH GOD AND OTHERS
E. James Wilder et al., *Joyful Journey* (Life Model Works)
Passing the Peace booklet and app (Life Model Works)
E. James Wilder and Chris M. Coursey, *Share Immanuel* (Life Model Works)
Dallas Willard, *Hearing God* (InterVarsity)
David Takle, *Forming* (Deeper Walk)
Victor A. Copan, *Changing Your Mind* (Cascade Books)
Ann Voskamp, *One Thousand Gifts* (Zondervan)
Sarah Young, *Jesus Calling* (Thomas Nelson)

GROUP IDENTITY
Marcus Warner and Jim Wilder, *Rare Leadership* (Moody)
E. James Wilder et al., *Joy Starts Here* (Life Model Works)
Timothy Johns, *Micro-Church Families on Mission* (Jesus Tribes)

HEALTHY SPIRITUAL MATURITY
James G. Friesen et al., *Living from the Heart Jesus Gave You* (Life Model Works)
Michel Hendricks and Jim Wilder, *When the Church Fails* (Moody)
E. James Wilder, *The Complete Guide to Living with Men* (Life Model Works)
Terri Sullivant, *The Divine Invitation* (Morgan James)
Peter Scazerro books: *The Emotionally Healthy Church* (Zondervan); *The Emotionally Healthy Leader* (Zondervan); *Emotionally Healthy Spirituality* (Zondervan)
Charlotte Mason, *Parents and Children* (Living Book)

RELATIONAL SKILLS FOR CHURCH (BOOKS)
Marcus Warner and Chris Coursey, *The 4 Habits of Joy-Filled Marriages* (Northfield)
Chris Coursey books: *Transforming Fellowship*, *Relational Skills in the Bible* (with Amy Brown; Deeper Walk), *30 Days of Joy for Busy Married Couples* (with Jennifer Coursey; Deeper Walk)
Barbara Moon books: *The Pandora Problem Companion Guide*, *Joy-Filled Relationships*,

Handbook to Joy-Filled Parenting, Joy-Filled Parenting with Teens, Re-Framing Your
  Hurts, Living Lessons on Intimacy with Christ, Jewels for My Journey, and more
Ed Khouri books: *I'm Wired for Relationships, Becoming a Face of Grace*, and more
Karl and Charlotte Lehman books/videos: *Outsmarting Yourself, Immanuel Approach
  for Emotional Healing and for Life, Immanuel*, and many more
Tom Anthony, *Building Better Community* (Life Model Works)
E. James Wilder, *The Pandora Problem* (Deeper Walk)
Barbara Moon with E. James Wilder, *The Pandora Problem Companion Guide*
  (Deeper Walk)

RELATIONAL SKILLS FOR CHURCH (TRAINING)

THRIVE training (intensive or online), available at thrivetoday.org
Journey Groups from Deeper Walk International, available at
  deeperwalkinternational.org
Help! I Live with a Narcissist (web course from Ed Khouri)
Life Model XP course (Life Model Works)
Connexus (Life Model Works)
Training/web-directed growth through Deeper Walk International

WEBSITES (LIFE MODEL RELATED)

lifemodelworks.org (all categories)
deeperwalkinternational.org (all categories)
thrivetoday.org (relational skills for the church)
alivewell.org (relational skills for the church)
barbaramoonbooks.com (all categories)
immanuelapproach.com and kclehman.com (mutual mind)
jesustribes.com and rocktribe.com (group identity)
presenceandpractice.com

WEBSITES (OTHER RESOURCES)

amblesideschools.com (all categories)
jesuscalling.com (mutual mind)
onethousandgifts.com (mutual mind)
thebibleproject.com (group identity)
charlesstone.com (relational skills for the church)

APPRECIATION

Deep thanks to Dallas, Jane, Becky, and the Willard Estate for providing the content, encouragement, perseverance, and generosity that brings this book project to fruition nine years after it began. Although Dallas is not listed as an author on this book, his contribution constitutes the central core of this project. "Mom Jane's" enduring attachment with my wife, Kitty, has been transformative to our lives. The blessings of the Willards go deeper than words can say.

My wife, Kitty, was the on-site coordinator for the Heart and Soul Conference. She has read and corrected every version of this text. Her sister Karen Mertes transcribed the audio recordings of the original lectures to begin the editing process.

Pastor Chris and Jen Coursey from THRIVE developed and managed the Heart and Soul Conference. Their work started in 2011 and continued well beyond the conference in 2012. All speakers, schedules, materials, books, meals, and the banquet honoring Dallas was under their direction. Many volunteers worked with the Courseys to create and run this event. They also reviewed this work in progress.

David Zimmerman has been my editor for NavPress. David edited the text from the live lectures, thus converting Dallas's speaking into a style that reads well. David has provided clarity for this project at every stage of development. This project presented complexities I have never encountered and David has humbly, cleverly, and directly guided the project through them all.

Timothy Wilder, my brother, has helped me think through the

history, philosophy, and theology. He has reviewed the manuscript to remove my most egregious errors.

Shepherd's House Board was quick to seize the idea of a dinner honoring Dallas and Jane Willard. They moved rapidly (for a board) to create an event and banquet. For the next six years, the board worked to provide time and opportunity to write this book. Perry Bigelow has been a special encouragement on this project. As COO of Life Model Works, Jim Martini provided direction that produced the agreements and contracts needed to publish this book. His negotiations and friendship created a reality from a dream. Pastor Nik Harang volunteered a year of his life to work for Life Model Works and develop the Life Model. During that year, he corrected the transcript of Dallas's talks and created most of the book proposal for NavPress that culminated in publishing this work. Pastor Michael Sullivant became the director of Life Model Works (Shepherd's House) about the time that writing began. Not only did Michael relieve the organizational burdens but he engaged with me on the concepts in this book.

Duane Sherman helped guide the road toward publication through many negotiations for clear rights and agreements. His desire to see deeper transformation in serious disciples helped move this project from a book everyone wanted to a reality.

Mark Anderson, Misa Garavaglia, Marilyn Grant, Michel Hendricks, Sean Harte, Bob Howey, Francis Hymel, Laurie Kayne, Ed Khouri, Sungshim and John Loppnow, Dave Mead, John Messer, Amy Pierson, Ken Smith, Betsy Stalcup, Marcus Warner, and Esther Wakeman provided stories or were test readers.

NOTES

CHAPTER 1: SALVATION IS A NEW ATTACHMENT

1. Jane worked at Shepherd's House Inc. in Van Nuys (Los Angeles, California) as supervisor, assistant director, and director of training. The Life Model was developed at Shepherd's House. In 2013, Shepherd's House began to go by the name Life Model Works.
2. Dallas Willard, *Hearing God: Developing a Conversational Relationship with God* (Downers Grove, IL: InterVarsity Press, 1984).
3. Shepherd's House staff held a Renovaré group in the office to practice spiritual disciplines.

CHAPTER 2: SPIRITUAL AND EMOTIONAL MATURITY

1. Jane's research includes, among other things, a lengthy paper on the role of the imagination in prayer, to which Dallas contributed a section on a theology of imagery in prayer. Jane presented that paper in 1988 to the Christian Association of Psychological Studies at their western regional conference in California.
2. Dallas's talk has been transcribed and edited so that it reads smoothly. What sounds wonderful to a live audience rarely reads as well.
3. Matthew 4:17.
4. Luke 6:20.
5. John 6:67-68, author's paraphrase.
6. 1 Corinthians 11:1, author's paraphrase.
7. Philippians 4:4, NET.
8. Philippians 4:5-7, author's paraphrase.
9. Philippians 4:6, KJV.
10. Philippians 4:7.
11. Philippians 4:8.
12. Phillippians 4:11.
13. See Romans 12, 1 Corinthians 13, Colossians 3, 1 Peter 1, 2 Peter 1, and so on.
14. Morris Albert, "Feelings," *Feelings* © 1974 RCA Victor.
15. James 4:1, author's paraphrase.

16. Galatians 5:19-21.
17. Romans 8:28, author's paraphrase.
18. 1 John 2:16, author's paraphrase.
19. John 3:16.
20. 2 Peter 1:3.
21. 2 Peter 1:3.
22. 2 Peter 1:4, emphasis added.
23. 2 Peter 1:4.

CHAPTER 3: THINKING *WITH* GOD

1. For more on trauma resolution, see Benjamin B. Keyes, E. James Wilder, and Sherry Todd, "Treating Trauma: Model Development, Comparison, and Analysis of Three Divergent Models," *The Journal of Christian Healing* 34, no. 2 (Winter 2018): 22–61.
2. Daniel Siegel, *Mindsight: The New Science of Personal Transformation* (New York: Bantam Books, 2011).
3. Allan N. Schore, *Affect Regulation and the Repair of the Self* (New York: W. W. Norton, 2003), 12–15. Schore has been called the Einstein of psychiatry and the leading thinker on the neurobiology of attachment.
4. Charles Stone, *Holy Noticing: The Bible, Your Brain, and the Mindful Space between Moments* (Chicago: Moody Publishers, 2019).
5. Gregory Bottaro, *The Mindful Catholic: Finding God One Moment at a Time* (North Palm Beach, FL: Beacon, 2018).
6. Dallas Willard in chapter 8.
7. Curt Thompson, *Anatomy of the Soul: Surprising Connections between Neuroscience and Spiritual Practices that Can Transform Your Life and Relationships* (Carol Stream, IL: Tyndale, 2010).
8. Michael Polanyi, *The Tacit Dimension* (Chicago: University of Chicago Press, 1966), 18.
9. Iain McGilchrist, *The Master and His Emissary: The Divided Brain and the Making of the Western World* (New Haven, CT: Yale University Press, 2009).
10. Marcus Warner and Jim Wilder, *Rare Leadership: Four Uncommon Habits for Increasing Trust, Joy, and Engagement in the People You Lead* (Chicago: Moody, 2017).
11. Mark 4:35-41, author's paraphrase. Mark was the catechist for Saint Peter and likely tells this story from Peter's experience.
12. Identity includes both *personal* and *group identity* when we are dealing with a brain that is over twelve years old. This change at twelve is part of the transformation of the brain at puberty.
13. This disruption of the right-brain fast track has been extensively described by Dr. Karl Lehman, so we will not examine the details here. See Karl Lehman, *The Immanuel Approach: For Emotional Healing and for Life* (self-pub., Immanuel, 2016).
14. Karl Lehman, *Outsmarting Yourself: Catching Your Past Invading the Present and What to Do About It* (Libertyville, IL: This Joy! Books, 2014), 24–31.
15. Richard Clark et al, "Cortical Desynchronicity Problems in PTSD" (Cognitive Neuroscience Laboratory, Flinders University, Adelaide, Australia).
16. See chapter 1's comments on *In Search of Guidance* (later titled *Hearing God*) by Willard.

CHAPTER 4: COMPONENTS OF THE HUMAN PERSON

1. Matthew 26:31-35, author's paraphrase.
2. Romans 7:14-25.
3. Matthew 26:69-75.
4. Romans 12:1, author's paraphrase.
5. 1 Corinthians 9:27, ASV.
6. In *Renovation of the Heart* Dallas writes about what happens to a person after departing from the truth: "When the light of the fundamental truth and reality, God, is put out in the heart and the soul, the intellect becomes dysfunctional, trying to devise a 'truth' that will be compatible with the basic falsehood that man is god; and the affections (feelings, emotions, even sensations) soon follow along on the path to chaos. . . . The mind is now uprooted from reality. It is committed to the truth of a falsehood." Dallas Willard, *Renovation of the Heart: Putting On the Character of Christ* (Colorado Springs, CO: NavPress, 2002), 52–53.
7. Matthew 22:36-40, author's paraphrase.
8. In *Renovation of the Heart* (p. 29), Dallas writes, "When we set aside contemporary prejudices and carefully examine these two great sources [ancient Greek and Judeo-Christian wisdom traditions], I believe it will become clear that 'heart,' 'spirit,' and 'will' (or their equivalents) are words that refer to one and the same thing, the same fundamental component of the person. But they do so under different aspects."
9. Author's paraphrase.
10. 1 Thessalonians 5:18, author's paraphrase.
11. Romans 12:2.
12. But if you go to church to worry about whether the song leader or preacher is doing the right things, it probably won't do you much good.
13. Romans 12:1.
14. Romans 12:1, author's paraphrase.
15. Mark 12:30.
16. John 15:15, author's paraphrase.
17. Romans 6:12.
18. Romans 6:13-14.
19. See Aristotle, *The Politics* 1.2.1253a1: "One who is incapable of participating or who is in need of nothing through being self-sufficient is no part of a city, and so is either a beast or a god."
20. Hebrews 13:5-6, author's paraphrase.
21. Romans 8:31, NIV.
22. Philippians 2:3, author's paraphrase.
23. Psalm 23:3.
24. Psalm 1:3, author's paraphrase.
25. Matthew 6:33, author's paraphrase.

CHAPTER 5: NEUROSCIENCE AND DEVELOPING CHARACTER

1. René Descartes, *Discourse on Method*, 4.32.
2. Emphasis mine.
3. There were two Reformed views of salvation in the century up to and including the Synod of Dort (two years before the *Mayflower* sailed). The view gaining momentum was the voluntarist view. See Robert W. A. Letham, "Saving Faith and Assurance in Reformed Theology: Zwingli to the Synod of Dort" (PhD diss., University of Aberdeen, 1979).

4. E. James Wilder and Marcus Warner, *The Solution of Choice: Four Good Ideas that Neutralized Western Christianity* (Carmel, IN: Deeper Walk, 2018).

5. Psalm 42:1.

6. Matthew 17:5, NLT.

7. Dallas Willard, *Life without Lack: Living in the Fullness of Psalm 23* (Nashville: Nelson Books, 2018), 85.

8. Luke 22:42.

9. Allan N. Schore, *Affect Regulation and the Origin of the Self: The Neurobiology of Emotional Development* (Hillsdale, NJ: Erlbaum, 1994).

10. John 15:9.

11. John 15:1.

12. Karl Lehman, *Outsmarting Yourself: Catching Your Past Invading the Present and What to Do About It* (Libertyville, IL: This Joy! Books, 2014), 5–16.

13. The brain as a whole highlights some experiences as more significant than others. This is done by a combination of quieting signals and attention-getting signals known as "value systems" that tell large areas of the brain that something important is underway. Two of these value systems have a strong effect on attention: (1) norepinephrine, which triggers attention for novelty; and (2) dopamine, which triggers attention for personally meaningful things. The brain's attention can be captivated by fast-moving, novel images of a video game, pornography, or other entertainment of no personal significance through norepinephrine. If the result is pleasurable, the dopamine system will create personal significance around the stimuli. Thus, focused attention is really two separate phenomenon with different (but potentially overlapping) value systems in the brain. See Gerald M. Edelman and Giulio Tononi, *A Universe of Consciousness: How Matter Becomes Imagination* (New York: Basic Books, 2000).

14. Discovered by the Nobel Prize–winning Gerald Edelman and further described by Guilio Tononi.

15. Ephesians 3:17.

16. Ephesians 3:14-19.

17. Wilder and Warner, *The Solution of Choice*, 68–73; Warner and Wilder, *Rare Leadership* (Moody, 2017), 134–137; Wilder, *The Pandora Problem* (Deeper Walk, 2018), 20–85.

18. For more on enemy mode and attachment see: E. James Wilder, *The Pandora Problem: Facing Narcissism in Leaders and Ourselves* (Carmel, IN: Deeper Walk, 2018).

19. Neither Dallas nor I would accept that the cingulate is the soul. The cingulate is in the body. We would both believe that the body should harmonize with the soul.

20. Ephesians 3:17.

21. Revelation 2:4, author's paraphrase.

22. Learn about Father Ubald in *Forgiveness: The Secret of Peace* (documentary film) available here: Secretofpeace.com.

23. See "The Voice of the Martyrs," accessed August 15, 2019, www.persecutionblog .com/colombia/.

24. Martin Mosebach, *The 21: A Journey into the Land of Coptic Martyrs* (Walden, NY: Plough, 2019).

25. 1 Thessalonians 3:5-7.

CHAPTER 6: SPIRITUAL FORMATION TOWARD WHOLENESS IN CHRIST

1. Author's paraphrase.
2. John 14:13, author's paraphrase.
3. John 8:51, author's paraphrase.
4. John 11:25-26, author's paraphrase.
5. Luke 6:28.
6. Matthew 28:19, author's paraphrase.
7. Matthew 18:20, author's paraphrase.
8. Colossians 3:9-10 and Ephesians 4:22-24, author's paraphrase.
9. Colossians 3:1-4, author's paraphrase.
10. Luke 14:26, author's paraphrase.

CHAPTER 7: TRANSFORMED BY LOVING ATTACHMENT

1. "The faith by which Jesus Christ lived, his faith in God and his kingdom, is expressed in the gospel that he preached. That gospel is the good news that the kingdom rule of God is available to humankind here and now." Dallas Willard, *Hearing God: Developing a Conversational Relationship with God* (Downers Grove, IL: InterVarsity Press, 2012), 202.
2. Dallas Willard, endorsement to E. James Wilder et al., *Living from the Heart Jesus Gave You* (Peoria, IL: Shepherd's House, 2013).
3. Both focused attention and loving attachment are always needed when dealing with creatures who are using human brains—that would be most of us.
4. 1 Corinthians 12:31.
5. NIV.
6. Romans 8:35-39, NKJV.
7. The characteristics come from Schore, but the simplified wording is mine.
8. 1 Peter 2:2.
9. A parent who is not hesed and breaks and injures bonds can be replaced. When we have a strong attachment, we do not allow anyone else to replace the one we love. This can even be true for our attachment to pets.
10. John M. G. Barclay, *Paul and the Gift* (Grand Rapids, MI: Eerdmans, 2015).
11. John 15:11.
12. Ecclesiastes 2:26.
13. Matthew 11:28, author's paraphrase.
14. Ephesians 2:8-10, emphasis added.
15. Psalm 96:4 (1 Chronicles 16:25 is almost identical).
16. 1 Peter 2:10.
17. Joshua 2:12-13.
18. Proverbs 20:6.
19. Leviticus 20:17.
20. Leviticus 19:18, translated in Matthew 5:43.
21. Hosea 6:6, NKJV.
22. Micah 6:8.
23. *Passing the Peace: After a Crisis* (self-pub., Life Model Works, 2015), available at lifemodelworks.org.
24. Karl and Charlotte Lehman's books, videos, and resources are available at kclehman.com.

25. Ed and Maritza Khouri's books, videos, and resources are available at equippinghearts.com.
26. Darrell Brazzell's recovery resources are available at newhope4si.com.
27. Chris and Jen Coursey's books, videos, training, and resources are available at thrivetoday.org.
28. Marcus Warner's books, videos, training, and resources are available at deeperwalkinternational.org.
29. 2 Corinthians 5:14-16.
30. Ecclesiastes 4:9-10, 12.
31. In time, Gary's wife died, he remarried, and he moved to Israel, where he also died. His body now awaits the Resurrection in the same cemetery as Oskar Schindler of *Schindler's List* is buried. Schindler's story and the Holocaust remind us that we most need people when it is hard to be a people. We also notice that when we do not see others as our people, we become exceedingly dangerous and deadly.
32. See Chris M. Coursey, *Transforming Fellowship: 19 Brain Skills that Build Joyful Community* (self-pub., THRIVEtoday, 2017); Amy Brown and Chris Coursey, *Relational Skills in the Bible: A Bible Study Focused on Relationships* (self-pub., Deeper Walk, 2019); and Tom Anthony, *Building Better Community: 12 Exercises to Strengthen Your Relational Muscles* (self-pub., Life Model Works, 2018).
33. John 21:15-17.

CHAPTER 8: DISCIPLINES FOR TRANSFORMATION

1. Matthew 5:14, ASV.
2. Ephesians 4:26, NIV.
3. Dallas elaborates on this function of the church in *Renovation of the Heart*: "This seems to have been Paul's idea. . . . Identification with Christ and the emerging community of Christ obliterated all other identities, not by negation, but by its new and positive reality" (p. 233).
4. Colossians 4:6, KJV.
5. Dallas Willard, *The Spirit of the Disciplines: Understanding How God Changes Lives* (New York: HarperCollins, 1991), 158.
6. ASV.
7. James 3:2, author's paraphrase.
8. Dallas Willard, *Spirit of the Disciplines*, 165.

CHAPTER 9: THE SCIENCE OF SPIRITUAL MATURITY

1. I would reword this to say, "You cannot count on Christlike, human maturity without spiritual maturity." Many non-Christians have far better emotional maturity than people claiming spiritual maturity.
2. Emphasis added.
3. Matthew 23:14.
4. Matthew 23:23.
5. Acts 3:6, author's paraphrase.
6. Brother Lawrence, *The Practice of the Presence of God* (New Kensington, PA: Whitaker House, 1982).
7. Acts 4:8.
8. Jim Wilder et al., *Joyful Journey: Listening to Immanuel* (East Peoria, IL: Shepherd's House, 2015).

9. Personal correspondence. This and other testimonials in the book are used with permission.

10. Richard Rohr's daily meditation, "The Face of the Other," January 31, 2019, https://cac.org/the-face-of-the-other-2019-01-31/.

11. Mark 3:1-6.

12. Amy H. Brown and Chris M. Coursey, *Brain Skills in the Bible: A Transforming Fellowship Bible Study* (Deeper Walk, 2019).

13. Chris M. Coursey, *Transforming Fellowship: 19 Brain Skills that Build Joyful Community* (self-pub., THRIVEtoday, 2017).

14. Marcus Warner and Jim Wilder, *Rare Leadership: Four Uncommon Habits for Increasing Trust, Joy, and Engagement in the People You Lead* (Chicago: Moody, 2017).

15. Marcus Warner and Chris Coursey, *The 4 Habits of Joy-Filled Marriages: How 15 Minutes a Day Will Help You Stay in Love* (Chicago: Northfield, 2019).

16. 1 Thessalonians 5:14, author's paraphrase.

17. Exodus 34:6-7.

18. Mark 2:9-11.

19. Matthew 15:14; 23:24.

20. The left brain, slow track, has corresponding feelings of the same name that come in response to a thought or idea, like *He just dissed me!*

21. We will ignore the body's systemic quieting systems so we will not have to explore how muscles, glands, organs, and organ systems keep themselves free from toxins, inflammation, infection, and other extremes.

22. The fast track contains two quieting systems—vegetative and interactive quieting—both relational.

23. E. James Wilder et al., *Joy Starts Here: The Transformation Zone* (East Peoria, IL: Shepherd's House, 2013).

CHAPTER 10: THE CHURCH THAT TRANSFORMS

1. David Takle, *Forming: A Work of Grace* (Kingdom Formation Ministries, 2013), 13–14.

2. 1 Peter 4:8.

3. Resources for addressing narcissism include: Wilder, *The Pandora Problem* (2018); Barbara Moon, *The Pandora Problem: Companion Guide* (2019); Ed Khouri, *Becoming the Face of Grace* (2019); Michel Hendricks and Jim Wilder, *When the Church Fails* (2020); and Marcus Warner and Jim Wilder, *Rare Leadership* (2016).

4. Resources on spiritual disciplines include: Dallas Willard, *The Spirit of the Disciplines* (1988); Dallas Willard and Don Simpson, *Revolution of Character* (2005); Dallas Willard, *Eternal Living*, Gary W. Moon, ed. (2015); F. B. Meyer, *Secret of Guidance* (2010); Dana Hanson, *Reboot: 70 Life Lessons with Dallas Willard* (2015); Richard J. Foster, *Celebration of Discipline* (1983); Jan Johnson, *Abundant Simplicity* (2011); Dallas Willard, *Hearing God through the Year*, Jan Johnson, ed. (2015).

CONCLUSION: TAKING DALLAS DEEPER

1. Michel Hendricks and Jim Wilder, *When the Church Fails* (Chicago: Moody Press, 2020).

2. Matthew 6:24.

3. 1 Timothy 6:9-10.
4. Ecclesiastes 5:10.

APPENDIX A: IDEAS FOR HESED ATTACHMENT AT CHURCH

1. Richard Gillard, arranged by David Hass, "The Servant Song," *We Give You Thanks* © 1998 GIA Publications; and Jim Gilbert, "I Love You with the Love of the Lord," in *Songs of the Church*, 21st century ed. (West Monroe, LA: Howard Publishing, 1990), no. 725.
2. Romans 12:15.

THE NAVIGATORS® STORY

T HANK YOU for picking up this NavPress book! I hope it has been a blessing to you.

NavPress is a ministry of The Navigators. The Navigators began in the 1930s, when a young California lumberyard worker named Dawson Trotman was impacted by basic discipleship principles and felt called to teach those principles to others. He saw this mission as an echo of 2 Timothy 2:2: "And the things you have heard me say in the presence of many witnesses entrust to reliable people who will also be qualified to teach others" (NIV).

In 1933, Trotman and his friends began discipling members of the US Navy. By the end of World War II, thousands of men on ships and bases around the world were learning the principles of spiritual multiplication by the intentional, person-to-person teaching of God's Word.

After World War II, The Navigators expanded its relational ministry to include college campuses; local churches; the Glen Eyrie Conference Center and Eagle Lake Camps in Colorado Springs, Colorado; and neighborhood and citywide initiatives across the country and around the world.

Today, with more than 2,600 US staff members—and local ministries in more than 100 countries—The Navigators continues the transformational process of making disciples who make more disciples, advancing the Kingdom of God in a world that desperately needs the hope and salvation of Jesus Christ and the encouragement to grow deeper in relationship with Him.

NAVPRESS was created in 1975 to advance the calling of The Navigators by bringing biblically rooted and culturally relevant products to people who want to know and love Christ more deeply. In January 2014, NavPress entered an alliance with Tyndale House Publishers to strengthen and better position our rich content for the future. Through *THE MESSAGE* Bible and other resources, NavPress seeks to bring positive spiritual movement to people's lives.

If you're interested in learning more or becoming involved with The Navigators, go to www.navigators.org. For more discipleship content from The Navigators and NavPress authors, visit www.thedisciplemaker.org. May God bless you in your walk with Him!

Sincerely,

DON PAPE
VP/PUBLISHER, NAVPRESS

NavPress
www.navpress.com

CP1308